Illustrations

Figures

Table

Notes on contributors

Peter Dean is the course manager for the BA(Hons) Media Production degree in the Department of Media Arts at the University of Luton, UK. He has recently supervised a Teaching Company Programme in e-commerce. He teaches digital media production and is currently completing an article on the regulation of strong encryption. He is also a consultant to a company developing a novel information security product funded by a DTI Smart award.

Luke Hockley is Head of the Department of Media Arts at the University of Luton, UK. He has published on various aspects of multimedia and is currently researching the relationship between media theory and new technologies.

Jeanette Steemers is a Senior Lecturer in the Department of Media Arts at the University of Luton. She has a professional background in international television, having worked as a senior researcher for the market research agency, CIT Research Ltd., and as Research Manager for HIT Entertainment plc, a London-based TV distributor and co-producer. She has written several articles on digital television policy and is editor of and a contributor to *Changing Channels: The Prospects for Television in a Digital World* (John Libbey, 1998).

Richard Wise is a Senior Lecturer in multimedia in the Department of Media Arts at the University of Luton. He has conducted research in the pedagogic uses of computers in higher and further education at the Cambridge Institute of Education, UK, and has published several pieces on critical issues associated with multimedia.

Acknowledgements

I wish to thank Jeff Taylor without whom this book would never have been started but who unfortunately was not able to be there at the end. Most particularly I wish to give my profuse thanks to Jeanette Steemers for her diligence in editing my words and for writing Chapter 5 with me. Without Jeanette the book would not have been finished. I would also like to thank my colleague Manuel Alvarado for his wise words of support and my colleagues Peter Dean and Luke Hockley for agreeing to contribute chapters at a late stage in the project. I would also like to thank Rebecca Barden at Routledge for being a patient and supportive commissioning editor. Finally, I wish to thank my wife, Zett, and my children, Thomas and Louise, for putting up with my dark moods during the writing of this book.

Introduction

Origins of this book

As a teacher of economics and politics I was an early adopter of computer technology, being both exhilarated and fascinated by its possibilities. Keen both to use the technology and to proselytise it amongst my colleagues, I acquired an embarrassingly unwarranted reputation as a Mac 'guru'. This reputation meant that I was asked to devise a multimedia pathway for a media degree. From the start I was determined that the course should teach students not only how to produce multimedia artefacts, but also to be reflective and critical with regard to the wider societal implications of the technology. It was in the process of writing this course together with my colleagues that the 'critical issues' of the title emerged.

Defining multimedia

Defining multimedia, however, is problematic. The word is controversial, with competing definitions and diverse origins, and it was only in the 1980s that the term came to refer to a marketing niche for specialised products of the computer industry. The counter-culture computer pioneer Ted Nelson was scathing about this development and saw 'multimedia' as 'a resurrected term from the 1960s, when it meant slide shows with sound. Why bring back such an irrelevant term?'[1] Indeed, I can recall coming across dusty 'multi-media' packages in a liberal studies store-room in a further education institution in the 1970s. Such packages consisted of 'magic lantern'-type film-strips and accompanying audiotapes on such subjects as 'The Suffragettes' and 'The Industrial Revolution'. During the 1960s, 'multimedia happenings' involving music, light shows and tactile experiences had been a feature of both the artistic avant-garde and the hippy counter-culture. In yet another sense, global capitalist conglomerates with diverse media interests are sometimes called 'multimedia' corporations.

However, the sense in which 'multimedia' is used in this book refers specifically to the application of computer technology to human communication. Feldman has defined this sense of multimedia concisely as 'the seamless integration of data, text, images and sound within a single digital information environment'.[2] Such a definition concentrates on technologies and applications like electronic mail, on-line publishing, CD-ROM, the Internet, and digital television. However, we define multimedia in a less strictly technical way than this. Indeed, as far as the purposes of this book are concerned, such terms as 'cyberspace', 'new media technologies', 'computer-based media', 'digital technologies' and 'information and communications technologies' are adequate synonyms.

The key concept and technology behind multimedia has been digitisation: the conversion of images and sound to numbers, making them amenable to manipulation by a computer. Because multimedia machines have the capacity to manipulate symbols according to predetermined rules they can emulate all existing media forms. For this reason we see multimedia as the latest phase in the history of the mass media and so it is implicated in the history and culture of telecommunications and broadcasting institutions.

Ultimately multimedia has taken on a symbolic value in discourses about the very future of our civilisation. Consequently a central aim of this book is to examine these technologies from cultural and social perspectives. To do this we must trace the specific historical and institutional circumstances in which both the technology and the idea of multimedia arose. We conclude by examining the ideological implications of multimedia and its functions and purposes in civic life.

The origins of multimedia

A number of different political, economic, cultural and technological forces have contributed to the development of multimedia. The technical elements which make multimedia possible (fast microprocessors; high resolution screens; audio and video digitising and compression techniques; high capacity storage, etc.) were each developed by different agencies for different purposes. The main technical and conceptual innovations behind multimedia were formed in the 1960s and 1970s, although a number of individual elements predate this period. The history of multimedia may be seen as a reciprocal relationship between three institutions: the state through its military and intelligence agencies, the computer and media industries, and various (counter-) cultural elements.

Military origins

In Chapter 1 we examine the contribution of the military to the development of multimedia. The military had been interested in computer technologies since the Second World War, initially as a method for producing artillery range tables and controlling anti-aircraft guns and subsequently as a means of deciphering enemy codes. The application of electronic computing to warfare continued to be lavishly funded during the Cold War when the development of nuclear weapons and computer-guided strategic missiles was a priority. It was this state-funded effort that produced the microchip and thus laid the foundation for the mass production of computing power upon which were built all subsequent developments in multimedia technology.

Although the microchip, the foundation of the multimedia industry, arose from weapons development, it was in the application of the computer to information processing that the military made the largest contribution to multimedia. This occurred in three main areas: aircraft simulation, image analysis and battlefield command and control.

Aircraft simulation

Simulators arose out of the military's need to find cost-effective ways of training personnel in the use of sophisticated weapons systems. This was particularly so when it came to aircraft, which by the 1960s had become complex and expensive. The development of simulators for training pilots required using computers to reproduce realistic three-dimensional visual representations of situations in which pilots might find themselves. Moreover, these visualisations were interactive and able to respond in real-time to the actions of the user.

Image analysis

One aspect of military intelligence that has had particular relevance for the development of multimedia technologies has been photo reconnaissance and analysis. The need to automate the analysis and interpretation of masses of images taken from satellites and aircraft has generated the image processing techniques that are now key multimedia technologies.

Battlefield command and control

Computerised interactive visualisations were also developed for the military to assist commanders and individual fighters in battlefield situations at both the tactical and strategic levels. This led to the development of visual display devices such as the head-up display (HUD) and the graphical user interface (GUI) which are the forerunners of the virtual reality headset.

Probably the single most important contribution by the military to multimedia technology has been the Internet. The Internet has its origins in the US military's requirement for a global control and command network that could survive a nuclear attack. The result was a decentralised network that uses the global telephone system to enable digital data to be sent to anyone in the system (at least in theory).

Counter-culture origins

In Chapter 2 we examine another important influence on the development of multimedia: the, mainly North American, counter-culture of the 1960s. This movement has contributed two main themes to the discourse around multimedia technologies, neither of which excludes the other. One stresses the democratic and enabling potential of the computer while the other sees it primarily as an aid to spiritual evolution. Both of these perspectives have been adopted to various degrees by those in politics, commerce and education, who promote multimedia technologies as the herald of a new age. Most significantly, it was out of the counter-culture computing movement that the personal computer emerged as a consumer product and commercialism supplanted radical idealism.

The birth of the multimedia market

In Chapter 3 we trace how a hobbyist market for personal computers, emerging from the activities of counter-culture 'hackers', evolved into a mass market. By the early 1980s the personal computer had a widespread presence in commerce and education. However, these early machines could not be described as multimedia since they used text-based 'command-line' operating systems and did not provide an integrated environment of sound and images. Initially genuine multimedia machines were costly and restricted to commercial applications such as arcade games, training and information, and sales 'kiosks'. The breakthrough for multimedia as a commercial product came with the development of graphical user interfaces (GUI) for personal computers and the CD-ROM. By the 1990s the computer and publishing industries were vigorously promoting multimedia PCs to a home market by targeting families with children. However, despite the success of a few titles such as Microsoft's *Encarta*, the market never took off and by the end of the 1990s many publishers have considerably reduced their commitment to multimedia. The future of multimedia is seen to lie with increasingly powerful and sophisticated network technologies rather than delivery via CD-ROMS and stand-alone PCs.

The evolution of mass media

Digitisation means that any of the transmission methods that constitute the telecommunications infrastructure may be used to deliver multimedia. This infrastructure utilises wired and wireless technologies that have been developed since the nineteenth century. Current developments in multimedia should thus be seen in the context of the history of these network technologies. Chapter 4 traces the evolution of these telecommunications from the early days of the telegraph, telephone and radio to the current era of digital television and the Internet. What becomes clear in this survey is that there is no necessary connection between a transmission method and its content. At the beginning of the twentieth century radio was seen as a one-to-one method of personal communication and the telephone as a one-to-many method for distributing entertainment into the home. By the middle of the century a ubiquitous telephone network and the growth of TV ownership meant these roles had reversed. However, by the end of the century, with fibre optic cable, digital satellite and mobile phones, the picture is much more mixed.

What becomes clear from this survey is that the advent of digital multimedia represents both continuity and change. It represents continuity in the sense that it is the latest stage in a century-old process of technically improving the telecommunications infrastructure. On the other hand digital technologies in general and multimedia in particular represent a qualitative change in what the telecommunications infrastructure can deliver. Digitisation brings about a significant improvement in what may be transmitted into households: firstly, in the quality of representations that may be experienced, and secondly, in the range and quality of information to which individuals have access. It is generally accepted that these technological developments are such that they will inevitably have a profound influence on our whole culture. However we would argue that, in comprehending the social and cultural impact of multimedia, it is not enough to concentrate on the technology alone; the political and institutional context of technological change should be taken into account also.

Chapter 5 examines the relationship between telecommunications and the state as it has evolved in the UK and US during the twentieth century. Before the 1980s telecommunications and broadcasting systems were heavily regulated and limited in number. State policy was based on the assumption that the telecommunications spectrum, both wired and wireless, was a scarce resource. The telephone was seen as a natural monopoly that needed to be regulated to ensure that no citizen was disadvantaged by either income or geographical location. In the same way the state regulation of broadcasting in the early years was concerned with preventing anarchy on the airways, for which a centralised frequency allocation and licensing system appeared the best solution. Within this context the regulation of the content of broadcasting to maintain publicly defined standards of taste and decency appeared a straightforward, if sometimes controversial, exercise.

With the advent of digital technologies, and the possibility of unlimited transmission capacity, many of the certainties surrounding telecommunications regulation appeared to be undermined. In contrast to the old regime of limited spectrum and a few monopolistic providers, the digital era promises an age of telecommunications plenty with many diverse providers using a wide variety of transmission methods. With this new situation it appeared to some that the old regulatory regime was no longer relevant or indeed appropriate, and from the 1980s, governments began to dismantle their regulatory systems through a process of privatisation and deregulation. However, although digital technologies provided the rationale for this process, this book argues that the main motive for telecommunications restructuring was political and financial rather than technological. The governments that came to power in the US and UK during the 1980s were driven by an ideological commitment to free markets which informed all their policies. This political shift led to a resurgence in the power and influence of large capitalist corporations. It was these political developments, rather than the new media technologies, that explain the changes in the relationship between the state and the main media institutions after the 1980s.

The rhetoric that accompanied the deregulation and privatisation of telecommunications and broadcasting claimed that it would result in more competition and an accelerated introduction of new technologies. Chapter 6 examines the responses of media corporations to the new deregulated environment and concludes that the 'multimedia heaven' promised by the legislators has been slow to materialise. Far from increasing, competition has declined as media corporations have become involved in a process of mergers, acquisitions and strategic alliances on an international scale. The global media system that is emerging from this process is one that is increasingly dominated by an oligopoly of giant, mostly US-based, transnational media conglomerates. Even the promise of technological innovation has not been as rapid as predicted. Companies appear to be reluctant to embark on investment in the face of uncertain consumer demand and the high cost of interactive multimedia technologies.

This is not to say that digital multimedia do not have special implications for our society, but they may not be the same as those predicted by the conventional wisdom. For example, in Chapter 7 Peter Dean, taking as his starting point Nicholas Negroponte's four-dimensional view of the implications of the information age (decentralising, globalising, harmonising, empowering),[3] discusses some of the ethical issues arising from the introduction of digital multimedia technologies. In particular, Dean examines what happens when existing legal systems, based on the nation state, are used to control digital telecommunications systems. Highlighting the implications of widely available and sophisticated forms of computerised encryption, Dean concludes that traditional notions of jurisdiction, censorship and privacy are becoming increasingly difficult to sustain, as digital technologies become more prevalent.

Multimedia and cinema

Multimedia technologies have not only had an impact on telecommunications and broadcasting, they have also revolutionised cinema. This aspect of multimedia technology is addressed in Chapter 8 in which Luke Hockley considers the impact of the new digital technologies upon special effects in the movies. In considering digitised special effects, Hockley regards them as existing within a set of social, industrial, (sub-)cultural and economic relationships, and at the same time as part of an unfolding historical discourse. Hockley takes a position that synthesises the views of political economists such as Schiller,[4] who see special effects as integral to capitalism's commodification of the image, and cultural critics such as Philip Hayward, who see the value of special effects as lying in the creation of spectacle.[5]

The ideology of multimedia

Since the 1980s it has become widely accepted that the new technologies of cyberspace are the harbingers of a new 'information age', a digital renaissance in which individuals will become increasingly empowered and knowledge will become the new source of wealth. Chapter 9 argues that this view is ideological and has been used to legitimise and promote a major restructuring of capitalism during the 1980s and 1990s. This restructuring has resulted in an increase in the power and wealth of capitalist enterprises and a parallel reduction in that of working people. This concluding chapter locates the origins of the ideology of the information age in two intellectual traditions. One tradition, with its roots in the ideas of the seventeenth-century enlightenment and, more particularly, in the classical economics of the eighteenth and nineteenth centuries, sees the systematic application of knowledge to production as a means of increasing social welfare. One of the most influential exponents of this view has been the American sociologist Daniel Bell, who first characterised our era as the post-industrial age. Another tradition sees advances in media technologies as having the potential to lead to a spiritual transformation of our society. This latter view is more recent and owes much to the ideas of the Canadian thinker Marshall McLuhan as modulated by various counter-culture and 'New Age' writers. The ideology that results from the blend of these two strands is typified by Alvin Toffler's contention that we are entering a historical 'third wave' following the previous two waves of agriculture and industry.[6] Chapter 9 challenges as unhistorical the view that we are entering an information age since it is impossible to envisage any human activity at any time that did not involve knowledge in some form. The chapter examines claims that multimedia technologies, in particular the Internet, will lead to a reinvigoration of the public sphere and a consequent increase in democracy and civic participation. However, while there is evidence that some repressed and dissident groups have been able to make their voices heard by using the Internet, the book argues that there are still formidable obstacles to be overcome before multimedia can become the vehicle for a genuine participatory democracy. Not least of these is that the principal agents promoting the technology are the global media conglomerates who are more interested in promoting pay-per-view entertainment than in creating a democratic forum in cyberspace where their activities might be scrutinised. We cannot rely on multimedia technology and market forces to enhance democracy; that can only come about by an act of political will, informed by critical reflection on the technology in the context of human values. It is hoped that this book will make a modest contribution to that process.

Notes

1   T. Nelson, *Literary Machines*, Sausalito, California, Mindful Press, 1980 (1992 edition).
2   T. Feldman, *Multimedia in the 90s*, London, Blueprint, 1991, p. 6.
3   N. Negroponte, *Being Digital*, London, Hodder and Stoughton, 1995, p. 229.
4.   H. Schiller, *Information Inequality: The Deepening Social Crisis in America*, London, Routledge, 1996, pp. 59–73.
5   P. Hayward, 'Industrial Light and Magic – Style, Technology and Special Effects in the Music Video and Music Television', in P. Hayward (ed.), *Culture, Technology and Creativity in the Late Twentieth Century*, London, John Libbey and Company, 1990.
6   A. Toffler, *The Third Wave*, London, Collins, 1980.

Chapter 1

Digitisation and war

This chapter examines the ways in which multimedia technologies evolved from the needs of the military to produce more accurate weapons and gain intelligence advantages over opponents. It explores the role of multimedia technology in the development of simulators for training and strategic and tactical planning as well as the military rationale for the development of networks.

The military origins of multimedia

Multimedia, in common with all microelectronics-driven technology including the microprocessor and personal computer, is in part a by-product of military research and development (R&D). The key components of today's multimedia, the computer itself, microcircuits, the Internet, two- and three-dimensional imaging, simulation and so on, were originally developed under the auspices of the military. Although the list of military-funded developments that have led to multimedia is long, it is productive to our understanding to explore the actual historical circumstances in which these technologies were devised and developed.

Weapons

The science of ballistics occupies an important place in western scientific thought and is closely connected with the later development of the computer. When the cannon was introduced into Europe in the fourteenth century no one really understood how a cannon ball moved through the air. The first people to think about the problem were soldiers and military engineers such as Roberto Valturio (*c.* 1450–80) who needed to develop practical methods for targeting their weapons accurately, and the first mathematical treatise on ballistics was written by Nicolo Tartaglio in Venice in 1537. However, Tartaglio subsequently burned his notes after becoming conscience-stricken at the thought of slaughtering fellow Christians more efficiently. Yet when Italy came under threat of invasion from the 'infidel' Turks, his Christian scruples were overcome and he reworked his calculations and published the book.[1]

During the sixteenth and seventeenth centuries, such eminent scientists as Leonardo da Vinci, Galileo and Isaac Newton also turned their minds to the problem of ballistics. For Galileo these investigations led to speculation about the motions of the planets which led him into conflict with the Church.[2] In England Sir Isaac Newton went on to refine Galileo's ideas and developed the differential calculus to calculate the motion of the planets around the sun. It was this work which was to provide the mathematical tools by which the motions of all moving bodies could be calculated. However, the lack of standardised manufacture of either cannon or cannon balls, and the difficulty of allowing for the vagaries of the wind, meant that these theories were not of much practical use. It was not until the twentieth century, with the development of rifling and other improvements to ordinance, that artillery became more accurate. It then became practical to use the differential calculus to calculate the trajectories of projectiles.

By the time of the Second World War, ballistic tables could be calculated for any given explosive charge, size of projectile and angle of gun elevation by teams of human 'computers' applying the differential calculus. Their collective results were collated and then printed out to be used by gunners on the battlefield. However, this was an extremely slow and labour intensive operation, and mistakes were frequent. It became obvious that mechanisation would improve the process in terms of cost, speed and accuracy.

There had been attempts in the nineteenth century to mechanise the calculation and typesetting of mathematical tables – most notably astronomical tables for navigation. In the 1830s Charles Babbage (1791–1871) designed such a machine with funding from the British Government. However, his Difference Engine could not be built in his day because of the inability of manufacturing to the necessary precision. Babbage's claim to be

FIGURE 1.1 Charles Babbage's uncompleted Analytical Engine, designed in 1840
Courtesy of the Science Museum/Science and Society Picture Library

the father of the computer rests in fact on another unbuilt machine, the Analytical Engine, which was capable of mechanising any conceivable mathematical problem.[3]

In the US in the 1930s Vannevar Bush, Director of F. D. Roosevelt's Office of Scientific Research and Development, designed the differential analyser, an analogue calculus computer, to produce artillery range tables, but this proved to be frustratingly slow.[4] So even by the 1940s, artillery tables were still being calculated by organised teams of human computers working with desk calculators.[5] Meanwhile, weapons were being developed faster than their performances could be computed.[6]

Yet the development of new weapons, particularly anti-aircraft weapons and the atomic bomb, made faster techniques of calculation a matter of urgency. The answer was seen to lie in electronic digital computers rather than analogue ones. By the end of the Second World War both the US Navy and the US Army had digital computers for calculating ballistics tables. One such computer was the US Navy's Harvard–IBM Automatic Sequence Controlled Calculator, later known as the Mark I. The Mark I was not a completely electronic computer since it had moving parts in the form of 3,304 electromechanical relays which acted as on-off switches.

The first fully electronic computer designed to calculate artillery range tables was the US Army's Electrical Numerical Integrator and Calculator machine (ENIAC). ENIAC's task 'was to simulate the trajectories of shells through varying conditions of air resistance and wind velocity, which involved the summation of thousands of little pieces of trajectory'.[7] ENIAC made use of an unprecedented 19,000 electronic valves, and although it did not become operational before the Second World War ended, it demonstrated the feasibility of working with such a large number of electronic switches.

The ballistic problems involved in shooting down aircraft provided another example of the impetus that military needs gave to the development of the computer. Control systems were developed for anti-aircraft guns and missiles during the Second World War which made use of feedback to adapt the trajectory of the missile to changes in the path of the moving target.

An added impetus to the development of computers by the US military was the 'Manhattan Project' to develop the atomic bomb. The atomic bomb utilises the energy released when the nucleus of an atom of fissile material such as uranium is split. This releases neutrons which then split the nuclei of adjacent atoms and the process continues to repeat itself. This chain reaction proceeds with such speed that the number of neutrons doubles every 10 billionths of a second, and the entire reaction may be completed in just a few billionths of a second. The result is the production of energy millions of times greater than the initial reaction that started the chain. This chain reaction only starts when the fissile material reaches a 'critical mass'. The designers of the first atomic bomb achieved this by compressing the fissile material by means of a chemical explosion which created a symmetrical shock wave known as an 'implosion lens'. However, in order for the shock wave to be the right shape, precise calculations were required which stretched the capabilities of human computers working with mechanical desk calculators. It was in order to do these calculations that the military turned to electronic computers.[8]

These developments continued with increased vigour after the Second World War as tension between the United States and the Soviet Union led to the Cold War, the arms race and the space race. The computer made possible the hydrogen bomb, the intercontinental ballistic missile, multiple guidable warheads, precision guided cruise missiles, the 'Star Wars' strategic defence system, the 'Stealth' bomber and all the other 'Baroque' features of the arms race (as Mary Kaldor describes in her book *The Baroque Arsenal*).[9] As George A. Keyworth II, President Reagan's Chief Science Advisor testifying at US Congressional Hearings on the 'Star Wars' strategic defence system, pointed out:

It has been the incredible leaps in data processing, as much as any single area which has fuelled this explosion. . . . The very existence of today's and tomorrow's ability to solve complex problems on incredibly small machines, and fast has opened up the development of our entire national technical base. . . . It was data processing which overcame John von Neuman's scepticism of ever making the ICBM[10] work in the first place. It was data processing at the heart of MIRVing.[11] It was data processing which has provided the ICBM accuracy necessary for pre-emptive strikes. And it is data processing which will be at the heart of any defence against ballistic missiles.[12]

It was the work undertaken on these computers for the purpose of making more deadly ordinance that laid the foundations for the computing science upon which all modern digital media are based, but the crucial development which led to today's multimedia was the microchip.

Microelectronics

One particular concern of the US military in the post-war period was the need to stay ahead of the Soviet Union in the development of thermonuclear intercontinental ballistic missiles (ICBMs). The aim was to ensure that the US would always be able to retaliate with deadly reliability and accuracy against any nuclear assault from the USSR. The US was perceived to have a disadvantage in that the power of its rockets was less than that of the Soviet Union's. The Soviets excelled in solid fuel technology, which could launch larger payloads, whereas US expertise lay in less powerful liquid fuel propulsion. The Soviet ability to launch missiles with larger and more sophisticated computer guidance systems fuelled the US drive for smaller yet powerful on-board computer guidance equipment. The answer to perceived Soviet superiority was to miniaturise the components for the computers which controlled the navigation and guidance of the missiles. This would also make them process data more quickly.

The invention in 1948 of the transistor by Bardeen, Shockley and Brattain demonstrated that the hot fragile vacuum tubes which had powered the ENIAC could be substituted by a smaller, faster and more robust component. The US military financed the development of integrated circuits which embedded many thousands of transistors onto a slice of silicon. In the early 1970s, three engineers from the Santa Clara Valley electronics company Intel produced a 'microprocessor', the equivalent of a computer CPU (central processing unit), on a single chip of silicon. By the mid-1980s integrated circuits made with the most advanced technology could carry as many as a million individual transistors, each only a few microns on a side. (A micron is a thousandth of a millimetre, or 0.00004 inch.) It was this development more than any other which made possible the rapid advances in computer technology since the 1970s. In particular the microchip made possible the mass production of computing power without which the creation of a consumer market in digital multimedia would have been inconceivable.

Interface

By the 1950s the problem facing military intelligence was that the masses of data that electronic instruments produced created an 'information overload'. The general problem of information overload had been recognised as early as the 1930s by Vannevar Bush, Director of F. D. Roosevelt's Office of Scientific Research and Development, which was responsible for directing the scientific aspects of the US war effort.

Described as a 'visionary technocrat',[13] Bush came from an American tradition of rational administration dating back to the early nineteenth century. He was worried that the very growth in scientific knowledge, as represented by published books and articles, was making it more difficult to utilise the information available, claiming that: 'The summation of human experience is being extended at a prodigious rate, and the means we use for threading through the consequent maze to the momentarily important item is the same as was used in the days of square rigged ships.'[14]

Bush was concerned that library cataloguing systems made it difficult for a researcher to retrieve information in a way that would allow him or her to follow common ideas through several publications. He believed that classification systems should be based on the way the brain works, which he perceived to be by association, stating that: 'Man cannot hope fully to duplicate this mental process artificially, but . . . [S]election by association rather than by indexing, may yet be mechanised.'[15]

Bush had formulated his ideas by 1934, and eventually published them in 1945 in *Atlantic Weekly*, in an article titled 'As We May Think'.[16] Here he described a machine which he called the Memex. The Memex (memory expander) was meant to be built into a desk at which the user would sit. Images from microfilm inside the desk could be projected onto a pair of screens on the top of the desk. The user could classify material as it came in front of him or her. Once classified, individual microfilm frames could be rapidly searched using an electrically-powered optical recognition system. A major innovation was that Bush devised a system by which the person using the Memex could register links between different pieces of information. These links could be named and added to, giving the possibility of recalling a whole 'trail' of associated articles at a later date. The user could add annotations by writing with a stylus on a photosensitive screen. Bush even contemplated the use of a voice recognition system.[17]

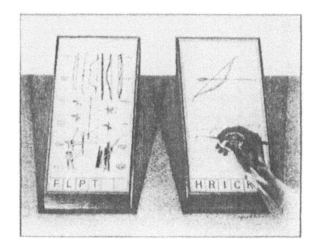

FIGURE 1.2   Memex screens. Images could be projected on to these twin desk-top screens which anticipate the windows of modern graphical user interfaces
Source: Life 19 (11), p. 124

A number of researchers working on problems of information management for the US military were greatly influenced by Bush's ideas. One such researcher was Douglas Engelbart working at the Stanford Research Laboratories in California. Engelbart's report titled *Program On Human Effectiveness*, for the US Air Force's Office of Scientific Research, drew heavily on Bush's ideas. Engelbart's aim was, as he wrote in correspondence with Bush, 'to increase significantly the effectiveness of human problem solvers by augmenting abstract symbol manipulation'.[18]

Like Bush, Engelbart believed that the way to amplify human intellectual capabilities was by means of a mechanised associative classification system that allows 'non-sequential writing – text that branches and allows choice to the reader, best read at an interactive screen'.[19] The type of information management system that Engelbart developed from Bush's ideas has since come to be known as 'hypertext', a term first coined by Ted Nelson in his 1965 paper, 'A File Structure for the Complex, the Changing and the Indeterminate'.[20] Hypertext systems were first used by the US military for the management of information. For example, in 1982 the nuclear-powered aircraft carrier *USS Carl Vinson* had its data-management system and maintenance manuals installed on a hypertext system named ZOG, developed at Carnegie-Mellon University in 1972.[21]

As we shall see, the concept of hypertext (and its elaboration into hypermedia) has been crucial to the development of interactive digital multimedia. Hypertext was arguably the inspiration behind the first multimedia applications including Apple's HyperCard and the first web browser, Mosaic (the forerunner of Netscape's Navigator and Microsoft's Internet Explorer).

These were the 'killer' applications which helped to establish the Internet as a consumer medium.

Battle control

On the battlefield the individual fighter or commander needs to make decisions quickly. This applies at both the tactical and strategic level. In the 1950s the US military built the North American Air Defence System (NORAD), a ring of radar stations deployed to give early warning of Soviet nuclear bombers and missiles coming over the North Pole. The commanders of NORAD needed to have information instantly and, more important, in a form which could be interpreted quickly.

This led the US Air Force to research into video displays. Visual displays for radar had been used during the Second World War. These, however, were rudimentary oscilloscopes which simply showed the time when the radar pulse was sent and when it was received back after bouncing off an aircraft. Much more information was needed to be displayed on the NORAD screens. As De Landa points out:

> Making data patterns emerge was the initial motivation behind the military and intelligence development of computer displays. It was useless to have large banks of information if access to that data was slow and cumbersome.[22]

At the same time, there existed a parallel problem connected with how humans should interact with computers. In the 1950s and 1960s the main method of inputting information and getting it out again was 'batch processing'. The large expensive computers of the 1950s were regarded by their owners as capital which needed to be worked to their fullest extent and so an industrial mode of using them developed which precluded any one person monopolising the computer.

Information was input from punched cards that were collected into batches which then had to be entered into the computer by teams of computer technicians – a priesthood of people who had exclusive access to the computer. One of the characteristics of batch-processing was that errors only became apparent after the program had been executed and reams of print-out delivered to one's desk. Typically these errors were the result of a typing mistake – the omission of a space or period for example. This resulted in much frustration and inefficiency, and these methods were seen as inappropriate for the military's needs.

In 1958 the United States Department of Defence established the Advanced Research Projects Agency (ARPA) to fund research at civilian research centres. One of the main objectives of the new agency was to look for alternatives to batch-processing. Among the fruits of this research were time-sharing and graphical interfaces. Time-sharing, as the name implies, allows many users, sitting at individual terminals, to share a computer's time.

Recognising that computers can execute commands at enormously faster speeds than any one human user can enter them, researchers were able to design a system whereby one central computer simulates many small computers. This allowed each individual user to interact directly with the computer and have the experience of having the machine to themselves. Time-sharing allowed the individual operator to interact with the computer in 'real-time', without the delays entailed by batch-processing. The first interactive visual interfaces for a computer were used for NORAD which used light-pens and joy-sticks for input.

In the development of graphical interactive computer interfaces there are two pioneers who stand out: Douglas Engelbart and Ivan Sutherland. As early as the 1950s Engelbart had recognised that a computer screen could not only display the computer's output, but could also be used as a means of input. Thanks to his radar experience during the war, Engelbart realised that the computer display had become the surface of contact between humans and machines. As De Landa comments:

> Now the screen had to be transformed into a tool allowing users not only to display data but to control the machine. The future of interactivity would depend on the events that took place at the surface of contact: the computer screen could be turned into a new way of enslaving people (allowing the machine to pace and discipline the user) or transformed into a means to augment man's intellect . . . [h]e aimed at transforming the computer display into a surface of contact between humans.[23]

The development of the interactive visual interface was advanced further by the work of Ivan Sutherland, regarded by many as the 'father of computer graphics' for his role in devising many of the techniques which now form the basis of computer graphics.[24] The light-pen used by the US Air Force for its early warning systems was based on an interactive computer system called Sketchpad which Sutherland developed at the Massachusetts Institute of Technology (MIT) in 1962. During the 1960s General Motors had used a system similar to Sketchpad to design car bodies.[25] Such systems were to form the technological basis of the computer aided design (CAD) industry – one of the first commercial applications of the 'microchip revolution'.[26] The techniques pioneered by Sutherland in Sketchpad were also to lead to painting applications such as the Quantel Paintbox and Adobe's Photoshop which have been the mainstays of the multimedia graphic production industry.

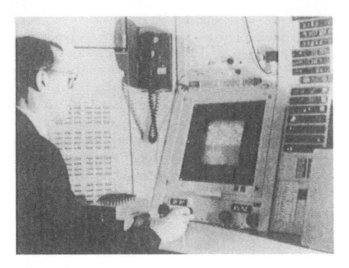

FIGURE 1.3   Sketchpad, Sutherland's innovative graphical user interface (GUI), built in 1962
Courtesy of the MIT Museum, Cambridge, Mass.

Simulation

A pressing need of the military was to find effective ways of training personnel in the use of sophisticated weaponry. This was particularly the case when it came to aircraft, which by the 1960s had become complex and expensive. This was not a new issue as the first flight simulator had been patented in 1910, and by the 1930s the American Link Corporation was producing trainers in quantity.[27] These early flight trainers could simulate the motion of an aircraft by mechanical means, but they could not reproduce the view from the pilot's cockpit. By the 1950s it was possible to do this by having the pilot's actions control the movement of a small television camera as it moved over a scale model of a landscape. Sutherland knew that computers could be used to generate such images, and he had already created simulations of aircraft landing on carriers. As Pimentel and Teixeira explain:

> Instead of constructing scale models from paint, foam and glue, the computer constructed images using stored data. Any 3-d object could be digitised and entered into the computer. For example, an airport could be represented as a large number of 3-d points with lines connecting each point. After a series of calculations, a view from any vantage point could be constructed.[28]

The technologies that permit a user of these systems to apparently move through a coherent simulated environment make use of intellectual tools that have been known for many hundreds of years. These are scientific linear perspective and the Cartesian coordinate system. Systematic techniques to create illusions of reality date back to ancient Greece. Classical painters created the illusion of depth by means of geometrical rules, and the Florentine architect Fillipo Brunelleschi (1377–1446) is credited with having rediscovered these laws of scientific linear perspective.

Descartes in his treatise *La Géométrie* demonstrated how geometrical theorems could be expressed in an algebraic form using what we now call the Cartesian coordinate system. Descartes' great insight gave scientists a mathematical language with which to describe the movement of objects through space. The Cartesian coordinate system allows any object in space to be described in terms of three numbers corresponding to a distance from a common origin. It is this same conversion of space into numbers that allows computers to simulate real and imaginary scenes and display them to a viewer.

Commercial organisations were not slow to see the potential of Sutherland's work and by 1963 computer-generated wire frame animations were being produced by Bell Laboratories.[29] In 1968 Sutherland together with David Evans established a company to sell the first computerised scene generators, and the first flight simulator to make use of these computerised techniques was built for the US Navy in 1972 by the General Electric Company (GEC).[30] Meanwhile the US Army had been funding the virtualisation of Aspen, Colorado since the 1970s. This demonstrated the potential role of simulation to provide functional familiarity with a foreign city through computer-orchestrated 'walk-through' techniques, especially useful in training US invasion forces.[31]

This work on simulation and 'interfacing' was to form the basis of subsequent research and development to create 'virtual reality' machines in which the user may interact with a computer-generated environment as if it were everyday 'real' space and time.

Military intelligence

Apart from the enhancement of weapons, the other important reason for the development of computers by the military was the need for intelligence about the enemy. Both the US and the Soviet Union had entered the Second World War after they had been the victims of surprise attacks by Japan and Germany respectively. This experience had affected their behaviour during the period of the Cold War balance of terror. Both countries began to devote huge resources to the computerisation of intelligence gathering and in particular to the decipherment of the enemy's coded radio transmissions.

The use of electronic computers to break codes was pioneered during the Second World War at the British Government's Code and Cypher School at Bletchley Park, Buckinghamshire. The main problem had been to crack German military codes quickly enough to provide operationally useful data. The Germans used a machine called Enigma which employed a system of rotors and electrical wiring to encode messages prior to transmission. Bletchley Park's solution to the problem was to construct an all-digital electronic computer called Colossus which used 1,500 electronic valves, making it much faster than previous machines which incorporated mechanical elements.[32] However, of as much importance as Colossus was the abstract principle on which it operated. This was based on the ideas of the mathematician Alan Turing, one of the leading figures at Bletchley Park. In his 1936 paper entitled 'On Computable Numbers', Turing had described an abstract general model for a logical machine, which has subsequently become known as the 'Turing Machine'.[33] This machine could calculate any problem capable of mathematical formulation and also simulate all other computing machines.[34]

After the war these efforts continued with renewed vigour under the auspices of the National Security Agency (NSA) in the US and the General Communications Headquarters (GCHQ) in the UK, and the most powerful computers continue to be those used for decipherment by the state security services. As De Landa points out,

> military computers evolved following two different sets of pressures. Their components had to become smaller to allow the development of navigation and guidance systems for missiles, and they had to become faster to join the number crunching race in which cryptological devices were locked.[35]

Image analysis

Another aspect of military intelligence which has particular relevance for the development of multimedia technologies is photo reconnaissance and analysis. Photo reconnaissance had been widely used in both the First and Second World Wars. In the Cold War period, with the threat of nuclear weapons raining out of the sky with little warning, the need for accurate intelligence about the enemy's dispositions and intentions became imperative.

Computer analysis of aerial and satellite photos was developed in the US during the 1970s under the auspices of the National Photographic Interpretation Centre (NPIC). As De Landa puts it:

> The imaging apparatus of overhead reconnaissance entered a new era when images ceased to be simple replicas of their objects, and began to be treated as pure data, graphic information on which the full simulation capabilities of the Turing machine could be brought to bear. ... [D]ifferent forms of image degradation could now be corrected

through the use of computers . . . by simulating the conditions under which its information was degraded.[36]

As with the decipherment of codes, the main reason for wanting to mechanise the process of image analysis was to ensure that relevant information could be made available to commanders in enough time to make a difference on the battlefield. Efforts were made to develop technologies which would incorporate the accumulated knowledge of human photo-analysts into the computer – to endow the machine with a degree of artificial intelligence (AI). With the image converted to digital form, the individual picture elements (pixels) which make up the image could be analysed by applying special algorithms.[37] Edge detection algorithms were used to detect discontinuities in the intensity of groups of pixels in order to establish boundaries between features. Region-growing or splitting algorithms grouped clusters of pixels with similar optical properties (for example, colour hue and intensity) and then 'grew' them by applying certain statistical measures to neighbouring pixels.[38] Since the enemy's military equipment is measurable in terms of numerically quantifiable features or 'signatures', such as the ratio between a tank's length and width or the characteristic shadow of a particular fighter, these features can be programmed into the computer's memory. Where the human photo-analyst makes use of his or her experience to interpret fuzzy images, the machine photo-analyst 'tries' to match patterns programmed into its memory with the patterns of pixels which make up the image. The program then calculates the probability that a particular image represents a given object. As De Landa explains in more detail:

> Once an image has been broken down into areas bounded by common edges, an effort is made to fit these shapes into 3-D templates. These include not only explicit geometric representations of objects (like flight simulators), but also knowledge regarding the ways in which objects project into flat images: knowledge regarding the depth cues that may be derived from texture and illumination, relational models depicting the possible combinations in space and so on.[39]

These capabilities are now a common feature of commercial paint packages such as Adobe Photoshop which permit the user to manipulate existing images, for example by changing colours or by adding, rearranging or removing elements.

Networks

We have already seen how time-sharing allowed many people to use a single computer at the same time, each sitting at their own terminal. In fact, the terminal connected to the computer did not have to be near to it; it could be at the end of a corridor or at the end of a telephone. It was then recognised that a computer with links to many users could be used as a medium through which these users could communicate with each other. This was seen as a means of encouraging co-operation between geographically separated teams working in similar defence research areas. The Advanced Research Projects Agency (ARPA) under its first director, J. C. R. Licklider, actively promoted time-sharing and interactive computing, and in 1969 the Advanced Research Programs Agency Network (ARPANET) was established to enable academics working on ARPA-funded projects to share their findings.

With the advent of the ICBM (intercontinental ballistic missile), the US military became concerned that their communications systems could be disabled by a nuclear first strike. The design of ARPANET was based on the principle,

> that the strongest communication system would be a distributed network of computers having several properties: it would have sufficient redundancy so that the loss of subsets and nodes would not isolate any of the still-functioning nodes; there would be no central control and each node would contain routing information and could automatically reconfigure this information in a short time after the loss of a link or a node.[40]

ARPANET was based on work undertaken by Paul Baran of the Rand Corporation, funded from a grant by the US Air Force. Baran's answer to the problem of the survivability of the network was packet switching, a technology which is now an essential feature of computer networks.

Packet switching works by splitting data up into small packages. Each packet is addressed and carries information about its sequence in the total message. The packet is routed by packet-switching exchanges which dispatch the packets according to the state of other data traffic. By this method the fragments are sent by many routes to their final destination where they are reassembled into the original message. In this way the system can self-organise. The organisation comes from the messages themselves, 'which contain enough "local intelligence" to find their own destination without the need of centralised traffic control'.[41]

As we shall see in Chapter 5, ARPANET was to form the technical basis of the Internet which is seen by many as a crucial element in the development of multimedia into the twenty-first century.

Conclusion

It is impossible to understate the significance of military expenditure in laying the foundations of today's multimedia industries. None of the technologies that make multimedia possible – fast powerful computers, imaging and simulation techniques – would exist today had it not been for the Cold War and the space race. But in Chapter 2 we shall see how, as well as this military research and development, there is another side to the genesis of multimedia. The history of multimedia involved another partner crucial to its further development, popularisation and commercial penetration: the American 'counter-culture' of the 1960s and 1970s.

Notes

1 J.D. Bernal, *The Extension of Man*, St Albans, Paladin, 1973.
2 Ibid., p. 179.
3 A. Hodges, *Alan Turing: The Enigma of Intelligence*, London, Counterpoint, 1983, p. 297.
4 M. De Landa, *War in the Age of Intelligent Machines*, New York, MIT Press, 1991, p. 36.
5 Hodges, op. cit., p. 300.
6 C. Evans, *The Mighty Micro*, Oxford, OUP, 1983.
7 Hodges, op. cit., p. 301.
8 Ibid., p. 300.
9 M. Kaldor, *The Baroque Arsenal*, London, Abacus, 1982.
10 Intercontinental ballistic missile.
11 Multiple Independently Targeted Re-entry Vehicles.
12 Cited in V. Mosco and J. Washo (eds), *The Political Economy of Information*, Madison, University of Wisconsin Press, 1988, p. 14.
13 De Landa, op. cit., p. 119.
14 V. Bush, 'As We May Think', *The Atlantic Monthly*, July 1945, reprinted in T. Nelson, *Literary Machines*, Sausalito, California, Mindful Press, 1983, p. 1/40.
15 T. Nelson, *Literary Machines*, Sausalito, California, Mindful Press, 1983, p. 1/50.
16 Reprinted in ibid., pp. 1/39–1/54.
17 J.M. Nyce and P. Kahn, *From Memex to Hypertext*, Boston, Academic Press, 1991.
18 Ibid., p. 237.
19 Nelson, op. cit., p. 0/2.
20 Ibid., Preface to 1992 edition, unnumbered page.
21 P. De Bra, *Hypertext Systems*, Eindhoven University of Technology Website. Available on-line at http://wwwis.win.tue.nl/2L670/static/zog.html (4 May 1998).
22 De Landa, op. cit., p. 220.
23 Ibid., p. 216.
24 K. Pimentel and K. Teixera, *Virtual Reality Through the New Looking Glass*, Pennsylvania, McGraw Hill, 1993, p. 32.
25 A. Darley, 'Abstraction to Simulation' in P. Hayward (ed.), *Culture Technology and Creativity in the Late Twentieth Century*, London, John Libbey, 1990, p. 42.
26 Pimentel and Teixeira, op. cit., p. 33.
27 B. Wooley, *Virtual Worlds: A Journey in Hype and Hyperreality*, Oxford, Blackwell, 1992, p. 42.

28 Pimentel and Teixeira, op. cit., p. 35.
29 Darley, op. cit., p. 42.
30 Pimentel and Teixeira, op. cit., p. 35.
31 Ibid.
32 Hodges, op. cit., p. 268.
33 Turing conceived the machine firstly as a long tape divided into squares which could either be blank or contain a symbol, secondly as a scanner which would scan one square at a time and either read, write or erase the contents and thirdly as a set of instructions or program. The machine was capable of four steps: move the tape one square to the left or right, alter the symbol in the square or stop. Turing demonstrated that by including the instructions on the tape any calculation could be executed. Ibid., pp. 96–99.
34 Ibid.
35 De Landa, op. cit., p. 214.
36 Ibid., p. 262.
37 An algorithm is a procedure or set of instructions for solving a particular problem on a Turing Machine.
38 De Landa, op. cit., p. 262.
39 Ibid., p. 202.
40 Ibid., p. 120.
41 Ibid., p. 120.

Chapter 2

The computer counter-culture

The personal computer revolutionaries were the counter-culture
... Apple cofounder Steve Jobs had traveled to India in search of
enlightenment; Lotus 1-2-3[1] designer Mitch Kapor had been a
transcendental meditation teacher. They were five to ten years
younger than the hippies but they came out of the zeitgeist of the
1960s, and embraced many of the ideas of personal liberation and
iconoclasm championed by their older brothers and sisters. The
PC was to them the talisman of a new kind of war of liberation:
When he hired him from Pepsi, Steve Jobs challenged John
Sculley, 'do you want to sell sugared water to adolescents or do
you want to change the world'.[2]

Introduction

In the previous chapter it was argued that multimedia could not have existed
in its present form without the technological developments prompted by the
arms and space races of the Cold War. However, multimedia is more than just
a set of technologies for communicating images and sound. It is an idea that
also plays an important part in current political and cultural discourses: the
multimedia computer as a revolutionary artefact with the potential to change
the course of human history. This chapter will identify the origins of some

aspects of these discourses in the social revolt among middle-class young people in the US during the 1960s and 1970s that has come to be known as the 'counter-culture'. It is argued that to fully appreciate multimedia as a cultural phenomenon, rather than simply as a technological one, requires an examination of the issues that concerned the counter-culture in the 1960s and 1970s.

Counter-culture influences on current discourses are of two main kinds. These approximate firstly to the political and secondly to the cultural 'wings' of the counter-culture. The political wing was known as the New Left. Members of this group believed that cheap computing power in the hands of citizens could be a powerful resource for democracy and a weapon against overbearing government and big business. For the cultural wing of the movement (originally the 'hippies', but now fragmented into a variety of 'New Age' persuasions), the multimedia computer's capacity to both provide windows to artificial realities and link the world into a 'global village' prefigured a new stage in the evolution of human consciousness.

Counter-culture

The term 'counter-culture' was first used by Theodore Roszak in his book *The Making of a Counter Culture* (subtitled *Reflections on the Technocratic Society and its Youthful Opposition*).[3] The counter-culture as a social 'movement' began in California in the 1960s and flowered worldwide in the late 1960s and early 1970s. Roszak characterised the counter-culture as a revolt against technocratic society, identifying influences as diverse as the anti-industrialism of the nineteenth-century Romantic movement, the spiritual values of Zen Buddhism and the 'beat' writers of the 1950s such as Alan Ginsberg and Jack Kerouac. The issues it was concerned with 'stemmed from a dissenting sensibility as old as the lament that the Romantic poets had once raised against the Dark Satanic Mills'.[4]

The counter-culture had both political and cultural aspects. The cultural revolt stressed the need for a new consciousness and its participants were the hippies. This cultural wing rejected traditional family relations in favour of communal ways of life. They were also advocates of psychedelic drugs and various forms of mysticism as a means of attaining higher forms of consciousness. The political wing of the counter-culture, the New Left, was strongly influenced by Marxist and anarchist philosophies. Groups such as Students for a Democratic Society (SDS) pursued the ideal of participatory democracy and led protest demonstrations in support of the civil rights movement and against the Vietnam War.

In fact, what unified the movement and gave it much of its energy during the 1960s was its opposition to the Vietnam War. But the war was not the only political concern of the counter-culture: civil rights, racism and environmental issues also motivated political action. But most significantly the counter-culture represented a profound challenge to the materialistic world view of 'straight' culture. This was manifested, on the one hand, in a denial of the arid, instrumental values of the technocratic state, and on the other, in an affirmation of humanistic and holistic values. In considering the role of counter-culture in the evolution of multimedia discourses one cannot help but be struck by the irony that the computer, the highest achievement of technocratic and militaristic strivings, should become an icon for a movement which opposed those self-same values.

In the 1960s and 1970s the vanguard of the computer revolution consisted of young men and women imbued with counter-culture values who, recognising that microcomputer technology would eventually make unprecedented computing power accessible at low cost, wanted to create 'insanely great'[5] machines. They saw computers as tools that might both aid the fight for social justice and trigger a spiritual renaissance that would sweep away the technocratic state.

At the same time the high-tech economic boom generated by military spending and the space race was concentrated mainly in the Bay area around San Francisco (Silicon Valley) which also happened to be the birthplace and main centre of gravity of the counter-culture. It was therefore not surprising that many computer students and workers should hold counter-culture values. Two not mutually exclusive principles can be discerned within the counter-culture tendencies: one was concerned with political justice and the other with augmenting and extending human intellectual and spiritual potential. Both of these tendencies have had a major influence on the development of multimedia.

Computing for the people

It might be thought that the counter-culture would have totally rejected the computer as a symbol of the technocratic society it disdained. Many in the movement regarded technology as a means of repression by the state and big business, a 'fetter of liberation' in the words of the influential New Left philosopher, Herbert Marcuse.[6] However, for others technology represented a means of empowering the individual to take on the state and big business. This attitude towards technology has roots in the American radical tradition that had always been interested in machines and systems that would empower people and encourage a self-reliant citizenry. In this tradition many in the counter-culture espoused what Murray Bookchin described as 'liberatory technology'[7] and what Ivan Illich called 'tools for conviviality'.[8] This ambivalence towards technology has been noted by Bruce Sterling:

The counter culture of the 1960s was rural, romanticised, anti-science, anti-tech. But there was always a lurking contradiction at its heart, symbolised by the electric guitar. Rock music was the thin end of the wedge.[9]

Many of those who both identified with counter-culture values and were familiar with the potential of computers were aware that computing could also be used as a human-centred, or 'soft' technology which could support the communal styles of living espoused by many in the movement. Thus David Dickson in his influential 1974 book *Alternative Technology* discusses how the activities of decentralised 'relatively autonomous and self-sustaining communities' could be co-ordinated through a complex computer.[10]

This view of technology as potentially liberating was reflected by Ted Nelson, a leading counter-culture figure, and the inventor of the term 'hypertext', when he proclaimed in 1974 in his counter-culture computer text *Computer Lib/Dream Machines* that, 'You can and must learn about computers now'.[11] This counter-culture perspective was also expressed by the *People's Computer Company* (PCC), the first 'popular' computing magazine which stated on the cover of its first issue in 1972: 'Computers are mostly used against people instead of for people, used to control people instead of to free them. Time to change all that – we need a . . . people's computer company.'[12] Part and parcel of this notion of democratic independence was the general 'do-it-yourself' survivalism aimed at encouraging a self-reliant citizenry. This was represented perhaps most comprehensively by the *Whole Earth Catalog*, published first in 1968 in Sausalito, California by founder-editor Stewart Brand.

The Whole Earth Catalog, which Brand edited and published between 1968 and 1971, was a counter-culture compendium of 'appropriate' technology and

FIGURE 2.1 The photograph of Ted Nelson seen on his website
Source: http://www.sfc.keio.ac.jp/~ted/TedPicPermish.html, reproduced by permission of Ted Nelson

alternative techniques, and was a commercial success.[13] It was inspired by the systems philosophy of the unorthodox, but internationally respected, American engineer Buckminster Fuller (1895–1983). Fuller's work combined the pragmatic, hard-headed approach of the engineer with a commitment to a holistic view of the universe which was very much in harmony with counter-culture philosophy. In his essays and lectures Fuller argued for a technology which would harness human ingenuity to create a sustainable and convivial future for the species:

> We now know scientifically that for the first time in history there can be enough to support continually all of expanding humanity at previously undreamed-of and ever-advancing standards of living and intellectual satisfaction in effective participation in the evolutionary processes.[14]

Symbolic of the resonance of Fuller's ideas with counter-culture values was his best known and most widely used invention: the geodesic dome that became a movement icon.[15]

Roszak identifies in publications such as *The Whole Earth Catalog* and *Rolling Stone* a synthesis of traditional 'reversionary', i.e. bucolic, and 'technophile' versions of utopia with high-tech science-fiction versions. In this vision the computer would,

> undergird a new Jeffersonian democracy based, not upon equal distribution of land, but upon equal access to information: . . . the new technology would be contained within an organic and communitarian political context, just as would be geodesic dome technology, electronic music production and soft drug technology.[16]

Computer activism

It was against this background that some counter-culture activists began to see the computer as a potential technology of liberation. According to one such activist, Lee Felsenstein, the movement was motivated by the failure of the 1960s 'underground press' and community broadcasting movement to challenge mainstream media and, as he put it, 'serve the cause of decentralisation in society'.[17] Another activist who helped to create the 'counter-computing' movement was Pam Hart. Hart, disillusioned with her job as a programmer at Berkeley, 'dropped-out' to devote her skills to the anti-war movement, and recounts that: 'during the Cambodia invasion demonstrations in Berkeley a group of us got together and designed a retrieval program for co-ordinating all of the actions on campus'.[18] Eventually Hart got together with Felsenstein and others to set up a community resource based on a surplus second-generation computer, the mainframe XDS 940, donated by the private company, Transamerica. The group described itself as comprising those 'who believe that technological tools can be tools of social change when controlled by the people'.[19]

The project, dubbed 'Resource One', provided computer services to other non-profit organisations working for social change. Resource One was one of the very few public computer centres in the US – a non-profit corporation, devoted to charitable and educational uses of data-processing technology.

By 1974 the Resource One founders, in order to give the community more access to computers, began putting terminals in stores and libraries. The new system was designed as a bulletin board and was called the Community Memory Project (CMP).[20] The aim was to build an electronic public space, which Felsenstein referred to by the ancient Greek name for assembly: the agora. In the electronic agora human relationships, suppressed and alienated by the centralised mass media, could be once again revived. In a description reminiscent of much 1990s rhetoric about the Internet, another of the project's workers commended its potential as a 'radical social artefact':

> Community Memory . . . is convivial and participatory. Such a system represents a precise antithesis to the dominant uses both of electronic communications media, which broadcast centrally-determined messages to mass passive audiences; and of cybernetic technology, which involves centralized processing of and control over data drawn from or furnished to direct and indirect users.[21]

CMP was built as a communal resource, an arrangement that was appropriate both ideologically and technically, because it was based on terminals connected to a mainframe computer.

With the development of the personal computer (PC) it seemed that hopes for the widespread manifestation of this particular 1960s vision of social interactive computing would be eroded. However, there were still many who kept the dream going. In 1978 a bulletin board system (BBS) was opened in Chicago[22] and, although the original Community Memory Project was turned off in January 1975, it was subsequently revived and technically enhanced by a number of the original founders during the 1980s.[23]

One of the most successful endeavours to keep the dream of the electronic agora alive was instituted by the founder of *The Whole Earth Catalog*, Stewart Brand, with the establishment of the WELL (Whole Earth 'Lectric Link) in 1985. Brand and his collaborator, Larry Brilliant, were both heavily involved in many of the more controversial activities of 1960s counter-culture and hoped that the WELL would become a vehicle for social change through the establishment of a communal 'cyberspace' of virtual communities.[24]

Tools for thinking

Integral to the idea of liberatory technology that inspired the counter-culture was that technology should be easy to use and improve the life of the user. Previously this had meant removing the burden of physical toil. Now with the invention of what Ted Nelson termed 'literary machines',[25] it was the burden of mental toil in categorising and sorting symbols according to systematic procedures that became the problem. For the early pioneers of 'thinking machines' these procedures had mostly been mathematical. The French thinker Blaise Pascal (1623–62) had designed and built a mechanical calculator for his tax collector father in 1645;[26] while Charles Babbage's Difference and Analytical engines were designed to reduce the mental labour of scores of human 'computers' (people who spent all their time working with numbers) calculating navigational tables in the 1820s.[27] However, during the 1960s many people working in the field realised that the computer's ability to produce actual and imaginary audio-visual representations of the real world meant that it could be used as a communication tool as well as a calculating tool. As we saw in Chapter 1 the idea that machines could aid non-mathematical thinking had been discussed by Vannevar Bush in the 1940s. In his 1945 paper, 'As We May Think', Bush saw his Memex machine as augmenting the human mind's natural tendency to work by association – something that traditional systems of pedagogy and research failed to do. These ideas were taken up by Douglas Engelbart and Ted Nelson during the 1950s and 1960s. And as we saw in Chapter 1, Engelbart had speculated whether computers could automate symbol-handling tasks, and thus help people to solve complex problems easily and effectively. Engelbart presented these ideas in a report to the United States Air Force's Office of Scientific Research. In the report he outlined a project to increase significantly the effectiveness of human problem-solvers by augmenting abstract symbol manipulation.[28] Speaking later of his insight Engelbart said,

> When I first heard about computers, I understood, from my radar experience, that if these machines can show you information on punch-cards and printouts on paper, they could write or draw that information on a screen. When I saw the connection between a cathode-ray screen, an information processor, and a medium for representing symbols to a person, it all tumbled together in about a half an hour.[29]

The idea that people could use computers to amplify thought and communication, as tools for intellectual work and social activity, was a very potent one. The development of this style of computing was carried out under the auspices of the US Department of Defence's Advanced Research Projects Agency (ARPA) by unorthodox young programmers influenced by counter-culture notions.[30] However, after 1970 the locus for this work moved from ARPA to the Xerox Corporation and many of the young ARPA researchers moved with it, taking with them their vision of the computer as an instrument for creating a better world.

Xerox PARC

It would not be fanciful to say that the Palo Alto Research Center (PARC) was a key link between military research, counter-culture computer idealism and the emergence of a commercial market in multimedia. By the 1960s the Xerox Corporation was a market leader in the office equipment business by virtue of its patents on the Xerography dry printing process. However, Xerox had become concerned that the advent of cheap business computing would threaten profits in the copier market that it dominated. The obvious course was to diversify into the computer industry and to this end the company set up a research group in Palo Alto near the University of California's Stanford campus.

Even with the move from batch-processing to direct input via a keyboard and screen, computers were still difficult to use. Xerox, like the military, recognised that the key to successfully harnessing the power of the computer was the human–computer interface.

By 1969 as the Vietnam War escalated, the military was becoming a less welcome research sponsor in academia. The passing of the 'Mansfield Amendment' in 1970 by a US Congress keen to curtail 'frivolous research' prevented ARPA from funding projects that were not directly or obviously linked to a specific military objective. The community of computer scientists that had grown up in the 1960s began to break up.[31] Xerox took this opportunity to recruit a number of the key ARPA researchers for PARC.[32]

The main project that PARC worked on was the Alto computer, a machine conceived as a model for the personal computer of the 1980s. Using earlier developments by ARPA, it had a mouse, a high-resolution screen and a keyboard that sat on a desktop. The software team, led by Alan Kay, who had worked with Ivan Sutherland, the 'father of computer graphics' at ARPA, developed the Alto's WIMP (Windows Icons Mouse Pointer) screen environment on a 'bit-mapped' screen that allowed the free interchange of text and graphics. This 'revolutionary' graphics and object-based 'programming environment' was being developed to enhance the creative use of the Alto. Xerox's Learning Research Group based this on what they believed to be the most powerful and natural way possible to communicate with the computer short of ordinary spoken language. Outlining the philosophy behind the design of the Alto's interface the leader of the research team, Bob Taylor, explained that 'People can give commands to a computer much more rapidly and easily by seeing and pointing than by remembering and typing, so we adopted and then adapted the mouse.'[33]

One of the projects that fed into the development of the Alto was Alan Kay's 'Dynabook'[34] (a contraction of Dynamic Book) which included many of the features that reached maturity with the laptops of the 1990s. The Dynabook was intended to be a general purpose electronic *Whole Earth Catalog*. It would have a built-in high-resolution flat screen, a graphical interface that could support animation, input and output devices supporting visual and audio communication paths, and network connections to shared information resources and other Dynabook users. The Dynabook concept epitomised the counter-culture values that pervaded research at Xerox PARC, and which were described by Stewart Brand as, 'soft, away from hugeness and centrality, toward the small and the personal, toward putting maximum computer power in the hands of every individual who wants it (and allowing) you to "fly" formerly unreachable breadths and depths of your information matrix'.[35]

Virtual reality and cyberspace

Popular media discourses about multimedia have tended to stress the power of the computer as a quasi-magical device for empowering its users – a view encapsulated in Microsoft's advertising slogan for its Windows 95 operating system: 'Where are you going today?' These ideas have become crystallised in the concepts of 'cyberspace' and 'virtual reality' which have come to be seen in the popular imagination as symbols of the bright future which information and communications technologies are about to bring us. However 'cyberspace' and 'virtual reality' are in fact constructs which are 'as much figments of a (sub)cultural imagination as they (are) "real" phenomena'.[36] None the less the concepts of 'cyberspace' and 'virtual reality' have had a powerful resonance in popular discourses, involving an enthusiastic hyping of the new media by journalists in the 'old' media. Furthermore, the efforts of computer scientists working for the military to create computer-constructed worlds or 'virtual realities' excited many in the counter-culture who saw this, like psychedelic drugs, as a route to a new consciousness.

Cyberspace, a term that was first used in William Gibson's science-fiction novel *Neuromancer* (see p. 35), refers to the 'data space' of a network of computer systems – the numerical encoding of a real or imaginary Cartesian space. The most significant aspect of cyberspace to users is that it gives them the impression of actually being in a synthetic world rather than simply observing things and events. In current usage the term has also come to be used to describe the 'Internet' – the network of computer networks linked by the telephone system.

Virtual reality refers to the subjective experience of the 'data space' of the computer system when the computer translates numerical co-ordinates into a visual, aural and tactile display. It is the apparent world the user enters while using the system. The essential feature of virtual reality is that it lets the user look around the virtual world by head movements. The user can also move through the virtual world and manipulate virtual objects by the use of devices such as the data glove.

Some commentators, such as computer interface expert Brenda Laurel, see the origins of cyberspace and virtual reality as being rooted in the origins of human culture. Laurel has argued that:

> The notion of Virtual Reality is actually on a continuum that's older than science fiction by a lot. Enactments around pre-historic campfires, Greek theatre, performance rituals of aboriginal peoples the world over have all been aimed at a similar goal, and that is heightened experience through immersive, multi-sensory represen-tations.[37]

Rebecca Coyle, looking at more recent history, traces the origins of virtual reality to a range of entertainment devices designed to create an immersive effect. In the nineteenth century stereoscopes were the most popular method of viewing photographs. Other more recent examples are 1950s 3D movies and Morton Heilig's 1957 Stereoscopic Television Apparatus for Individual Use (STAIU) and Sensorama Simulator dating from 1961.[38]

Hayward argues that the idea of cyberspace technologies and virtual reality have been largely promoted, popularised and constituted by a group of advocates who,

> belong to a specific social group comprising individuals who have clung to residual 'counter-cultural' notions, most often articulated within terms of a loose Green-Libertarian rhetoric, while being assimilated into certain sectors of the American professional classes. This group is most notably represented by the computer industries, the culture of Silicon Valley itself and key generational figures such as Apple founder Steve Job [sic].[39]

Hayward locates the source of popular ideas of cyberspace and virtual reality in science fiction, psychedelia, rock music and New Age mysticism.

Science fiction

The notion of a computer-generated world into which a person could enter had been explored by John Brunner's 1975 sci-fi novel *Shockwave Rider*.[40] The 1982 film *Tron*[41] also featured a computer-generated virtual world that the video-game-playing hero had to enter and compete in.

The term 'cyberspace' was first used in the Canadian science-fiction writer William Gibson's 'cyberpunk' trilogy: *Neuromancer, Count Zero* and *Mona Lisa Overdrive*. Gibson conceives of cyberspace as a vast, three-dimensional electronic environment that spans the globe, consisting of corporate databases, artificial intelligences and all manner of information, both static and dynamic. In *Neuromancer* (1984) Gibson described cyberspace as:

> A conceptual hallucination experienced daily by billions of legitimate operators in every nation . . . a graphic representation of data abstracted from the banks of every computer in the human system. Unthinkable complexity. Lines of light ranged in the nonspace of the mind, clusters and constellations of data. Like city lights receding.[42]

As Hayward has pointed out, Gibson came to be seen as something of a prophetic guru to a computer counter-culture already excited by the work of Ivan Sutherland and others (see Chapter 1) on computer-generated worlds.

Psychedelic computing

One of the characteristics of the counter-culture since its beginnings in the 1960s has been its championing of psychedelic or mind-expanding drugs as an instrument of cultural change. Before he became involved with *The Whole Earth Catalog*, Brand had been involved with The Merry Pranksters. This was an anarchistic group which proselytised the use of psychedelic drugs from a garishly-decorated bus which travelled from town to town giving out LSD to local youth – an adventure described vividly in Tom Wolf's book *Electric Kool-Aid Acid Test*.[43]

The most prominent advocate of the liberating properties of psychedelics was Dr Timothy Leary. During the 1940s and 1950s Leary worked as a psychologist. He began to use LSD on his patients in 1960 whilst working at the Harvard psychology department. However, when LSD was declared illegal, Leary was forced to resign from Harvard and continue his work with private funding. As a result of his experiences he became an advocate for LSD and as the drug gained popularity with the counter-culture he became notorious in the popular media as the 'LSD Guru'.[44]

In 1966 he established a 'Church of LSD' based on the assumption that 'the modern civilization [as exemplified in American culture] is insane, destructive, warlike, materialistic, atheistic – a meaningless set of repetitious robot responses'.[45] The project of the Church was to use LSD as a 'sacrament', to return man to a life of harmony with his own divinity – with his mate and family, with his fellow human beings, and with other natural energies – organic and inorganic – of this planet. A complete and rapid evolution of society is intended.[46]

The psychedelic path had in fact been followed a decade earlier by another major influence on counter-culture ideas, the British writer Aldous Huxley. Huxley, who settled in California during the 1940s, was interested in Eastern religions and ways of knowledge and in this spirit experimented with psychedelic drugs in the 1950s, recording his experiences in his 1954 book *The Doors of Perception*.[47] Huxley even requested and was given LSD on his deathbed. In a curious symmetry the leading 1960s advocate of LSD, Timothy Leary, had his death transmitted 'live' on the Internet in 1996. For during the 1980s Leary had moved smoothly from evangelising psychedelics to evangelising computers as tools of intellectual and spiritual liberation arguing that 'personal computers and recreational computers, personal drugs and recreational drugs, are simply two ways in which individuals have learned to take power back from the state'.[48] Leary described William Gibson as 'the provider of the underlying myth of the next stage of human evolution',[49] and 'the Cyberpunk Person [as] the newest, updated, top of the line model of our species, homo sapiens sapiens, cyberneticus'.[50]

This link between the 1960s psychedelic counter-culture and later mutations of the computer counter-culture can be clearly seen in the evolution of *Mondo 2000*. *Mondo 2000* started out as a magazine for drug users called *High Frontiers*, and morphed into *Reality Hackers*, before finding its niche as the first popular magazine dealing with 'cyberspace' issues.[51] Even after the transition, *Mondo 2000* still dealt with drug issues with the editor, science-fiction writer Rudy Rucker, arguing that 'the point of being pro-psychedelic is that this means being AGAINST consensus'.[52] For Rucker, the power of the computer is that it represents a microcosm of a world that is 'a huge parallel computation that has been running for years'. Rucker confessed that 'this was the big transformation I was needing to make – to think of every thing as a computer — and talking about things like the enlightenment and the theory of relativity struck me as a waste of time, dead-horse topics left over from the past'.[53]

New Age

New Age is a term popularised in the mid-1980s to describe a nebulous, quasi-religious set of beliefs that are an outgrowth of the 1960s counter-culture and the 1970s 'human potential movement'. Adherents believe that a new age is dawning in which humans will realise higher, more spiritual selves. Some elements of the 'New Age' movement in the US have come to see virtual reality as an aid to expanding spirituality. As Hayward comments: 'The pertinence of cyberspace to New Age sensibility lies in its perceived capacity to complement and extend . . . meditation and spiritual development.'[54] Because it appears as a revolutionary technology, cyberspace also reflects the millenarian aspects of the New Age movement. One manifestation of this is the Technopagan movement which consists of 'Dionysian nature worshippers (who) embrace the Apollonian artifice of logical machines'.[55] One of the leaders of the movement, Mark Pesce, 'read William Gibson's breathtaking description of cyberspace as a call to arms'.[56] Pesce is the inventor of the Virtual Reality Markup Language (VRML), a technical standard for creating navigable, hyper-linked 3-D spaces on the World Wide Web, which attempt to make Gibson's 'consensual hallucination' a reality.[57] Virtual reality and cyberspace appeal strongly to New Age consciousness. According to Brenda Laurel:

> pagan spirituality on the Net combines the decentralizing force that characterizes the current stage in human development, the revitalizing power of spiritual practice, and the evolutionary potential of technology. Revitalizing our use of technology through spiritual practice is an excellent way to create more of those evolutionary contexts and to unleash the alchemical power of it all.[58]

McLuhan and new consciousness

Support for this belief in the evolutionary potential of new electronic communications technologies came from the ideas of one of the most unlikely of the influences on the counter-culture and subsequently on multimedia discourses, Marshall McLuhan. McLuhan was a conservative Canadian professor of literature whose ideas on the role of media in history resonated strongly with many counter-culture notions. McLuhan appealed to the counter-culture because his ideas were rooted in spiritual concerns about the nature of humankind. The most distinctive aspect of McLuhan's thought is his assertion that 'the medium is the message', by which he meant that the change that any new medium brings about is of more significance than its actual content. He stated:

> All media work us over completely. They are so pervasive in their personal, political, economic, aesthetic, psychological, moral and ethical, and social consequences that they leave no part of us untouched, unaffected, unaltered. The medium is the massage. Any understanding of social and cultural change is impossible without a knowledge of the way media work as environments.[59]

McLuhan believed that throughout history the media have had a profound, but imperceptible influence on how people see themselves in the universe. History, in McLuhan's model, has gone through three stages: the preliterate, characterised by oral communication; the age of literacy and print; and the present age of electric communication, which began with the telegraph and is now characterised by television and computerised communications. It was McLuhan's contention that, with the advent of writing and printing, humankind had been forced into a way of looking at the world that resulted in the loss of spiritual knowledge and experience that had been the birthright of preliterate peoples.[60] But now with electronic media we are to reclaim that aspect of our humanity that had been lost with printing. In a phrase that was to become adopted by promoters of new media of all shades of political opinion, McLuhan argued that, with electronic media, we were all now living in a 'global village':

> Ours is a brand-new world of allatonceness. 'Time' has ceased, 'space' has vanished. We now live in a global village ... a simultaneous happening. . . . We have begun again to structure the primordial feeling, the tribal emotions from which a few centuries of literacy divorced us.[61]

For McLuhan this process went deeper than just an improvement in the quality of life – it represented a real spiritual transformation. He made this clear in a 1969 interview with *Playboy* magazine:

> The computer holds out the promise of a technologically engendered state of universal understanding and unity, a state of absorption in the logos that could knit mankind into one family and create a perpetuity of harmony and peace. Psychic communal integration, made possible at last by the electronic media, could create the universality of conscious-ness foreseen by Dante when he predicted that men would continue as no more than broken fragments until they were unified into an inclusive consciousness. In a Christian sense, this is merely a new interpretation of the mystical body of Christ; and Christ, after all, is the ultimate extension of man.[62]

Conclusion

The theme of this chapter has been to argue that important aspects of multimedia technologies and the discourses around them have their origins in the 1960s counter-culture when 'even the technology that was the dominant culture's pride came in for rethinking and remaking'.[63] Multimedia technologies since the 1960s have come to be associated with two types of rhetoric. On the one hand the 'New Left' rhetoric sees cheap, powerful machines in the hands of 'the people' as an irreversible advance for democracy, community and a decentralised society. On the other hand the New Age vision sees the computer as a means to a higher plain of being – a view given intellectual support by McLuhan's ideas on the social, cultural and spiritual effects of media. As we shall see in subsequent chapters, the 1960s counter-culture has not been the only source of this discourse 'that identifies ... electronics and cybernetics, computers and information with a new birth of community, decentralisation, ecological balance, and social harmony'.[64] However, what is different about counter-culture influences is that they have had the most influence on those individuals who have actually shaped and built the mass-market computer and multimedia industry. In the next chapter we shall look at how hippies became businessmen and a revolution became a market.

Notes

1 A popular spreadsheet program.
2 H. Rheingold, 'The Virtual Community', Chapter 2 in *Daily Life in Cyberspace: How the Counter Culture Built a New Kind of Place*. Available on-line at http://www.rheingold.com/vc/book/2.html (28 May 1998).
3 T. Roszak, *The Making of a Counter Culture. Reflections on the Technocratic Society and its Youthful Opposition*, Berkeley, University of California Press, 1995.
4 Ibid., p. xiv.
5 This is how Steve Jobs described the Apple Macintosh computer. In S. Levy, *Insanely Great. The Life and Times of Macintosh, the Computer That Changed Everything*, London, Penguin Books, 1995.
6 H. Marcuse, *One Dimensional Man*, London, Sphere, 1968, p. 131.
7 M. Bookchin, *Post-scarcity Anarchism*, Berkeley, Ramparts Press, 1971, p. 83.
8 I. Illich, *Tools for Conviviality*, London, Calder Boyars, 1973.
9 B. Sterling, *Mirrorshades, the Cyberpunk Anthology*, London, HarperCollins, 1986, p. x.
10 D. Dickson, *Alternative Technology and the Politics of Technical Change*, London, Fontana/Collins, 1974, pp. 138–40.
11 T. Nelson, *Computer Lib/Dream Machines*, Redmont, Microsoft Press, 1987, Title page.
12 Quoted in T. Roszak, *The Cult of Information*, London, University of California Press, 1994, p. 138.
13 Ibid., p. 143.
14 R. Buckminster Fuller, *Utopia or Oblivion. The Prospects for Humanity*, London, Penguin, 1972, p. 176.
15 The geodesic dome was invented by Fuller as a low-cost and efficient method of construction based on scientific principles. Geodesic domes were supported by standardised, interconnected self-supporting members of high structural efficiency made from a range of materials. Their low cost and ease of construction made them particularly popular with those seeking to set up alternative communities in the 1960s. I. Tod and M. Wheeler, *Utopia*, New York, Harmony Books, 1978, p. 146.
16 Roszak, *The Cult of Information*, op. cit., p. 152.

17 L. Felsenstein, 'The Commons of Information', *Dr. Dobbs' Journal*, May 1993. Available on-line at http://bliss.berkeley.edu/impact/speakers/speakers_page.html (4 February 1998).

18 S. Brand, 'Spacewar: Fanatic Life and Symbolic Death Among the Computer Bums', *Rolling Stone*, 7 December 1972. Available on-line at http://www.baumgart.com/rolling-stone/spacewar.html (1 June 1998).

19 Roszak, *The Cult of Information*, op. cit., p. 139.

20 Felsenstein, op. cit., p. 3.

21 Michael Rossman quoted in Roszak, *The Cult of Information*, op. cit., p. 140.

22 Felsenstein, op. cit., p. 3.

23 Ibid., p. 35.

24 Rheingold, op. cit.

25 T. H. Nelson, *Literary Machines*, Sausalito, California, Mindful Press, 1992.

26 C. Evans, *The Making of the Micro. A History of the Computer*, Oxford, Oxford University Press, 1983, pp. 13–16.

27 Ibid., pp. 23–34.

28 'Program On Human Effectiveness Report for USAF Office of Scientific Research', in J. Nyce and P. Kahn (eds), *From Memex to Hypertext*, Boston, Academic Press, 1991, p. 237.

29 Rheingold, op. cit., Chapter 3.

30 Ibid., Chapter 10.

31 Ibid., Chapter 11.

32 Ibid., Chapter 10.

33 Ibid.

34 Brand, op. cit.

35 Ibid.

36 P. Hayward, 'Situating Cyberspace: The Popularisation of Virtual Reality' in P. Hayward and T. Wollen (eds), *Future Visions: New Technologies of the Screen*, London, BFI, 1993, p. 182.

37 Quoted in R. Coyle, 'The Genesis of Virtual Reality', in Hayward and Wollen (eds), ibid., p. 151.

38 Ibid., p. 151.

39 Hayward, op. cit., p. 180.

40 J. Brunner, *Shockwave Rider*, New York, Harper & Row, 1975.

41 Director/Screenwriter, Steven Lisberger, 1982, Walt Disney/Lisberger-Kushner Productions.

42 W. Gibson, *Neuromancer*, London, Grafton Books, 1986, p. 51.

43 Rheingold, op. cit., Chapter 2.

44 Available on-line at http://www.leary.com/Biography/QuickBio.html (7 July 1998).

45 Available on-line at http://leary.com/archives/text/Archives/Millbrook/ChurchofLSD.html (7 July 1998).

46 Ibid.

47 A. Huxley, *The Doors of Perception and Heaven and Hell*, London, Penguin Books, 1963.

48 R. Rucker, *Mondo 2000. A User's Guide to the New Edge*, London, Thames and Hudson, 1993, p. 84.

49 Hayward, op. cit., p. 185.

50 T. Leary, 'The Cyberpunk: The Individual as Reality Pilot', in L. McCaffrey,

Storming the Reality Studio, Durham, North Carolina, and London, Duke University Press, 1991, p. 247.

51 Rucker, op. cit., p. 9.
52 Ibid., p. 10.
53 Ibid., p. 11.
54 Leary, op. cit., pp. 199–200.
55 E. Davis, 'Technopagans', *Wired*, July 1995. Available on-line at http://www.wired.com/wired/3.07/features/technopagans.html (16 July 1998).
56 Ibid.
57 Ibid.
58 Quoted in ibid.
59 M. McLuhan, *The Medium is the Massage*, London, Penguin, 1967, p. 26.
60 M. McLuhan, *Understanding Media: The Extensions of Man*, London, Sphere, 1964, p. 44.
61 McLuhan, *The Medium is the Massage*, op. cit., p. 63.
62 P. Marchand and M. McLuhan, *The Medium and the Message*, New York, Ticknor & Fields, 1989, p. 205.
63 T. Roszak, *The Making of a Counter Culture*, op. cit., p. xxvii.
64 J. Carey, *Communication as Culture*, London, Routledge, 1989, p. 114.

Chapter 3

The birth of multimedia

Introduction

In the previous chapter we traced how the computer, as a machine for augmenting human capabilities, became a potent counter-culture icon. Young computer workers and enthusiasts who identified with counter-culture values sought to create machines that would change the world into one more conducive to those values. Throughout the 1960s and 1970s the cream of American computing talent had pursued a project of using computers to augment human capabilities: first under the auspices of the military and then as employees of Xerox PARC. However, during the mid-1970s another group consisting of young computer hobbyists came to see that the wide availability of microprocessors – computers on a chip – made possible a computer cheap and small enough to be owned by an individual. In the process of following this vision they created the personal computer market. At this point commercialism replaced radical idealism in the history of multimedia. Radical 'hackers' now became entrepreneurs and, as the market developed, established capitalist media corporations were drawn in.

The PC arrives

Altair

The first personal computer, the Altair, went on sale as a kit aimed at the small hobbyists' market. The Altair had been conceived and built by a computer counter-culture veteran, Ed Roberts, who had hit on the idea of taking one of the new microprocessors and supplying the components and instructions necessary for hobbyists to build a personal computer. The Altair, 'a computer you can build yourself for $420', was launched with a cover story in the January 1975 edition of *Popular Electronics* magazine. Roberts was hoping for 200 orders, to keep the enterprise alive, but he received more than that with the first mail delivery that arrived after the issue went on sale.[1] The Altair was 'an absolute, runaway, overnight insane success'.[2]

The Altair had demonstrated that the state of development of micro-electronics had reached a point where the cheap personal computer could be built. It also demonstrated that there was a demand for such devices. This runaway success of the Altair occurred despite the fact that it was sold without a keyboard, display screen, printer or any software. However, the absence of these components served to initiate a new era of counter-culture computing very different from the rarefied ethos of the computer engineers working on ARPA projects or at PARC. As there was no software for the Altair many enthusiasts got together in clubs, like the Homebrew Club in Berkeley, California, to provide mutual assistance in order to get the most from their new machine. This was to prove a key development. However, there was a striking contrast between the amateurism and counter-culture whimsy of the young hobbyists and the well-financed professionalism of the PARC scientists. The latter tended to treat the Homebrew members with disdain – an attitude exemplified by PARC scientist Larry Tesler's reaction when he attended a Homebrew meeting in 1975: 'I watched guys carrying around boxes of wires and showing programs that generated flashing lights. My neighbor said, "this is the future!" . . . I told him, "Forget it."'[3] However, the elitist PARC scientists grossly underestimated the members of the do-it-yourself computing clubs, particularly when a number of them attempted to make money out of their hobby by starting up companies. Among these were computer science students Bill Gates and Paul Allen who spotted the market created by Altair's lack of software and wrote an Altair version of the public-domain language BASIC (Beginners All-purpose Symbolic Instruction Code). Gates and Allen went on to found Microsoft, which by the 1990s was the world's most successful software company. Other Homebrew hobbyists went on to design and build their own personal computers. The most successful of these were Steve Jobs and Steven Wozniac, the co-founders (with Mike Markkula) of Apple Computer.

Apple

Steve Jobs and Steven Wozniac became all-American heroes in the late 1970s by turning their garage workshop operation into the million-dollar business that initiated the era of the mass-produced personal computer in the United States. Apple were not only first off the mark in producing a consumer-oriented personal computer, they also produced innovative software for people to use on it (such as word-processing and spreadsheets). On the back of this impetus Apple were able to gain a significant foothold in the academic and business markets.

IBM PC

From the 1950s to the 1970s one company had dominated the world computer industry: IBM. IBM had made its fortune by building and servicing large 'mainframe' computers and was an exemplar of the corporate world that the counter-culture rejected. The men running IBM had at first disdained the personal computer, but the success of the Apple II obliged them to change their strategy. In 1981 IBM entered the personal computer market. The IBM PC and its later clones were primarily miniaturised versions of the types of mainframe with which IBM was already familiar. Essentially IBM conceived the PC as a marketing strategy to exploit an unexpected new market and defend its existing corporate heartlands. Unlike the machines Xerox PARC had been working on, little thought was given to the PC's interface which 'was squarely of the old school – a command line operating system that failed to make computers one iota friendlier'.[4] The PC was in no way conceived as a multimedia machine. In fact so little thought had been given to its software design that the choice of operating system was almost an afterthought. A computer's operating system (OS) controls the way in which it executes commands, manages programs, memory, input and output devices, and receives and presents data to the user.

Microsoft

Paul Allen and Bill Gates had created Microsoft to supply the market created by the Altair's lack of a high-level programming language. Microsoft now performed a similar service for the IBM PC operating system, providing it with MS-DOS – Microsoft Disk Operating System. Crucially IBM did not have exclusive rights to the PC's key technologies. As well as relying on the MS-DOS operating system, IBM also had to rely on Intel for the microprocessors that would power the PC. This meant that other companies, starting with Compaq in 1982, were able to license these technologies to produce cheap 'IBM clones'. Consequently IBM was not able, for all its marketing might, to dominate the new market and Intel and Microsoft emerged as the financial winners. Microsoft benefited most since each time someone bought a PC they also had to buy a copy of Microsoft's system software. Since the costs of each extra copy of software produced is close to zero, Microsoft's profits soared. Essentially Microsoft was able to collect a tax on each PC sold.

Multimedia arrives

The term 'multimedia' in its current usage was born as a marketing concept. According to the head of Apple's Multimedia Lab, Sueanne Ambron, when Apple was planning to sell its new Macintoshes to schools and colleges on the basis of their ease of handling graphics and sound, the Marketing Department wanted to call the concept 'hypermedia': 'Everyone at Apple wanted to call the technology "hypermedia" . . . but I knew teachers wouldn't feel comfortable about "hyper" anything. So I suggested multimedia, because teachers would be more comfortable with that word.'[5] Multimedia had already entered the education arena as a term from the 1960s and 1970s when it applied mainly to tape-slide technology.

Business multimedia

The development of a personal computer market was a necessary condition for the birth of a consumer multimedia market. However, it was some time before the power of consumer personal computers was sufficient to deliver multimedia. In the 1980s genuine multimedia machines were still costly and so were mostly restricted to business users. During this period businesses made use of multimedia to provide entertainment, training and information.

Entertainment

The games industry was quick to exploit the multimedia potential of the microchip with arcade games. The first widely successful game was 'Pong', which was introduced in 1972. Other games such as 'Space Invaders', 'Lunar Lander' and 'Asteroids' followed throughout the 1970s. As the power and speed of microchips increased during the 1980s and 1990s, arcade games such as 'Firefox' and 'Dragon's Lair' began to employ photo-realistic three-dimensional graphics and interactivity.[6]

Training

Some of the earliest business multimedia systems were employed for training. Initially computer-based training (CBT) was fairly expensive and mainly used by large multinational corporations with distributed workforces such as airlines[7] and large financial institutions.[8] American Airlines incorporated laser disk-based multimedia into its training scheme for flight attendants. Many firms, such as Bethlehem Steel in Pennsylvania, have seen a benefit in the flexibility of multimedia training systems particularly for 'just in time training' (JIT) that can be accessed at any time. JIT systems are designed to allow workers to obtain on-line instructions just when they need it – for example when faced with a particular problem.[9]

Kiosk applications

The general public, in the main, first came into contact with multimedia in the late 1980s in the form of kiosks: stand-alone enclosed consoles, containing point-of-sale (POS) and point-of-information (POI) systems. A variety of institutions including banks, travel agents, museums and art galleries began to deploy interactive multimedia systems. One of the most successful and technically accomplished of these was the National Gallery Micro-gallery.[10] The Micro-gallery consisted of a cluster of Apple Macintosh computers with touch-screens that permitted the visitor to explore the collection by either theme, artist or period. It was also possible to design an itinerary through the gallery and have it printed out as a guide. This package was eventually marketed as the Microsoft Art Gallery, one of the most popular of the CD-ROMs aimed at the domestic market. As the costs of multimedia hardware and software fell in the 1990s more and more businesses began to see multimedia as an attractive and cost-effective adjunct to their marketing efforts.[11] One of the first companies to use interactive multimedia in retailing was the US-based Florsheim shoe company which installed kiosks in most of its outlets, and claims to have sold millions of pairs of shoes through this method. Customers are able to use the system to choose the colour/size/style combination that they want.[12]

Estate agents in the UK and Europe were among the first commercial organisations to make use of multimedia systems to help potential house buyers to view interior and exterior images of houses and see the location of the property on a map.[13] In Denmark, the leading real estate company, Home, installed such a system in its 120 branches in 1990. This led to dramatic increases in business with the number of people visiting outlets increasing fourfold and its market share rising by up to a quarter.

In 1995 British Airways began trials of an in-flight interactive multimedia system for its long-haul flights. This was designed to provide each passenger with an individual screen and a choice of up to twenty-four film and entertainment channels as well as games. The system is designed to allow passengers to use their credit cards to make purchases by means of a magnetic card reader in the handset. Passengers not only have a choice of movies, games and music, but are also able to follow the progress of their aircraft on a map or to view live video footage taken from cameras fixed to the aircraft's exterior.[14]

Consumer multimedia

Apple, again

Apple had always aimed to produce a personal multimedia machine and the company was confident it would sweep the market when it did so. When it saw how poorly designed the IBM PC was, Apple decided to take out an advertisement in the *Wall Street Journal* declaring 'Welcome, IBM'.[15] The reason Apple felt so confident that it would prevail over IBM was the fact that it had already begun to develop a personal computer that made use of much of the PARC research on graphical interfaces. In December 1979 Apple co-founder Steve Jobs took a delegation to Xerox PARC. The aim of the visit was to look at PARC's work on graphical interfaces to incorporate into Apple's new computer the Lisa. Jobs had been fascinated by the rumoured developments in computing research at Xerox PARC. As we have seen, these interface features were based on bit-mapped screen displays. A computer screen consists of thousands of individual picture elements of pixels, and in a bit-map display each pixel corresponds to data bits in the computer's memory, thus allowing the display and control of any image. The incorporation of

Welcome, IBM.
Seriously.

Welcome to the most exciting and important marketplace since the computer revolution began 35 years ago.
And congratulations on your first personal computer
Putting real computer power in the hands of the individual is already improving the way people work, think, learn, communicate and spend their leisure hours.
Computer literacy is fast becoming as fundamental a skill as reading or writing
When we invented the first personal computer system, we estimated that over 140,000,000 people worldwide could justify the purchase of one, if only they understood its benefits
Next year alone, we project that well over 1,000,000 will come to that understanding. Over the next decade, the growth of the personal computer will continue in logarithmic leaps
We look forward to responsible competition in the massive effort to distribute this American technology to the world.
And we appreciate the magnitude of your commitment
Because what we are doing is increasing social capital by enhancing individual productivity
Welcome to the task. apple

FIGURE 3.1   Apple welcome the launch of the IBM PC with an advertisement in the *Wall Street Journal* in 1981. Apple were confident of the superiority of their computers and failed to anticipate that the PC's success would eventually threaten Apple's very survival
Courtesy of Apple Computer, Inc.

bit-map graphical displays made possible the graphical representation of files and folders (icons) which could be manipulated on screen by using a pointing device such as a mouse.

This approach contrasted with the IBM PC and its clones which used text-based displays and operating systems controlled by lines of arcane instructions that had to be typed in from the keyboard. Despite its years of research and investment in the Alto, Xerox had decided not to develop a personal computer of its own and had struck a deal with Jobs by which Apple would get to see PARC's technology and Xerox would buy 100,000 Apple shares for $1 million.[16] There was then an exodus of Xerox staff from Palo Alto to Apple to work on a multimedia computer for the people. The move from Xerox to Apple eventually included Alan Kay himself, who brought with him the Dynabook concept. The Apple/Xerox deal marked the convergence of the ARPA research of the 1960s and 1970s with the Homebrew Club culture at Apple. It was the catalyst that brought multimedia computing to a mass market. The first fruit of this convergence was the Lisa, the first commercial computer with a graphical user interface running Apple's version of Xerox's graphical operating system. However, Lisa – launched in 1983 – was not a success. At $12,000 per machine it was more than three times the cost of MS-DOS-based PCs and it ran very slowly.[17] But by then Apple had already started on a new project: the Macintosh.

Macintosh

The Apple Macintosh not only incorporated the counter-culture inspired technologies developed by PARC, it was also marketed with a campaign that echoed counter-culture concerns about 'big' technology repressing the individual, a position exemplified by the advertising slogan, 'The computer for the rest of us'. Apple announced the Macintosh with a controversial sixty-second television advertisement shown during the 1984 US Super Bowl. The commercial was directed by Ridley Scott in the 'cyberpunk' style of his film *Blade Runner*. It opens with a monochrome scene of rows of tramping grey-clad, shaven-headed people. Above them, on a giant screen, a menacing face is haranguing them. Intercut frequently and in colour is a young blonde woman with red shorts and T-shirt bearing the word 'Macintosh' running past the rows of people, pursued by helmeted police.[18] She stops before the giant screen, whirls around and throws a sledgehammer which smashes it to pieces. It is then announced: 'On January 24th Apple Computer will introduce Macintosh. And you'll understand why 1984 won't be like 1984.'[19]

However, initial sales of the Macintosh proved disappointing. This was for a number of reasons. Its price was high, $2,495 per machine, and early models had no hard-disk drive and lacked the storage and memory power necessary to support a bit-mapped screen. This made the first Macintosh frustratingly slow.[20] Software developers were slow to produce programs for the Mac and for many potential consumers the interface seemed too weird and different. Consequently the Macintosh failed to dislodge the IBM PC and its clones from the home and business market. The IBM brand image in the public mind and particularly in the mind of the business community was one of reliability and efficiency. Making skilful use of this image, IBM began to sell their PCs into the booming 1980s office computer market. Apple's confidence proved to be misplaced as they were relentlessly squeezed out of the personal computer market over the next decade. As the saying went, 'no one was ever fired for buying IBM'.

DTP

The Macintosh was, however, able to establish a new niche for itself with the invention of desktop publishing (DTP). It was able to do this thanks to two developments: Postscript, a page description language[21] based on technologies developed at Xerox PARC, and Aldus PageMaker, the first successful desktop publishing application. The Mac's bit-mapped screen together with the first laser printer, the LaserWriter, enabled the printing of a page layout exactly as it was displayed on the screen. Alan Kay called this capability 'WYSIWYG' – what you see is what you get.[22] The combination of the Macintosh, LaserWriter and PageMaker allowed small businesses and community groups to produce printed material comparable to that made by highly capitalised printers, but at a fraction of the cost. Desktop publishing seemed to be fulfilling the counter-culture dream of a cheap empowering technology. Arguably desktop publishing saved the Macintosh by creating a new market made up of small-scale desktop publishing bureaus. Apple was thus able to establish a secure niche for itself even while it was being relentlessly squeezed out of the mainstream PC market. By the mid-1980s, however, Apple had become a minor player in a personal computer market dominated by IBM clones and the Microsoft operating system (MS-DOS).

HyperCard

Even though Apple had become marginalised, it was still enamoured with the notion of the 'Dynabook' and the company's eventual aim was still to produce a cheap portable device that would bring to its users text, sound, images and video. In one of the early Macintosh development meetings Steve Jobs had announced the aim of 'Mac in a book in five years'.[23] This was a project that was pursued with zeal. When he first encountered this Apple ethos John Sculley commented: 'It was almost as if there were magnetic fields, some spiritual force, mesmerizing people. Their eyes were just dazed. Excitement showed on everybody's face. It was nearly a cult environment.'[24] One of the computer engineers at Apple, Bill Atkinson, designed a Magic Slate inspired by Kay's Dynabook. Magic Slate was to have a flat liquid crystal display, be the size of a very thick notepad and be controlled by a stylus through a touch-sensitive screen. You could view and 'turn' pages by swiping the screen with the stylus.[25] When the company declined to develop the idea Atkinson produced a software version that would run on the Macintosh. Atkinson changed the interface book metaphor to one based on 'stacks' of index cards that could be linked to each other in any number of possible ways. Atkinson called this program 'HyperCard', acknowledging his debt to the originators of the hypertext concept: Bush, Engelbart and Nelson.

HyperCard, introduced in 1987, fitted with Apple's aim of promoting the Macintosh as a multimedia machine. Initially bundled free with every Macintosh, it was designed to let the user combine text, graphics and sound, as well as control external devices such as videodisk players. Its easy to use programming language, Hypertalk, permitted the addition of links and interactivity within and between stacks. In this way HyperCard could be said to be the first 'user-friendly' multimedia application. Its ease of use made multimedia producers of a large number of users from a variety of professional fields who would otherwise not have touched a computer. A number of significant multimedia productions were developed using HyperCard including the commercially successful CD-ROM *Explora* by the rock musician Peter Gabriel. HyperCard gave a large number of users their first taste of multimedia. As Levy puts it: 'Macintosh in its bit-mapped refusal to discriminate between text and graphic, was the natural platform for this nascent (multimedia) technology.'[26] For these reasons it can be claimed that the Apple Macintosh, with HyperCard, was the first genuine multimedia capable personal computer. Unfortunately Apple, having first made extravagant claims for HyperCard's potential, then neglected it. The company failed to keep it up to date with other products, particularly Macromind's Director, and, although it proved popular in education, there was no explosion of commercial software based on HyperCard.

However, the Holy Grail for multimedia was to bring video-quality moving images to the personal computer. Apple began to address this with an extension of the Macintosh operating system called QuickTime. Introduced in 1991 QuickTime enabled the Macintosh to play audio, video or animation files without any additional hardware or software. However, the major technical problem in delivering video-quality multimedia to a consumer market is the sheer amount of digital information that is required to encode sound and pictures and particularly moving pictures. The problem of storing and delivering moving pictures found its initial solution with the videodisk that could store up to an hour of video on each side in analogue form. Among the most widely seen of these videodisk-based systems was the package that was produced to accompany the BBC's *Domesday Project* in 1986. This ambitious project involved schools, individuals and other organisations across the UK providing images and text of their locality. This was combined in a multimedia package, which the user could navigate by means of an input device called a trackball, essentially an inverted mouse. Unfortunately the project failed to fulfil its promise and some have argued that this was a setback, albeit short-lived, to interactive multimedia.[27]

CD-ROM

The breakthrough in bringing video-quality multimedia to a consumer market came with the CD-ROM (Compact Disk Read-Only Memory), developed by the Dutch electronics multinational Philips and launched in 1986. CD-ROM was an adaptation of the audio compact disks developed by Philips in the late 1970s. Each CD-ROM had a storage capability of 650 megabytes, equivalent to over 200,000 pages of printed text. Initially, CD-ROM was used for the storage of large text databases, giving personal computer users access to databases previously only available on large hard-disks attached to mainframe computers. However, it was always realised that this storage capacity, together with the low cost of production (they can be mass produced using the same production facilities as audio compact disks) and physical robustness, made the CD-ROM an ideal medium for the mass distribution of multimedia.[28] However, the consumer multimedia market was slow to get started, with development hampered by confusion over formats, and at one point there were six rival CD-ROM systems.[29]

Delivery platforms

Philips, as a major international electronics corporation, had to make decisions about its response to the impending convergence of computing, telecommunications and consumer electronics. It had been committed to the research and development of optical and digital storage and transmission technologies since the 1960s. The development of the personal computer market in the early 1980s had suggested that there were opportunities for selling digital media products to a mass home market. As mentioned above the development of such a market faced both technical and marketing problems. The major technical problem was that of compressing the large number of bits of data that comprise a television image. One second of colour video in digital form comprises more than 200 megabytes of data. Since a CD can store 600 megabytes of data this means that it can hold about three seconds of video. The technical problem was solved by the development of compression techniques, faster CD-ROM drives and specialised graphics microchips. The marketing problem was to try to define a consumer concept with mass appeal. After research Philips launched a product, CD-Interactive

(CD-I), which could sit alongside the television, video and audio equipment in the living room. Like these more familiar consumer electronics the CD-I player was encased in matt black rather than the grey of the personal computer. Philips was also very aware of the necessity of having sufficient titles to play on the machine if it was to be taken up on a large scale by the public.[30]

Apart from CD-I the other main multimedia platform was the console, a computer-based machine that plugs directly into a domestic television, but lacks a keyboard. Consoles have been marketed almost exclusively as game machines with the data input either from a cartridge or a CD-ROM. By 1998 the sole remaining cartridge console was the Nintendo 64, earlier cartridge consoles such as the Sega Mega Drive and Super Nintendo Entertainment System (SNES) having waned. CD consoles include the Panasonic REAL 3DO, Sony Playstation and Sega Saturn.

The multimedia PC

When Microsoft produced its own graphical interface, the Macintosh's early advantage as a multimedia machine, albeit in a small market, was rapidly eroded. Bill Gates had been an admirer of the Macintosh version of the PARC operating system and recognised that the future lay with operating systems with graphical interfaces. Gates realised that the development of a graphical interface was a necessary precondition for there to be a multimedia market based on the huge installed base of Microsoft-based PCs. From the early 1980s the main thrust of Microsoft's strategy was to produce its own graphical interface to enhance and then replace MS-DOS. In 1985, a year after the launch of the Macintosh, Microsoft launched Windows, a program that added a graphical interface to DOS. In 1988 Apple filed a lawsuit against Microsoft claiming that Windows copied many of the key features of the Macintosh operating system. Microsoft, who marketed an improved version, Windows 3.0, in 1990, contested this and the lawsuit was decided in Microsoft's favour in 1993. Early versions of Windows were slow mainly because the program was not a proper operating system but had to 'sit on top of' DOS. In 1995, however, Microsoft launched Windows 95 with an unprecedented advertising campaign and at last the company had found a multimedia operating system (OS) to challenge the Apple's Macintosh OS.

Existing suppliers of Intel/Microsoft (Wintel) personal computers now saw an opportunity to revitalise a market that had seen sales level off as the home and business market approached saturation with the end of the 1980s boom. By the winter of 1994 PC builders such as Compaq, Packard Bell and IBM were offering machines with stereo speakers, built-in telephone answering machines, fax cards and television tuners in a drive to expand the market by selling PCs as family machines.[31] Apple had failed to take advantage of the Macintosh's in-built multimedia features and by the mid-1990s it was Intel and Microsoft who dominated the consumer multimedia market.

CD-ROM-based multimedia markets

On the face of it the CD-ROM market, with its low entry and production costs, provided the ideal scenario for small-scale entrepreneurial innovators to create a vibrant new market.[32] However, despite much effort on the part of publishers and developers, a profitable market for consumer CD-ROMs never developed. It was estimated in 1995 that only about 10 per cent of American multimedia firms made any money on their CD-ROM products.[33] Initially the low technological barriers to entry did attract many small firms into the market. However, most produced titles with little or no commercial prospects. Firstly, the titles were too costly at £50 and upwards.[34] Secondly, the size of the market was limited by the small number of machines capable of making use of the technology, and thirdly, there was consumer confusion because of the existence of competing CD-ROM formats.

Multimedia publishing

In the late 1980s Apple promoted HyperCard as an easy authoring tool for education, and although this resulted in a lot of specialist educational titles, sold mainly through mail order, quality varied considerably and few if any titles made any money. Consequently both the market and the firms in it remained small.[35] Major publishers and developers did not begin to become interested in consumer multimedia until Intel-based PCs running Microsoft's Windows graphical user interface began to be promoted as multimedia machines. At first there was much confusion concerning multimedia hardware and software standards for Microsoft/Intel based-PCs, and this proved to be something of a hindrance to the development of the market. It was not until the early 1990s, with the setting up of a Multimedia PC Working Group and a Multimedia PC Marketing Council,[36] that the manufacturers of PCs and PC peripherals addressed this problem. In fact it was not until the mid-1990s that a mass market for domestic multimedia based on multimedia PCs developed[37] and it was the interests of the large existing publishers and developers which shaped that market.

Those who were initially drawn into multimedia CD-ROM production were software companies and print publishers. The software companies saw the technology as a natural extension of their existing activities, as a way to expand beyond a saturated business market into education and household markets. For established publishers this new market offered opportunities to repackage content that they already owned. For the print publishers CD-

ROM publishing had both advantages and disadvantages. Although development costs were higher than for print, CD-ROMs represent a much cheaper distribution method than paper (especially for illustrated reference works like encyclopaedias). One problem for the print publishers was that, although they were keen to get into electronic publishing, they lacked the expertise for multimedia production, particularly in the areas of design and programming. This lack of technical know-how led to many established print publishers entering into mergers and joint ventures with software developers. An early example of this trend was the American publisher Random House's 1993 tie-up with Broderbund Software to produce the *Living Books* series of educational CD-ROMs. With the hardware industry becoming increasingly an assembly operation combining standard components and with only two competing operating systems (the dominant Microsoft Windows and the declining Mac OS) the opportunities for adding value, and thus profits, were seen to lie with the production of content. For these reasons software companies, with Microsoft in the lead, were eager to acquire the content resources of publishers. Microsoft clearly saw potential in the multimedia market and set about a strategy of mergers and acquisitions to obtain financial rights to content. It was particularly active in buying up photographic libraries and the rights to museum and art gallery collections. An example of Microsoft's strategy at this stage was their partnership with the British publisher Dorling Kindersley to produce interactive multimedia titles such as *Inside the Human Body* and *Musical Instruments*. The most successful of the Microsoft CD-ROM titles has been the *Encarta* encyclopaedia (although sales figures for *Encarta* are distorted because it has been bundled free with multimedia PCs by many retailers). However, by the mid-1990s, despite a significant growth in the market for multimedia PCs, the CD-ROM market was visibly stagnating. The publishers Marshall Cavendish, Penguin and HarperCollins all decided to pull out of the multimedia market. Even the most profitable publisher of multimedia CD-ROMs, Dorling Kindersley, had, by the end of 1996, downsized its multimedia division by fifty staff.[38] The original promise of the medium, that it would create a new multimedia product that would lead to the death of the book, has not been fulfilled. The only titles that have sold in any numbers have been children's titles and reference works and these rarely made any money. A survey in 1996 indicated that less than half of owners of CD-ROM drives had actually bought a new title, contenting themselves with the discs bundled free with their computers.[39]

The future of portable multimedia

It seems possible, however, that the spread of multimedia-capable PCs and the development of new disk technologies may yet revitalise this market.

Further improvements were promised by the introduction of a new Digital Video (or Versatile) Disk standard (DVD) in December 1995, with an increase in optical disk capacity from 650-Mbyte to between 8.5-Gbytes and 9.5-Gbytes.[40] The primary commercial potential of DVD is seen as a video distribution system to rival the VHS videotape although, unlike VHS videotape, it is an ideal medium for interactive multimedia.[41] However, the development of multimedia, as we shall see in the next chapter, began to enter a new phase at the end of the 1990s based not on portable multimedia, but on the existing transmission networks of telephony, cable and broadcasting. Paradoxically this might revive the consumer CD-ROM market since it has led to the development of a hybrid of CD-ROM and network technologies. The CD-ROM stores the graphical interface and up-to-date information can be loaded over the network. By the mid-1990s Microsoft had abandoned development of most of its consumer CD-ROM titles to concentrate on this hybrid form, an example being its latest versions of the Encarta encyclopaedia.[42]

Conclusion

When the computer counter-culture took the military-industrial complex's technology and made it 'people friendly' they thought they were helping to create a new world in which money was not the primary motivation. However, although the mass-produced microchip made it possible to produce something like the counter-culture vision of the cheap 'Dynabook', it also created the circumstance for the personal computer to become a commodity. The personal computer may still have been a dream machine for the young bosses of Apple but after the success of Apple II it was a source of profit too. At first software companies and traditional print publishers attempted to exploit the market with portable, CD-ROM-based multimedia with mostly meagre results. However, the era of CD-ROM multimedia could be seen as only a precursor to a more significant phase in which there would be a convergence with the old network technologies. In this next phase the development of multimedia would come to be dominated by the plans of powerful, long-established capitalist media and telecommunications corporations.

Notes

1 H. Rheingold, 'Xanadu, Network Culture and Beyond', Chapter 14 in *Tools for Thought*. Available on-line at http://www.rheingold.com/texts/tft/14.html (28 May 1998).

2 T. Roszak, *The Cult of Information*, London, University of California Press, 1994, p. 143.

3 S. Levy, *Insanely Great. The Life and Times of Macintosh, the Computer That Changed Everything*, London, Penguin, 1995, p. 72.

4 Ibid., p. 124.
5 R. Garner, 'The Mother of Multimedia', *Wired*, April 1994, p. 52.
6 B. Cotton and R. Oliver, *The Cyberspace Lexicon*, London, Phaidon, 1994, p. 17.
7 J. Jeffcoate, 'Multimedia in the Business Market. Is There a Multimedia Market?', *Information Management and Technology*, vol.26, no.5, 1993.
8 F. Rickett, 'Multimedia', in P. Hayward and T. Wollen (eds), *Future Visions of the Screen*, London, BFI Publishing, 1994, p. 76.
9 J. Jeffcoate, *Multimedia in Practice. Technology and Applications*, London, Prentice Hall, 1995, p. 130.
10 Ibid., p. 79.
11 Between 1990 and 1993 the number of installed interactive kiosks in the US grew by almost 250 per cent to over 90,000, and in 1994 Inteco Corp estimated that there would be over 2 million such systems in the US by 1996, more than the total number of gasoline pumps in 1994. *Software Economics*, vol.3, no.8, August 1994, pp. 7–8.
12 No named author, *Justifying the Investment, Interact: Newsletter of Interactive Media in Retail Group*, London, IMRG, Spring 1995, p. 4.
13 Ibid.
14 Ibid., pp. 1–2.
15 Levy, op. cit., p. 125.
16 Ibid., p. 77.
17 Ibid., p. 102.
18 Roszak, op. cit., p. 153.
19 Levy, op. cit., p. 170.
20 Ibid., p. 185.
21 A page description language encodes pictures and text as a series of instructions stored as a mathematical formula. Issuing a print command sends these instructions to the printer. This is much faster and more flexible than printing from a bit-map which stores an image as a series of grid references.
22 Levy, op. cit., p. 211.
23 Ibid., p. 258.
24 Ibid., p. 142.
25 Ibid., p. 240.
26 Ibid., p. 250.
27 Rickett, op. cit., pp. 75–6.
28 Cotton and Oliver, op. cit., pp. 39–40.
29 CD-ROM XA; Intel's DV-1; Videologic's DV-1; Philips' CD-I; Commodore's CD-TV; Sony's Data Discman.
30 A. Cawson, 'In Search of the Interactive Consumer, the Design and Development of Compact Disc-Interactive', in K. Bjerg and K. Borreby, *Home-Oriented Informatics, Telematics & Automation*, Copenhagen, University of Copenhagen, 1994.
31 R. Perry, 'The Rise and Rise of the Family PC', *Guardian*, 20 October 1994.
32 See, for example, the special report on multimedia in the *Independent*, 13 October 1992.
33 D. Pullan, 'Processes and Partnerships in Interactive Entertainment', Paper delivered to the Multimedia Investment Conference, Le Meridien Hotel, London, 3 May 1995. Proceedings published by IBC Technical Services, 57–61 Mortimer Street, London, W1N 8JX.
34 Ibid.

35 Ibid.
36 The first Multimedia PC standard, announced in 1991, was based on an Intel 286 processor and two megabytes of random access memory and proved to be woefully inadequate. Consequently, specifications had to be raised in subsequent years. MPC-3, announced in 1994, specified an Intel processor running at 75 MHz, eight megabytes of RAM, a 16-bit sound card and a quad speed CD drive. The storage capacity of the CD-ROM plus improvements in processing power in the 1990s represented by Intel's Pentium and the IBM/Motorola Power PC RISC chip made it possible for manufacturers to make a major effort to target multimedia at the household. J. Schofield, 'Multimedia: Just a Standard Problem', *Guardian*, 6 July 1995, p. 6.
37 By 1995 the number of installed CD-ROM drives worldwide was estimated to be 23 million. Of these about 19 million were in the US while in the UK the number of drives was about 1.9 million, a figure which was estimated to grow to 7 million by the end of 1997. The value of the UK CD-ROM market, worth £130 million in 1995, was estimated to be worth £560 million by 1998 of which about a third were games titles. *Observer*, 1 October 1995.
38 'Death of the Disc', *Guardian*, 16 October 1996.
39 S. Geer, 'A Lifeline for CD-ROM', *Daily Telegraph*, 17 September 1996.
40 M. Fritz, 'Digital Video Disks. Compact Disks Pump Up', *Wired*, July 1996, p. 105.
41 P. Marks, 'The White City Heat of Technology', *Guardian*, 11 July 1996.
42 S. Geer, op. cit.

Chapter 4

The evolution of
network multimedia

Introduction

> You stay at home and listen to the lecture in the hall,
> Or hear the strains of music from a fashionable ball.
> > 'The Wondrous Telephone', popular song 1877[1]

> Whether channeled down wires or through the air, spectrum is
> spectrum.[2]

During the 1990s the development of multimedia entered a new phase. While
the first generation of multimedia in the 1980s had been built on stand-alone
personal computers accessing text, sound and images from CD-ROM disks,
the second generation in the 1990s was to be based on computers linked
to existing communications infrastructure. In this process the development
of new multimedia technologies became linked with a technological and institutional infrastructure established by the telecommunications industry over
the course of the previous century. This infrastructure is based on both wired
and wireless transmission technologies and in comparing these two different
transmission media, it is important to focus on their similarities rather than
their differences. In this context all radiant energy travels in waves, and, as
James Clerk Maxwell discovered in the 1860s, radio and light waves are both

electromagnetic radiation, travelling at the speed of light and differing only in the frequency at which they vibrate. Electric current is not the same as electromagnetic radiation. The electrons that constitute it move a lot slower than light. None the less information can be propagated along a wire by an electric current at the speed of light in the same way as radio waves can be radiated. When this is realised the distinction between wired and wireless transmission becomes less clear-cut.

This chapter will examine the evolution of network technologies starting with the electric telegraph and early telephony right through to the later developments of cable and satellite networks and the Internet. In doing so it will also look at the importance of compression, switching and optical fibre in enhancing the capabilities of network infrastructures. Surprisingly the chapter ends with a return to wireless broadcasting, underlining the fact that the means of transmission does not necessarily alter the opportunities offered by the spectrum.

The pre-digital era

Wired transmission

The electric telegraph

The idea of using electricity to communicate over long distances can be traced back to the eighteenth century, but early experiments by Lomond in France (1787) and Ronalds in Britain (1816) were hampered by the capricious nature of static electricity and the fact that it was adversely affected by humidity.[3] In 1800 Alessandro Volta invented the first battery which could produce a continuous flow of low-voltage electricity, the Voltaic Pile, and in 1820 Hans Christian Oersted in Denmark discovered that the passing of an electric current through a nearby wire could deflect a magnetic needle. These discoveries together made the electric telegraph a practical possibility. William Cooke and Charles Wheatstone patented the first practical telegraph in 1837 which,

> was an elegant instrument containing five vertical needles pivoted on horizontal axes and arranged across a diamond shaped dial marked with the letters of the alphabet. Each of the needles could be deflected to the right or left by depressing the appropriate keys on the front of the instrument and, by means of the wires which connected the instrument to another at the far end of the line, the corresponding needles at the receiver would be deflected in the same direction.[4]

The Cooke and Wheatstone telegraph was set up on the Great Western Railway in 1839 where it was used as a means of monitoring and controlling

FIGURE 4.1 The Cooke and Wheatstone telegraph, 1843
Courtesy of the Science Museum/Science and Society Picture Library

the movement of rolling stock and by 1852 more than 4,000 miles of telegraph had been installed by British railway companies.[5] There was little use by the general public or even commercial organisations until the middle of the nineteenth century, when the public became dramatically aware of the importance of the telegraph following the publicity given to its role in the capture of a notorious murder suspect in England in 1845.[6] After this the telegraph came to be increasingly used by both businesses and the general public.

The earliest telegraph networks needed many operators and the system, particularly near urban centres, found it increasingly difficult to cope with the huge growth in traffic. However, during the latter half of the nineteenth century these problems were addressed with the introduction of such innovations as the printing telegraph (which printed the transmitted message at the receiving machine) and multiplexing, the sending of several messages along the same wire simultaneously.

In the US Samuel Morse and Alfred Vail developed a system based on electromagnets. In the Morse receiver an electromagnet, energised by the pulse of current from the line, attracted a soft iron armature which inscribed the dots and dashes of the Morse code on paper tape for later interpretation by the operator.[7]

During the latter part of the nineteenth century the telegraph system was extended on a global scale with the introduction of submarine cables across the English Channel in the 1850s and the Atlantic in the 1860s. By 1900 all the major cities in the world were linked by telegraph and the basic infrastructure upon which the global multimedia networks of the late twentieth century would be based was already in place. However, telegraphy (literally, 'distance writing') was soon to be overshadowed by telephony ('distance speaking'), which would provide the populations of the industrialised nations with a richer and more accessible form of communication.

Telephony

The modern telephone arose out of Alexander Graham Bell's investigations, conducted in the 1870s, into how humans produce and receive sound. Bell, a Scottish doctor who later became an American citizen, specialised in the treatment of patients with hearing difficulties, and the unlikely origin of the telephone stems from his attempts to artificially reproduce human speech. Bell's inspiration for how this might be achieved came from the German scientist von Helmholtz, who had simulated speech sounds by using electric current to vibrate tuning forks.[8] On this principle Bell began to experiment with the electrical transmission of sound over a distance. While the telegraph worked on the digital principle (messages were transmitted in the form of discrete pulses of electricity), Bell's telephone worked on the analogue principle. The mouthpiece of the telephone (the transmitter) converted sounds into a fluctuating electric current that was the analogue representation of the wave that carries the sound, while the earpiece (the receiver) converted the current back into sound.

By the 1880s Bell had begun to market his new invention in the US as a mass medium, as a source of information and entertainment transmitted from a central source to subscribers. This conception of telephony, as a means of transmitting music, entertainment and information, had a wide appeal. For example, at the 1881 Paris Exposition Internationale d'Électricité there was great public interest in telephonic demonstrations where visitors were invited to listen to live musical, operatic and theatrical performances through headphones. At the same time the Théâtrophone Company of Paris was making telephonic entertainment available to a less affluent public through coin-operated machines.[9]

By the 1890s telephone companies in both North America and Europe were offering their customers subscription services of musical and theatrical entertainment as well as coverage of sporting events, political speeches and church services. In 1896 the Universal Telephone Company provided affluent London subscribers with access to several London theatres for £10 per year plus £5 installation fee. In 1891 a Théâtrophone system was installed in public rooms at the Savoy Hotel in London and during the same period the Wisconsin Telephone Company in the US transmitted continuous music to subscribers every evening and Sunday afternoon.[10]

In the early part of the twentieth century there were even instances of what we would now call 'teleconferencing'. In 1912 a gathering of newspaper executives in New York took part in a multiple telephonic link-up in which 'Taft spoke from Boston, Canadian Premier Borden spoke from Hot Springs Virginia, a Kipling poem was recited from Daly's theatre, and a vocalist performed a "Southern song" from another New York theatre'.[11] In Ontario, Canada in 1890 the telephone was even used to transmit the proceedings of a murder trial when a local publican installed telephone transmitters in the courtroom. The transmitters were linked to twenty receivers in his establishment that he rented to customers for twenty-five cents an hour.[12] However, with the coming of radio after the First World War, the telephone waned as a medium of information and entertainment. Bell and his financial backers realised that the telephone's commercial success would not be based on 'eerie music piped from nineteenth-century cyberspace',[13] but on its ability to facilitate personal communications. In 1878 Bell telephones were given a publicity boost when there was a train disaster in the town of Tarriffville, Connecticut. A local druggist was able to use one of the few telephones in the town to summon doctors from a nearby town to the crash-site.[14] The disaster gave the Bell Telephone Company widespread publicity which led to a significant rise in the number of subscribers. At first Bell established local switching systems, but then began to build lines to connect cities and in subsequent years the telephone system spread rapidly and covered the whole of the US by 1904.[15] The subsidiary set up by Bell to handle this long-distance business was the American Telephone and Telegraph Company (AT&T). Eventually AT&T became the main Bell organisation and the individual Bell companies became subsidiaries.

At the same time as the telephone became established as a means of personal communication, it declined as a medium of entertainment and news, particularly with the increasing popularity of the cinema, gramophones and radio. A notable exception to the decline of the telephone as a source of entertainment was the Hungarian telephone-based information service Telefon Hirmondo, established in 1893. Described by Marvin as 'the only example of sustained and systematic programming in the nineteenth century that truly prefigures twentieth century broadcasting systems', Telefon Hirmondo continued operations until after the First World War.[16]

Cable

Although by the 1920s the telephone had been replaced by the radio as the instrument through which entertainment entered the home, wires still played a significant role in the transmission of such programming because of technical distribution problems. The technical problems facing long-distance radio communications in the 1920s arose from the fact that radio transmissions are subject to atmospheric interference, particularly from water vapour. This proved to be a particular problem in the US due to its large geographical size (reliable long-distance radio transmissions only became possible in the 1940s when it was discovered that interference could be reduced if the frequency of transmission was increased). A solution was found in wired transmission. In the US one of the earliest radio stations, WEAF in New York, was established by AT&T, who naturally made use of their phone lines both for remote broadcasts and to link its stations in other cities, thus establishing the first radio network.[17]

Wired transmission of radio programming became established in Europe during the 1920s. In both the UK and Europe early radio broadcasts only served the major cities, leaving large pockets of the population unable to receive a satisfactory signal. Many businesses took the opportunity to set up tall aerials to receive faint broadcast signals from urban areas or foreign countries. They then relayed them over wires to subscribers.[18] The first such relay or rediffusion system was established in the Netherlands in the early 1920s and the first British one was set up in 1925.[19] By 1935 there were 343 such cable systems in Britain (although reaching only 3.1 per cent of radio licence holders). The most cabled nation was the Netherlands with 50 per cent of households connected by 1939.[20]

As radio receiver technology improved and the BBC's transmitter network expanded, wired broadcasting declined in the UK in the 1930s and a number of relay systems went out of business. That the industry managed to survive the 1940s was due to wartime restrictions on transmitter power, designed to prevent enemy bombers homing-in on their signals. In these circumstances relay systems prospered, doubling their number of subscribers by the end of the war.[21]

With the re-establishment of television broadcasting after the war, cable operators in the UK and Europe received another stimulus when they fulfilled the same role they had with early radio by relaying signals to households with weak television broadcast reception. In the US too, cable television developed as an *ad hoc* solution to the problem of bad broadcast television reception both in areas remote from the main centres of population and also in large cities, where multiple signal reflections and shadows cast by buildings made reception difficult. Private companies would provide a cable service to communities with poor reception by sending the signal down a wire from an antenna in an area where the signal was strong. These early systems were known as Community Antenna Television (CATV). One of the first CATV systems was set up in Lansford, Pennsylvania in 1950 by a local radio and television retailer who erected a mountain-top antenna linked by coaxial cable to each subscriber,[22] a practice known as 'distant signal importation'. By 1952 seventy distant signal importation companies were in operation in the US.[23]

At first the cable companies had used twisted pairs of copper telephone wire allowing 2-4 television channels, but as cable systems became more permanent, these were replaced by coaxial cable which reduced external interference by having one conducting wire wrapped around the other. Coaxial cables were able to carry electrical signals of higher frequency than open twisted-pair telephone wires, so cable companies were able to provide many more channels than were available over the air. Cable companies now began to augment existing broadcast channels with others from outside the local area.[24] Initially these were picked up by the cable company's local master antenna but increasingly, during the late 1960s and early 1970s, distant broadcast signals were beamed in using microwave transmission.[25]

Wireless transmission

Early radio

Wireless transmission had evolved from scientific advances at the end of the nineteenth century. In particular, James Clerk Maxwell's theoretical description of radio waves (1864) and Hertz's detection of them in the late 1880s, had led in 1896 to Marconi's first demonstration of radio transmission on Salisbury Plain in England over a distance of 1.75 miles. (It is interesting to note that, long before 'the digital age', Marconi was using digital technology in the form of the on-off pulses of Morse code.) Progress was rapid thereafter. In 1899 Marconi had achieved the first cross-Channel broadcast between France and England. The first transatlantic broadcast took place on 12 December 1901, from Cornwall, England, to Saint John's, Newfoundland. In 1902 the Canadian Reginald Fessenden broadcast the first analogue radio transmission sending voice and music over a distance of 25 miles. Fessenden had achieved this through the technique of modulating the amplitude, or magnitude, of 'carrier' radio waves with the sound waves generated by speech or music. The radio transmitter generated a carrier wave with constant characteristics, such as amplitude and frequency. The signal containing the desired information was then used to modulate the carrier. This new wave, called the modulated wave, contained the information of the signal.

During the first decade of the twentieth century other techniques were developed to improve the reception and transmission of radio signals. The most significant of these were the diode, or valve, produced by Sir Ambrose Fleming in 1905, which permitted the detection of high-frequency radio waves, and the audion, or triode, invented by Lee De Forest in 1907, which was able to amplify radio waves. By the early 1920s regular radio broadcasting of music, entertainment and news was taking place in Europe and America by both state-owned and commercial companies.

In the 1930s the American radio engineer Edwin H. Armstrong developed the technique of modulating the frequency of the carrier wave (FM) rather than its amplitude (AM), the method used since Fessenden. Frequency-modulated radio waves proved to be less prone to interference from both natural and artificial electrical sources because of their constant amplitude. This made them ideal for the transmission of television and high fidelity radio. FM was transmitted at a higher power and frequency than AM radio (30–300 MHz as against 0.3–3 MHz) giving it a wider bandwidth than AM. This very high frequency (VHF) wave had enough bandwidth to carry two or more channels to produce, for example, stereophonic or quadraphonic sound. When television became a mass medium after the Second World War it too was transmitted on the VHF part of the radio spectrum, although by the 1960s most TV broadcasters had begun switching to ultra high frequencies (UHF) transmission (300 MHz to 3,000 MHz).

By the 1960s even higher frequencies on the radio spectrum were beginning to be exploited for the purposes of relaying telephone calls rather than for broadcasting. US companies such as Sprint and MCI began to exploit super high frequency microwave transmissions (3,000 to 30,000 MHz) in order to challenge AT&T's monopoly on the transmission of long-distance telephone calls. This technological development was to have far-reaching institutional and political repercussions since it resulted in the first major challenge to the AT&T monopoly in long-distance telephony and the eventual break up of AT&T in 1980. (See Chapter 5.)

The cellular phone

This pattern of hybrid wired/wireless transmission has been a feature throughout the history of telecommunications. This is well illustrated by the development of cellular radio as a means of providing mobile, person-to-person telephony. Radio-telephones were not new, but before the 1980s had been bulky and expensive and only a limited number could operate in one area at a particular time.[26] Developed in the 1970s by AT&T's Bell Laboratories for use in cars, the cellular phone was marketed with great success to the public during the 1980s. The system divides an area into clusters of 'cells', each cell covering a radius of about 8 to 12 miles and each with its own radio transmitter with about 120 two-way radio channels. To eliminate interference, neighbouring cells do not use precisely the same radio frequencies, but the frequencies used in each cluster may be repeated in adjacent clusters. As the phone user moves away from one transmitter, the signal is switched automatically to that in the neighbouring cell.[27]

Interactivity

Leaving television aside, the multimedia potential of cable lies in the fact that the coaxial cables used by cable companies have some 416,000 times the capacity of telephone twisted-pair wires. This means that they can deliver not only scores of television channels, but also forms of two-way communication.

With this combination of microwave and coaxial cable some American cable operators were, by the 1970s, able to offer their subscribers 50–100 channels of television with fully active two-way capacity, permitting the user a degree of control over what is presented to him or her on the screen.[28]

A number of experiments in interactive cable have been conducted since the 1970s with varying degrees of success. The first, in 1977, was the Qube system which enabled users to make interactive responses by pressing buttons that sent signals back to computers at the cable head-end to be analysed and displayed.[29] The interactivity offered by Qube to its subscribers included competing against each other in quiz shows or voting for the most popular characters in soap operas as well as home shopping.[30] Even though the system gained widespread publicity it did not prove profitable and was discontinued in 1984.[31] During the 1980s the most important form of interactivity was pay-per-view where viewers were able to choose a programme for an extra fee.

In the UK cable never became as widespread as in the US because terrestrial transmission was generally better. In the 1950s nearly one million UK homes were connected in order to get better reception,[32] but as transmitters became more powerful the number of homes connected fell. During the 1970s the number of cable subscribers stopped growing and then began to fall. The industry lost 140,000 subscribers in five years,[33] and began to lobby for greater freedom to distribute additional programming, particularly films, in order to keep existing customers and attract new ones. Until this time, a strong lobby (by the BBC in particular) from the 1930s had restricted cable operators to simply relaying existing broadcasting channels.

Satellite

Surprisingly, the technological development that contributed most to the rapid growth in cable television, particularly in the US, was the communications satellite. In 1972 only 11 per cent of homes were connected to cable in the US.[34] By 1975, the year of the first satellite, this had risen to 12 per cent and by the 1990s, with the distribution by satellite of dedicated film and sports channels, over 63 per cent of US homes were connected to cable.[35] Cable in the US was becoming a multi-million dollar business, and its success inspired other initiatives around the world, particularly in Europe.

Satellite was originally conceived as a more cost-effective means of microwave distribution. The first communications satellite, the privately developed Telstar, was launched in 1962. The Communications Satellite Corporation (COMSAT) was incorporated on 1 February 1963 as a private US company to establish, in conjunction with the telecommunications administrations of other countries, a commercial communications satellite system. In mid-1964 the International Telecommunications Satellite Consortium (INTELSAT) was formed by 110 nations to manage international satellite communications. In 1965 INTELSAT launched Intelsat 1, better known as Early Bird, the world's first commercial geo-synchronous communications satellite (it had been preceded in 1963 by the experimental geo-synchronous satellite Syncom II).[36] A geo-synchronous satellite orbiting at a distance of 22,500 miles from the earth takes twenty-four hours to complete one orbit. Since this is the same time as the earth takes to turn once on its axis it appears to 'hover' over the same location, and can be used to transmit communications signals consistently to the same 'footprint'.

The first significant link-up between satellite and cable occurred in 1975 in the US. Home Box Office (HBO), a pay television channel, used satellite to bring the Mohammed Ali–Joe Frazier heavyweight championship boxing match from Manila in the Philippines to cable subscribers in the US. HBO had originally been set up to provide feature films to cable networks using ground microwave links, but after the success of the Ali–Frazier transmission it became clear that satellite provided a much more efficient and cost-effective means of distribution. HBO began to market its feature film service to cable companies across the US and was soon followed by other companies including the twenty-four-hour news service CNN, and Georgia's Superchannel, both owned by The Turner Broadcasting System of Atlanta.[37] The availability of these extra television channels made cable networks very attractive to the public and resulted in a great expansion throughout the 1980s with most major US cities awarding franchises to cable companies.[38] In 1975, the year of the Ali–Frazier transmission, 12 per cent of homes in the US could receive cable TV; five years later in 1980 that figure had more than doubled to 20 per cent. By 1985 43 per cent of US homes were cabled[39] and by the mid-1990s this had risen to over 63 per cent.[40]

Direct broadcast satellite (DBS)

In the US in the late 1970s a number of individuals bought their own satellite dishes in order to receive for free the programming that was being beamed down to the cable operators. The response of the satellite programme providers was to scramble their signals so that only cable companies with the necessary decoders could receive them. Eventually the satellite broadcasters allowed independent companies to sell decoders to dish-owners in the mid-1980s.[41] Having to pay for the service initially led to a fall-off in US dish sales and the prevalence of cable meant that DBS did not have a great impact, with less than 4 per cent of US households owning a dish by 1988.[42]

DBS in the UK began with the establishment of Sky Television in 1989 followed by British Satellite Broadcasting (BSB) in 1990.[43] (Sky had previously operated as a low-powered satellite to cable systems from 1982–9.)[44] The two companies merged in 1990 to form BSkyB (British Sky Broadcasting – although effectively BSB was taken over by Sky). In its early years BSkyB struggled to make a profit. However, this situation changed dramatically when the company won the contract to show live UK Premier League football in 1992. The satellite dish was taken up more enthusiastically in the UK than in any other country. And Sky's football programming revived a moribund cable industry (although the cable companies' ability to undercut British Telecom in telephony after 1991 also contributed to the growth in cable subscriptions).

The post-digital era

Computers and communication

The process of turning existing telecommunications networks into potential carriers of multimedia began in the 1960s when the first digital telephone exchanges were established using Pulse Code Modulation (PCM). PCM converted analogue voice signals into digital signals by digitising the wave form. At this stage the application of computer technologies to the telephone system was seen as simply a means of increasing the capacity of overworked circuits.[45] Later in the 1990s digitisation would drive the convergence of the telephone, cable and broadcasting industries as transmitters of multimedia to a mass market.

The modem

The crucial step in the process of digital convergence was the invention of the modem by Ward Christensen in 1977. This made it possible for computers to communicate with each other over the telephone system. In fact, commercial on-line databases had first appeared in the late 1960s, but they used dedicated lines to provide information to customers' remote terminals.[46] The database market only really began to take off after Christensen's invention.[47]

The modem (from the contraction of MOdulator, DEModulator) converts the digital signals of the computer into the analogue signal of the telephone line. These are then transmitted over telephone lines to another modem which re-converts the sound waves back into a bit-stream which the computer can 'read'. The modem dramatically reduced the cost of connecting computers over the telephone line, and by 1979, only two years after its invention, there were already 33 million data transactions per year between computers in the UK alone. By 1983 this had more than doubled to 74 million transactions.[48] During the 1980s a number of companies set up data bank services which made use of modems to deliver information to business subscribers, particularly in financial services, law and to libraries. The use of data bank services became a significant source of revenue for telephone companies.

The modem made it possible for computers to be connected via the world's most widespread network infrastructure, the telephone system. However, copper wire telephone systems, and the newer but less common cable networks, did not have sufficient bandwidth for the delivery of more sophisticated interactive multimedia of the kind available, for example, on CD-ROM. The on-line data systems developed during the 1980s could only transmit text or numeric data or, in some cases, simple line graphics.

The advantages of digitisation

The onset of digital transmission means that the limitations of copper wire, and indeed of all transmission media, can be overcome by computation. The main techniques used to improve the amount of information that can be transmitted over a given medium are firstly, digital compression which converts large amounts of digital information to a smaller amount for transmission, and secondly, packet-switching which has made possible the phenomenon of the Internet.

Bandwidth

Bandwidth is the term used in communications theory to define the capacity of a communication channel to carry information measured in Hertz or cycles per second. Voice telephony requires a bandwidth of 3–4kHz (thousands of cycles per second), whereas television pictures require 6–8MHz (millions of cycles per second).[49] The wider the bandwidth of a communication channel, the greater the range of frequencies, and therefore information, that can be sent along it at a given time. Voice transmission alone at normal telephone quality requires a bandwidth of 64,000 bits per second (64 kilo bits per second). To send sound and moving pictures requires the most bandwidth of all with the amount depending on the screen size and frame rate of the video. A three colour, 1,024 pixel by 768 pixel video image running at thirty frames per second would require a bandwidth of 566 Mbit/s (millions of bits per second).[50]

Compression

Compression techniques work by reducing the number of bits that have to be transmitted to convey a given amount of information. Rather than increasing the bandwidth of the transmission medium, compression uses the computing power available at both transmitter and receiver ends to reduce the number of bits that have to be transmitted. The principle of compression can best be understood by considering the case of digital video. To transmit a digital television picture requires a data rate of 217 megabits per second. However, it is not necessary to repeat this for every frame because from frame to frame large parts of the scene do not change. By transmitting only those portions of the picture that change, the amount of bits that have to be transmitted can be considerably reduced.

A number of compression standards have been adopted, the most important for motion video compression being those established by the Moving Pictures Expert Group (MPEG). MPEG-1 compression can reduce by between 50 and 200-fold the amount of data that needs to be transmitted to support a 320 pixels by 240 pixels video image with CD-quality sound at thirty frames a second.[51] The reduction will depend on how much change there is from frame to frame.

The rapid development of switching and compression software techniques in the research laboratories of the telephone companies meant that by the mid-1990s it was possible to transmit VHS-quality video down twisted-pair copper wires. As Gilder explains:

> Graphics and video might impose immense floods of bits on the system, but compression technology could reduce the floods to a manageable trickle with little or no loss of picture quality.[52]

As well as improvements in picture quality the extra capacity given to wired transmission by digitisation makes it possible for cable companies to offer their subscribers a high degree of interactivity. For example, in 1993 the cable compan Videotron, with franchises in London and southern England, introduced a system which allowed viewers to choose different camera shots of football matches as well as watch action replays.[53]

Switching

The earliest use of digital processing in communications, as we have seen, was in telephone exchanges with the introduction of electronic switching. The telephone network is a switched network: that is, the path, or circuit, needed to connect one telephone to another is created and maintained only for the duration of each individual telephone call. In the early days of the telephone system switching was performed by human operators who used switchboard plugs to 'patch' one telephone line to another.

By the beginning of the twentieth century automatic telephone exchanges began to replace manually operated ones. (The first public automatic telephone exchange in the UK opened in Epsom, Surrey in 1912.)[54] These automated exchanges used electromechanical relays and switches that were controlled by dialled digits, a system invented in 1889 by Almon B. Strowger, an undertaker in Kansas City.[55] Electromechanical switching reduced the need for operators, but was not flexible and needed considerable maintenance. However, Strowger exchanges were still operating in the 1990s. One of the last, a private exchange in Catford, England, only closed in 1995.[56]

However, with the introduction of electronic switches in the 1960s it became possible to computerise switching, effectively eliminating the distinction between electronic communication and computing since both switch bits of information around under the control of stored programs. With this development came the concept of the 'intelligent network' in which the telecommunications network could 'process, route and store information using digital switches and transmission links, computers and databases'.[57]

The initial advantage of these technologies for the telephone system was that they made it more efficient by enabling the detection and elimination of transmission errors. Digitisation also prevented the system becoming congested by re-routeing messages away from overloaded circuits. Only later was it appreciated that program-controlled digital switches enabled extra services to be offered to telephone users including virtual exchanges, answering services, alarm calls, call re-routeing and charge card billing.

But most crucially the digitisation of the telephone system raised the possibility for the telephone and cable companies of overcoming the bandwidth limitations of their existing copper infrastructure to deliver multimedia services to subscribers. As Gilder explains:

> If all else failed, powerful electronic switches could compensate for almost any bandwidth limitations. Switching could make up for the inadequate bandwidth at the terminals by relieving the network of the need to broadcast all signals to every destination. Instead, the central switch could receive all signals and then route them to their appropriate addresses.[58]

The most widely used method of digital switching for the integrated transmission of voice, data and images in digital form over telephone networks is the Integrated Services Digital Network (ISDN). An ISDN line can carry two 64-kilobits-per-second digital channels to a customer using two pairs of twisted copper wire.[59] The International Telecommunications Union established standards for ISDN as early as 1984.[60]

Subsequent technologies – such as the high bit rate digital subscriber line (HDSL) – dramatically improved on ISDN, delivering thirty channels (2 Mbit/s) over two or three copper lines to subscribers. Asynchronous transfer mode (ATM) technology is another switching technology under development by telecommunications companies, and it is claimed that it can further increase the maximum available bit rate to over 6 Mbit/s.[61] ATM permits VHS-quality video to households over copper telephone lines. In the US a number of trials using ATM were carried out, most notably the Time-Warner Cable/Silicon Graphics Full Service Network (FSN). This 1994 pilot study involved 4,000 households in Orlando, Florida being networked using the latest transmission, switching and compression technologies.[62] The system had an optical fibre trunk to neighbourhoods of 500 houses, and services entered the house by coaxial cable. In 1995 there was an ATM trial in East Anglia, England conducted by British Telecom (BT), Apple and Oracle in which families were able to select videos and other services for transmission into their homes over copper telephone lines.

Packet switching

The key switching technology for the development of a universal digital infrastructure has been packet switching. In Chapter 1 we described how scientists trying to ensure the survival of military communications systems in the event of nuclear war made use of packet switching. In a packet network, messages are divided up into uniform packages each with a header giving (a) the destination to which it is addressed, (b) the message to which it belongs and (c) its position in the message. At various nodes of the network computers read and route the different packages, and the whole message is then reassembled when it reaches its final destination.[63]

The first tests of packet switching were carried out by the National Physical Laboratory in the UK in 1968.[64] Packet switching formed the basis of the Pentagon-funded Advanced Research Programs Agency Network (ARPANET) which was established in 1969. It was ARPANET that was to become the foundation of the Internet.

The Internet

The significance of packet switching for the Internet is, as Howard Rheingold points out, twofold:

> First, [it] creates the building block for a communications system with no central control because you don't need a central controller when each packet and the entire network of routers all know how to get information around. Second, as the world's information becomes

digitized, those packets can carry everything that humans can perceive and machines can process – voice, high-fidelity sound, text, high-resolution color graphics, computer programs, data, full-motion video.[65]

Strictly speaking an 'internet' is any network of networks, and many commercial, military and academic organisations had already been linking their computers into local area networks (LANs) for a number of years. The process by which the Internet – with a capital 'I' – came into being is one in which these LANs were progressively able to talk to each other through the use of packet switching and common standards for exchanging digital information, known as protocols.

As we saw earlier, the origins of the Internet lie with ARPANET. ARPANET's backbone was based on PDP8 and PDP11 computers located in American universities that were all linked by permanently open telephone lines. Originally used to facilitate communications between the military and academic researchers working on military contracts, ARPANET, largely as a result of military cutbacks, underwent a major reorganisation in 1983. The main result was that it split into military and civilian sections. The Internet grew out of the civilian division of ARPANET. From ARPANET came the Internet Protocol (IP) designed to let any computer communicate with any other on the telephone system. In the US, under the auspices of the National Science Foundation Network (NSFNET), IP was adopted by academic and government organisations as a means of exchanging information between their mainframe computers and also as a method of scholarly communication using electronic mail.[66] Eventually education and research sites which had not formed part of the original ARPANET adopted IP as did, eventually, almost every other LAN in the world.[67]

Commercial interest in the Internet began in 1989 when CompuServe, a US company previously concerned with providing data bank services, began to offer Internet access to subscribers wishing to use e-mail. CompuServe was followed in 1993 by America Online and Delphi who offered access to data banks, electronic mail, as well as on-line chat services. These service providers also permitted their subscribers to receive and send software and computer files using the file transfer protocol (ftp), as well as use remote computers interactively (telnet).

Internet browsers

One problem in achieving acceptance of the Internet by the general public was the difficulty of using the associated software. In many ways this paralleled the difficulties faced by the early personal computers before the evolution and acceptance of the graphical user interface (GUI) in the 1980s. The development that did most to overcome this problem and begin to establish the Internet as a mass medium was the World Wide Web (WWW or W3). The World Wide Web was developed by Tim Berners-Lee, a physicist at CERN (the European Laboratory for Particle Physics) as a means of facilitating group work and information exchange with his colleagues. In 1991 Berners-Lee made his WWW program freely available on the Internet.[68]

The WWW is based on the concept of hypertext. Hypertext works on the principle of creating links between digital data so that clicking on a word on the computer screen with a mouse will bring on screen a definition, a picture, a related text article or a sound. On the WWW information is embedded in web documents using a hypertext format called Hypertext Markup Language (HTML), which the browser interprets as text, style or colour or as a link to another address somewhere else on the Internet. The World Wide Web uses a protocol called Hypertext Transmission Protocol (HTTP) which permits any computer to 'talk' to any other computer regardless of its operating system.

The World Wide Web runs on the client-server model where an information provider runs a server that holds the information made available to a client somewhere else on the Internet. The flexibility of the system enables the individual to use 'helper' programs to display animation or video or to play sound.

Client programs, which allow the user to 'surf' the WWW, are known as browsers and look and work very much like Apple's HyperCard application (see Chapter 3). The first successful web browser was Mosaic which was developed by Marc Andreeson and Eric Bine at the National Centre for Supercomputing Applications (NCSA) in the US. Andreeson left NCSA to set up a new company, Netscape, to develop his ideas. In 1994 Netscape's first product, the client browser Navigator, was distributed free by Netscape over the Internet to educational and non-profit making organisations and it soon overtook Mosaic in popularity.[69] Commercial organisations originally had to pay and this gave Microsoft the chance to gain a competitive edge when it released its browser, Internet Explorer, based on Mosaic, for free in 1996. Netscape had to respond by dropping the commercial charge for Navigator. In 1997 Netscape went one step further and released the source code for Communicator. The source code is the text of the program produced by the programmers in a language such as C++. Customarily the source code is proprietary and not accesible by the user. By making the source code freely available Netscape was saying to users that there were no hidden features in the software which might surreptitiously garner information from their PCs and it also gave software writers the opportunity to develop the program further.

By the late 1990s a number of so-called 'convergence' technologies were being developed to facilitate the transmission of television channels over the Internet.[70] Examples of convergence products include Microsoft's WebTV, a hybrid TV-PC intended to provide access to the Internet on cable systems. Another example of this trend was Apple's iMac launched in 1998. This is based on the Macintosh operating system and combines the functions of a WebTV-like Internet access device with a CD or DVD player.

Digital wireless transmission

One of the other features of digitisation and packet switching is that they can be applied as easily to wireless as to wired transmission. By the mid-1990s digital radio technologies were making it possible to transmit the same range of frequencies through the air as could be carried by coaxial cable. An important advantage of digital transmission in any medium, as we have seen, is that it can take advantage of compression techniques to provide many more channels at a given frequency. For satellite broadcasters this also means more cost-effective use of expensive transponder time. Digital television transmission has some other advantages too. It makes possible high definition wide-screen formats as well as permitting the downloading of code to be cached by the receiver to provide interactivity, for example for games. Digital transmission also promised to transform the most long established form of broadcasting: sound radio. In 1996 Germany's Bosch and Deutsche Telekom, the telecoms operator, demonstrated a DAB-TV system which was a radio/television hybrid, and in 1996 the BBC launched a digital Audio Broadcasting (DAB) service with CD-quality sound.[71]

Digital satellite television (DST)

By the 1990s direct analogue broadcasting via satellite was technically and financially established, but already it was becoming obvious that this was a passing phase and that the real excitement would come with the introduction of digital transmission. The first digital DBS system, the geosynchronous Hughes DirecTV satellite, was launched in 1994 offering 150 digital channels to the whole of North America. It quickly became one of the most successful consumer electronics products ever: in its first seven months sales of the eighteen-inch dish-antenna and set-top box were greater than those obtained in the first year by VCRs, CD players and wide-screen television sets put together.[72]

The US market is extremely competitive and DirecTV was soon joined by other digital direct-to-home (DTH) satellites EchoStar and PrimeStar.[73] In Europe a number of digital satellite services were started in the 1990s including DStv in Italy, CanalSatellite Numérique in France and DF1 in Germany. In the UK, BSkyB announced that it would be launching a 200-channel geosynchronous digital DBS satellite in late 1998.

Leaving television aside, and in a development that symbolises the independence of media form from content, wireless transmission is rapidly becoming the primary means of person to person communication. This process started with cellular radio, but was given an additional boost when digital satellite was seen to offer opportunities for voice and data traffic. Organisations who have set up new satellite-based digital communications systems include Inmarsat. This project, funded by 1,200 companies and eighty member countries, has launched a number of geosynchronous satellites to provide telephony to remote regions of the world.[74] However, a drawback of geosynchronous satellites has been that their orbit is too high for effective telephony and data transmission. The distance the signal has to travel means that there is always a slight delay in reception, and terminal equipment has been cumbersome and expensive.[75] To overcome these problems, several digital satellite systems were developed in the 1990s using a larger number of smaller, low-orbit satellites called 'constellations'. In 1990 Microsoft and the mobile phone company, McCaw Cellular, formed a joint company, Teledesic, to launch a system consisting of 840 small satellites operating in low earth orbit by 2001. In 1994 Motorola began work on a satellite system called Iridium which had placed 66 equally spaced satellites 420 miles above the earth by 1998.[76] As they orbit at low altitude these systems use less power to transmit and receive signals, permitting smaller sized sets for the user.

Digital terrestrial television (DTT)

DTT transmitters operate at much lower frequencies than DST – 0.6 gigahertz as opposed to satellite's 11 gigahertz – and have to transmit in a narrower frequency range. This means that digital satellite can transmit hundreds of channels, but digital terrestrial broadcasting will only be able to transmit a few dozen. Despite this disadvantage the British Government's Broadcasting Act of 1996 set out the basis for the introduction and licensing of digital terrestrial television services.

This is not to say that DTT has no advantages. It is cheaper to both receive and transmit than DST. Terrestrial is also more suitable for portable or mobile reception than satellite and cable and, since terrestrial digital transmitters use less power than PAL transmitters, it could lead to integration with cellular radio services.[77]

FIGURE 4.2 One of the satellites in the Iridium network

Courtesy of Slim Films

Increasing bandwidth by transmission

Optical fibre

Since the late 1960s the telecommunications industries have been able to make use of optical fibre. The optical fibre cable is a radical development in communications technology because it transmits photons (i.e. light) where cable or telephone wires transmit electrons (i.e. electricity). We have seen how digital technologies have increased the carrying capacity and efficiency of existing wired and wireless transmission infrastructures. Optical technologies promise an even greater expansion in the bandwidth of the telecommunications network. Optical fibre cables are hair-thin strands of pure, highly transparent glass through which pulses of light from a LASER (Light Amplification by Stimulated Emission of Radiation) are transmitted. The laser makes use of the fact that atoms hit with light at the right frequency will be stimulated to release an excess of energy in the form of photons or light particles. The electronic signal is encoded digitally and then converted into pulses of laser light by an 'emitter' which are then transmitted down the fibre to an optical detector which converts them back to electronic form.

The idea of using fibres as a transmission system was first suggested in 1966 when Charles K. Kao, a Chinese engineer working at Britain's Standard Telecommunications Laboratories,[78] proposed that it was possible to convert a telephone conversation into pulses of infra-red light which could be transmitted along a strand of pure glass and then converted back into speech. The main technical problem was that the glass needed to be perfectly transparent. However, within eleven years this problem had been overcome, and the first optical fibre link was working between Hitchin and Stevenage in Hertfordshire, England.[79]

Early attempts at optical communications were hampered by the need to use electronic amplifiers along the route. These amplifiers converted the photons into electrons, boosted them, and then changed them back into photons. This constituted a significant bottle-neck. The problem was solved with the development of all optical amplifiers by a team at the University of Southampton, England. The team discovered that by introducing the element erbium into a short length of fibre it could be made to act as an amplifier. By the 1990s all optical links, using erbium-doped optical fibre amplifiers, had been established between Cyprus and Israel (261 km) and between Naples and Pomezia on the west coast of Italy. Another important technical enhancement to photonic transmission technologies was the development of the soliton: a means of shaping pulses of light to prevent dispersal and distortion over long distances.[80] The significant thing about optical fibre, as far as communications is concerned, is that light has a much higher frequency than electricity and so can carry a much greater amount of information. In fact, operating at very high frequencies of infra-red light, optical fibre cable has an almost unlimited bandwidth and can actually carry many more signals than can be transmitted through the air over the entire radio spectrum. George Gilder calls this potential of optical fibre cable the 'fibresphere':

> consider all the radio frequencies currently used in the air for radio, television, microwave, and satellite communications and multiply by two thousand. The bandwidth of one fibre thread could carry more than two thousand times as much information as all these radio and microwave frequencies that currently comprise the 'air'. One fibre thread could bear twice the traffic on the phone network during the peak hour of Mothers' Day in the USA (the heaviest load currently managed by the phone system).[81]

By the 1990s data rates of 1,000 Gigabits per second had been achieved over optical fibre,[82] and telephone and cable companies in the industrially developed world have taken advantage of optical technologies to enhance their network carrying capacity. By the mid-1990s most of the advanced world economies were linked by undersea optical cable, and the main fibre trunk routes within each country are already laid. The gap has been between these fibre trunk routes and the 'local loop' into homes and businesses, which are still overwhelmingly connected by telephone copper wires and, to a lesser but rapidly increasing extent, by the coaxial lines of cable companies.

However, optical fibre does have some disadvantages. One of these is that glass, unlike copper, cannot transmit electricity and so may be put out of action by power failures – conventional telephones keep working during power cuts. Another problem is that the cost of converting signals between the electrical and optical domains has tended to rule out optical commun- ications for all but the largest and heaviest users. British Telecom's TPON system (Telecommunications over Passive Optical Networks) has sought to overcome this by starting with a single fibre at the exchange which is then progressively split, fanning out in the network so multiplying the number of terminations served by the original exchange fibre. In general, though, both cost and a perceived lack of consumer interest have hampered the expansion of fibre cable to households.

Conclusion

In this chapter we have seen how telecommunications technologies have undergone immense improvements in capacity and range since the invention of the telegraph in the first half of the nineteenth century. Throughout this process one lesson has been that media content has no necessary relation to the particular media technology employed to transmit it. At the end of the nineteenth century families were enjoying entertainment carried into their homes on a wire. Families at the end of the twentieth century are also receiving entertainment down wires. When radio was invented in 1896 it was seen as a future means of personal communication.[83] By the 1990s, with the development of digital mobile communications, the future of personal communication was again connected to wireless technologies. Yet in the intervening period, wireless was the main medium for the transmission of news and entertainment and wires were used for personal communication.

The convergence of the digital computer and the telecommunications system represents both continuity and change. Digital convergence can be seen either as the latest stage in a continual process of technical improvement or as a new qualitative stage in the history of human communications. Digital technologies represent a radical shift, not only in the 'efficiency' and organisation of communication networks, but also, potentially, in their cultural role. With digital technology the technical fidelity and range of the media representations that can be channelled into the household far exceeds anything that could have been imagined by previous generations of mass media consumers. Given the potency of the new digital communications technologies it is tempting to see recent dramatic changes in the media landscape as a consequence of these advances in digital technologies. However, in the next chapter we shall examine the proposition that it has been political rather than technological forces that have been instrumental in bringing about these changes.

Notes

1 E. Barnouw, *A Tower in Babel: A History of Broadcasting in the United States*, New York, Oxford University Press, 1966, p. 7.
2 G. Gilder, 'From Waves to Wires', *Forbes Magazine*, 5 June 1995. Available on-line at http://www.forbes.com/asap/gilder/telecosm13a.htm (1 August 1998).
3 G.R.M. Garrat, *The Communications Explosion in the Nineteenth Century: Some Contributions of Electrical Engineering*, Milton Keynes, Open University Press, 1973, p. 13.
4 Ibid., p. 16.
5 Ibid., p. 17.
6 Ibid., p. 18.
7 Ibid., p. 21.
8 Ibid., p. 33.
9 C. Marvin, *When Old Technologies Were New*, Oxford, Oxford University Press, 1988, p. 210.
10 Ibid., p. 215.
11 Ibid., p. 213.
12 Ibid., pp. 209–16.
13 B. Sterling, *The Hacker Crackdown. Law and Disorder on the Electronic Frontier*, London, Penguin Books, 1992, p. 7.

14 Ibid., p. 8.
15 Ibid.
16 Marvin, op. cit., pp. 223–8.
17 L.S. Gross, *Telecommunications*, Madison, Wisconsin, Brown and Benchmark, 1995, pp. 55–6.
18 T. Hollins, *Beyond Broadcasting: Into the Cable Age*, London, BFI Publishing, 1984, p. 36.
19 Ibid.
20 Ibid., p. 37.
21 Ibid., p. 41.
22 Ibid., p. 114.
23 Gross, op. cit., p. 134.
24 Ibid., p. 135.
25 V. Sparkes, 'Cable Television in the United States', in R.M. Negrine (ed.), *Cable Television and the Future of Broadcasting*, London, Croom Helm, 1985, p. 19.
26 Gross, op. cit., pp. 174–5.
27 Ibid.
28 T. Feldman, *Multimedia*, London, Blueprint, p. 6.
29 Gross, op. cit., p. 147.
30 Hollins, op. cit., p. 206.
31 Gross, op. cit., p. 150.
32 Hollins, op. cit., p. 41.
33 Ibid., p. 43.
34 Ibid., p. 117.
35 Research by A.C. Nielsen. Available on-line at http://www.classic-cable.com/history.html (20 July 1998).
36 Hollins, op. cit., pp. 24–5.
37 Gross, op. cit., pp. 140–2.
38 Ibid., pp. 142–3.
39 US Department of Commerce, quoted in Gross, op. cit., p. 142.
40 Research by A.C. Nielsen, op. cit.
41 Gross, op. cit., p. 154.
42 Ibid.
43 R. Collins, *Direct Broadcasting by Satellite in the UK*, London, ESRC, 1991, p. 6.
44 Collins, ibid.
45 R. Mansell, *The New Telecommunications. A Political Economy of Network Evolution*, London, Sage, 1993, p. 17.
46 T. Feldman, op. cit., p. 17.
47 J.S. Quarterman, *The Matrix: Computer Networks and Conferencing Systems Worldwide*, Cincinnati, Digital Press, 1990, pp. 58–9.
48 Hollins, op. cit., p. 22.
49 With the increasing importance of digital communication it has become more usual to measure bandwidth in bits per second.
50 E.X. Dejesus, 'How the Internet Will Replace Broadcasting', *Byte*, February 1996, p. 51.
51 Ibid., p. 54.
52 G. Gilder, 'Into the Fibersphere', *Forbes Magazine*, 7 December 1992. Available on-line at http://www.forbes.com/asap/gilder/telecosm13a.htm (1 August 1998).
53 S. Homer, 'Interactive Television For All', *Independent*, 5 April 1993.
54 M. Spalter (1996), BT website. Available on-line at http://www.btinternet.com/~fyneview/light.straw/about.html (1 August 1998).

55 Mansell, op. cit., p. 11.
56 Spalter, op. cit.
57 Mansell, op. cit., p. 2.
58 Gilder, 'Into the Fibersphere', op. cit.
59 Dejesus, op. cit., p. 51.
60 Mansell, op. cit., p. 25.
61 Dejesus, op. cit., pp. 51–2.
62 N. Mundorf, L. Kolbe and W. Brenner, 'Convergence of Media, Machines and Messages. The Case of the Time-Warner Full Service Network', *Convergence: The Journal of Research into New Media Technologies*, vol.3, no.1, 1997, p. 112.
63 I. Pool, *Technologies Without Boundaries*, London, Harvard University Press, 1990, p. 33.
64 H. Rheingold, 'The Virtual Community', 1985, at Howard Rheingold's website. Available on-line at http://www.well.com/user/hlr/vcbook/vcbook3.html (4 April 1998).
65 Ibid.
66 J.S. Quarterman, *The Matrix*, op. cit., p. 307.
67 Not all LANS use IP – Token Ring, for example, does not.
68 B. Cotton and R. Oliver, *Understanding Multimedia 2000: Multimedia Origins: Internet Futures*, London, Phaidon, 1997, pp. 35–6.
69 Ibid., pp. 36–7.
70 J. Davis, 'Apple's Columbus a Bold Bet', *CNET News*, 13 March 1998. Available on-line at http://www.news.com/News/Item/0,4,20057,00.html (13 March 1998).
71 P. Marks, 'Cue the Computer', *Guardian*, 16 May 1996.
72 Gilder, 'From Waves to Wires', op. cit.
73 D. Hancock, 'Digital Television: A European Perspective', in J. Steemers (ed.), *Changing Channels: The Prospects for Television in a Digital World*, Luton, University of Luton Press, 1998, pp. 125–6.
74 T. Phillips, 'Dial S for Satellite', *Guardian*, 29 January 1998.
75 Ibid. The smallest telephone that can send a signal to the Inmarsat satellite is the size of a laptop computer and weighs 2 kg.
76 M. Tran, 'Telecoms Space Race Starts', *Guardian*, 22 March 1994.
77 J. Forrest , 'Views of the Future of Digital Terrestrial TV', *Spectrum*, Autumn 1993, p. 14.
78 J. Hayes, *Fiber Optics Technician's Handbook*, Albany, New York, Delmar Publishers, 1994. Reproduced on Jeff Hecht's website. Available on-line at http://www.sff.net/people/Jeff.Hecht/history.html.
79 From BT website, 1998. Available on-line at http://www.education.bt.com/factfile/ff9text.htm (3 February 1998).
80 G.J. Mulgan, *Communication and Control: Networks and the New Economies of Communication*, Cambridge, Polity Press, 1991, p. 113.
81 G. Gilder, 'Into the Fibersphere', op. cit.
82 Speech by Robin Smith, Head of Research at British Telecom at 'The Information Superhighway Conference', Cumberland Hotel, London, 24 October 1994.
83 Marvin, op. cit., 1990, p. 157.

Chapter 5

Old media, new media and the state

Jeanette Steemers and Richard Wise

Introduction

In the previous chapter we saw how the rapid adoption of microelectronic components and the introduction of digital technology were, by the 1980s, beginning to transform the established media and communications industries. However, this transformation was not solely a technological one. It was just as much, if not more, a political one, and many of the recent transformations in media and communications actually precede the widespread introduction of digital technologies. This chapter argues that these transformations can only be understood in the context of the enormous changes which took place in the relationship between the state and the media and communications industries during the 1980s and 1990s. It outlines the history of state policy towards media and communications concentrating primarily on the US and the UK. After a survey of policy as it existed before the 1980s, when telecommunications and broadcasting systems were heavily regulated and limited in number, attention focuses on the changes in policy which occurred after the 1980s, when deregulation and competition based on free market ideology became the guiding principles for the governance of these industries.

Old media, new media

Ever since electromagnetic transmission became feasible in the late nine-teenth century the state has been intensely interested in its regulation. However, the technological changes described in the previous chapter have had important implications for the way in which the state has sought to regulate broadcasting and telecommunications. The most important implication was that, in a world of converging communications technologies, the electromagnetic spectrum could no longer be assumed to be a limited resource, as had been the case in the early days of broadcasing. When the telephone was introduced rival companies operated independent uncon-nected systems[1] – for example, in Michigan, 'two phones and two directories were necessary to reach all subscribers'.[2] As more people used the telephone the obvious disadvantages and inefficiencies of this duplication led to an eventual consolidation of companies into monopolies which came increas-ingly under the control of the state. Similarly when radio started there were only a few frequencies available for broadcast transmissions (the familiar long, medium and short waves) and so a centralised frequency allocation and licensing system was considered necessary to prevent stations interfering with each other. Thus in the old media world there were a limited number of broadcasting and telecommunications services run, in the main, by separate institutions using different transmission technologies (non-wired and wired) and in which the state took an increasing interest. However, although the regulation of communications has evolved in different ways in different countries, three main issues have emerged as the rationale for state intervention: the need to maintain common technical standards for reasons of safety and interoperability; a concern with the economic role of the communications industries; and a concern with the moral and political content of entertainment services.

However, the post-digital era promises almost unlimited transmission capacity (both wired and non-wired), and there is a general belief that state regulation must adapt according to these new circumstances. With the prospect of unlimited bandwidth and many service providers and network operators, the promoters of a free market in communications have argued that monopolistic public tele-communications providers are no longer needed.[3] According to this view cross-subsidies to achieve universal access, and common technical standards to preserve system integrity, are illegitimate devices used by the telecommunications companies to reinforce their dominant market position.[4] A free market in telecommunications would protect the consumer interest just as well and more efficiently than statutory regulation.[5] According to this argument, the concept of universal service, based on an assumption of communications scarcity, is irrelevant in a world where:

most homes will have a choice of connecting to five high-capacity networks: one built on the telephone system, one built on cable television, one built on the electric power network, a wireless network for personal communications devices, and another wireless network built from the spaces freed up in the radio spectrum as today's analogue television signals go digital.[6]

Old politics, new politics

At the same time as technological changes were taking place in the 1980s and 1990s, neo-liberal conservative governments in the US and Europe were radically altering the relationship between the state and the communications industries through the privatisation of telecommunications and broadcasting organisations, and the introduction of deregulatory policies. For many these deregulatory measures were a logical response to the information revolution: an unavoidable, multi-channel, multimedia world in which consumers will be king with a choice of hundreds of digital services from wireless (satellite and terrestrial), the Internet and narrow-casting. ('Narrow-casting' refers to programmes which may only be received by subscribers.) However, in this chapter it is argued that these changes in regulatory regimes, although on the face of it prompted by digital convergence, have primarily political rather than technological roots.

Regulating 'old' media

Early regulation of telephony

In the US and UK it was commercial companies who pioneered the introduction of the telephone. However, in both these countries the state took a keen interest in how the service developed. At this time state policy reflected the belief that the telephone system was a natural monopoly. A natural monopoly is said to exist when a product or service can only be delivered most efficiently by one organisation. For example, it would be an inefficient use of resources to have several parallel railway lines owned by different companies on every route. Similarly it would be inefficient to have wires from different telephone companies going into every household. There are also economies of scale to be gained by having a monopolistic telephone provider. These include non-duplication of management, marketing, purchasing and maintenance resources. The problem for regulators was how to gain the economic advantages of monopoly without allowing the commercial exploitation of monopoly power.

In the UK this was solved by the nationalisation of the telephone companies. Telephony became a state monopoly when it was placed under the control of the Royal Mail in 1880 following a High Court ruling that the telephone was a telegraph (the Royal Mail had run the telegraph system as a state monopoly since 1869). In fact, telephone companies were allowed some autonomy until 1912 when their assets were finally nationalised.[7]

In the US too the telephone system had become a monopoly by the 1920s, albeit a private one. In the early years the industry was dominated by the Bell Telephone Company, the company founded by the inventor of the telephone, Alexander Graham Bell. When the patents to Bell's invention expired in 1894,[8] many local telephone companies were established across the States. However, Bell's organisation was restructured into American Telephone and Telegraph (AT&T) in 1900,[9] and it developed and patented superior new technologies for long-distance telephony.[10] This control of long-distance lines gave AT&T a crucial advantage over its local rivals, who it then proceeded to buy out, and by the 1920s the American telephone system had essentially become an AT&T monopoly.[11] The resulting conflicting claims of capital and public interest were partially reconciled in 1913 when AT&T reached an accommodation with the US government. This accommodation was known as the 'Kingsbury Commitment', after the US Attorney General at the time.[12] Under the 'Kingsbury Commitment' AT&T would agree to submit to federal regulation in return for retaining its monopoly power – an arrangement that has been described by one commentator as 'an odd kind of American industrial socialism'.[13]

Monopolistic telephone companies, under state ownership or supervision, promoted social equity since the elimination of competition ensured that all users had equal access to the telephone irrespective of their location or economic status. This was achieved by cross-subsidy, using the profits from providing connections to densely populated urban areas to cover the losses from providing the same service to sparsely populated areas. Under a competitive system, without regulation, only the most wealthy or geographically accessible customers (i.e. the most profitable) would be likely to be served.

Early radio regulation

As radio was first used for ship-to-shore communications, it was initially seen as a form of point-to-point communications, a substitute for the telephone.[14] This view was reflected in early British radio legislation, when by an Act of Parliament in 1904, the regulation of radio was placed under the jurisdiction of the Postmaster General, the government minister responsible for telephony and telegraphs.[15] For governments the main use of radio was initially believed to be for shipping, military communications and for the purpose of maintaining contact with the colonies.[16] As with multimedia in the 1970s, the development of the 'new' technology of wireless was closely connected with national security, as illustrated by the British Navy's backing for Marconi's experiments in the 1890s.[17]

The adoption of radio by commercial shipping in these early years contributed to better safety at sea, but also gave rise to concerns that unregulated commercial and amateur transmissions could interfere with maritime transmissions thus compromising safety. Shortly after the sinking of the Titanic (1912) the US Congress passed the Radio Act aimed at keeping shipping broadcasts separate from the growing community of amateur radio enthusiasts. The Act required the owners of transmitters to obtain a licence from the Department of Commerce, who would allocate frequencies.[18] Security considerations were also important. The military especially feared interference to its own communications, and is known to have been a proponent of a monopoly broadcasting organisation in the UK.[19]

Voice and music broadcasts aimed at the general public became more widespread after the First World War. In this period there were many unregulated radio transmissions by both commercial operators (mainly set manufacturers and the stores which sold their products) and amateur enthusiasts. It was primarily a concern with preventing unregulated chaos of the radio airwaves that shaped policy when governments began to regulate wireless transmissions as a broadcast, rather than as a point-to-point technology.

Commercial radio broadcasting in the US began in 1922 when WEAF, owned by AT&T, began operating as a so-called toll station, charging a fee to transmit advertising messages.[20] To keep people listening WEAF broadcast music and entertainment programmes. AT&T successfully lobbied the Department of Commerce to assign WEAF its own frequency on the grounds that, unlike other stations, it was offering a service to the whole population and should not therefore be made to broadcast on the same frequency as everyone else.[21] AT&T created the first radio network by setting up 'toll' stations in other cities which it linked using its telephone network. AT&T's radio stations also broadcast sports commentaries from other cities, carried by AT&T's long-distance lines.[22] This 'networking' across a greater area greatly enhanced the value of AT&T's radio stations to advertisers. AT&T then used its monopolistic power to prevent the establishment of any rival networks by refusing other radio stations access to its phone lines. This led to government intervention in 1926 to allow other companies into commercial radio broadcasting. As a result, the National Broadcasting Company (NBC) was established in 1926, followed in 1927 by the Columbia Broadcasting System (CBS).[23]

Developments in the US in the 1920s were to have an influence on the early regulation of broadcasting in the UK where there was concern to avoid the technological chaos of the airwaves which was evident in the States.[24] In 1922 this fear of spectrum overcrowding prompted the British

Post Office to give just one company, the Marconi Company, a licence to begin regular broadcasts from its stations in London (2LO), Manchester (2ZY) and Birmingham (5IT).[25] When other manufacturers of radio receivers applied for licences in order to stimulate sales of their sets, the Post Office, still fearful of airwave anarchy, initially refused.

On the one hand the British government believed that radio waves were a scarce resource and that like the telephone system, radio constituted a natural monopoly. On the other hand it did not want to see a broadcasting monopoly in the hands of one company.[26] Therefore, in 1922, the Post Office licensed a consortium of six major radio manufacturers to form the British Broadcasting Company (BBC).[27] Although popular in its early years the British Broadcasting Company was dogged by financial problems.[28] The response of the government was to set up the Crawford Committee in 1926 to examine the future of broadcasting.[29] In 1927, following the Committee's recommendations, the Conservative government set up the British Broadcasting Corporation as an independent public monopoly funded by a licence fee paid by owners of radio sets.[30]

Social regulation of broadcasting

By the 1920s it became clear that anyone with the capital to build a radio station could reach and possibly influence many people simultaneously. Although, as we have seen, the initial concern was to bring order to the airwaves, the political establishment soon became concerned with the social and political implications of radio broadcasting. In the US there was from the beginning a tension between the perceived cultural value of the medium and its use as a vehicle for advertising. This concern was expressed in 1922 by the Secretary for Commerce (and future President) Herbert Hoover who commented '[i]t is inconceivable that we should allow so great a possibility of service to be drowned in advertising chatter'.[31] Demands for state regulation in the US led to the passage of the Radio Act in 1927, which proclaimed that radio waves belonged to the people, and that broadcasters had to obtain licences subject to the allocation of a frequency and a commitment to broadcast 'in the public convenience, interest or necessity'.[32]

In the UK policy on the social role of radio was largely shaped by the beliefs and character of John Reith, the first General Manager of the British Broadcasting Company, and later the first Director-General of the BBC. Reith saw the task of public service broadcasting as being to 'educate, inform and entertain'.[33] The BBC would be distanced from commercial influences, especially advertising, and would provide a wide and full range of programmes for the whole population, financed by the licence fee. Reith believed that the BBC should do more than simply give the public what they wanted, arguing in his 1924 book *Broadcasting Over Britain*, that: 'He who prides himself on giving what he thinks the public wants is often creating a fictitious demand for lower standards which he will then satisfy.'[34] Reith took the paternalistic view that it was the BBC's role to give the listener 'something better than she thought she wanted'.[35]

Monopoly became an essential part in maintaining this type of paternalistic control. Scarcity of airwaves is often given as the reason for early broadcasting monopolies like the BBC, but monopoly also offered the best way of controlling what was regarded as a persuasive medium. There were always more than enough frequencies to create several competing broadcasting organisations from the beginning, but numbers were limited for political, social, economic and cultural reasons.[36] The principle of monopoly was also applied to television broadcasting when it resumed after the Second World War in the UK and many European countries.

The principles of public service broadcasting, as they evolved from Reith's model, can be summarised as follows:

- independence from the state, commercial and other organisations;
- some form of public funding;
- geographical and social universality; anyone anywhere has access to broadcasting services;
- varied and balanced schedules containing a mixture of education, information and entertainment;
- an obligation to be impartial in the provision of news and public information;
- accountability to the public.[37]

Of course these elements can not be seen in isolation. They interact, overlap and may conflict. For example, the way a broadcaster is funded has a bearing on the level of its independence from the state or other organisations.[38] The funding of the BBC has been, since its inception in 1926, derived from a universal licence fee. In recommending the licence fee the Crawford Committee in 1926 had argued that not only would this provide a stable source of finance, but it would also guarantee its creative and political independence.[39] This hope proved to be somewhat optimistic, particularly after the 1970s when inflationary pressures and the decline in the growth of colour TV licences forced the BBC to ask the government for larger licence fee increases in order to keep pace with the rising costs of running the corporation.[40]

The UK government's political commitment to the principles underlying public service broadcasting was demonstrated in 1955, even when the BBC's television monopoly was broken with the establishment of the commercially funded Independent Television (ITV) network. ITV was bound by the same public service obligations as the BBC. It had a statutory duty to pursue public service principles, providing a broad range of cultural and regional programming and safeguards against political bias based very much on the Reithian model. As we shall see, this changed after the 1990 Broadcasting Act, which reduced the level of public service obligations that commercial broadcasters had to fulfil.

In the US the commitment to public service broadcasting was never as strong as it had been in the UK. This was despite the fact that in the early years there was strong awareness of the social implications of unrestricted commercialism in broadcasting. Pioneers of American broadcasting such as David Sarnoff (the radio operator who picked up the *Titanic*'s distress call, the inventor of radio as an entertainment medium, president of RCA and founder of NBC)[41] had expressed beliefs similar to those of Reith,[42] and the 1927 Radio Act had stated that the right to use public airwaves should be on condition that broadcasters served 'the public convenience, interest or necessity'.[43] The US Secretary of Commerce, Herbert Hoover, had expressed the hope that advertising would not pollute radio with all its promise for public enlightenment.[44] Yet it is an indication of the failure of Hoover's hope that when he died in 1964, 'NBC broadcast a tribute that was followed by a beer commercial, a political commercial, and a cigarette commercial'.[45]

Public service broadcasting in the US originated with early experiments in educational broadcasting.[46] In the 1920s a number of educational institutions set up radio stations primarily to support home-study students, and in 1922 there were seventy-four such stations in operation.[47] However, during the course of the 1920s these educational broadcasters were progressively bought out by commercial stations. Educational broadcasters organised to fight this trend but eventually hopes for public service broadcasting were dashed with the defeat of an amendment to the Communications Act in 1934. This would have reserved 25 per cent of broadcasting time for educational and non-profit broadcasts.[48] The principles of public service broadcasting in the US had been outlined in the Federal Communications Commission's (FCC) 1946 report *Public Service Responsibilities of Broadcast Licensees*.[49] However, the FCC was unable to prevent the progressive ditching of these principles as the quest for high audience ratings led to 'a steady trend away from "controversial" and modestly rated public service programs and towards entertainment'.[50] The failure of commercial media to provide adequate cultural and education provision led to the setting up of the Carnegie Commission and in 1967, with the Public Broadcasting Act, the establishment of a Public Broadcasting Service (PBS). However, the impact of PBS was small and by 1970 public interest coverage had fallen to 2 per cent of total US programming.[51] This situation was exacerbated by funding problems after PBS broadcast a number of programmes critical of the Nixon government. This resulted in the administration vetoing Congressional funding for the service in the early 1970s,[52] and this withholding of financial support by the federal government continued into the 1980s and 1990s. By the 1990s PBS had become increasingly dependent on sponsorship and imported programming, particularly from the BBC.

Early regulation of cable

Early regulation of cable in both the US and the UK was principally designed to protect established monopoly broadcasters. In the UK before the Second World War, the BBC, who already faced competition from overseas private radio stations, such as Radio Normandie and Radio Luxembourg (founded 1931 and 1933 respectively), regarded cable as a threat.[53] In the 1930s The Relay Services Association (the UK cable industry's trade association) lobbied the government to allow cable operators to originate programmes on local affairs, something the BBC stoutly resisted on the grounds that it would diminish its public service principles.[54]

In the US the main concern until the 1980s had been to protect local broadcasting stations from cable stations who wanted to import channels from outside the local broadcasting transmission area. Attempts by local TV stations to persuade the Federal Communications Commission (FCC) to regulate against the importation of signals failed when Congress refused to pass the necessary legislation in the late 1950s.[55] After this, it was state and local authorities that took on the role of regulating cable, issuing franchises and placing stipulations on how the cable companies should operate. A key condition for obtaining a franchise was how much the cable company was willing to pay a local authority for the privilege of holding the franchise.[56] Despite Congress's refusal to legislate the Federal government became involved in cable regulation in the 1960s when, following a 1963 Federal appeals court ruling (the Carter Mountain Case),[57] the FCC began to restrict local cable companies from importing programmes from outside their area.[58]

From intervention to *laisser-faire*

New Right philosophy

The election of the 'New Right' governments of Margaret Thatcher in the UK in 1979 and Ronald Reagan in the US in 1980 was a watershed in the history of the state regulation of communications. The media and communications landscape that had emerged in the inter-war and post-war years had been based on a general faith in the powers of rational public organisation:

> The BBC, like the telephone and broadcasting companies of most advanced countries was formed at a time ... of Fabian dominance in

Britain, progressivism in the US and corporatism in Europe. There was widespread faith in technology, and rationality in debate and organisation. There was also a belief in the virtues of scale, at least when it brought order to the untrammelled market. Both RCA and the BBC are products of this period, each with a national purpose, and each a creation of collaboration between State and private sector.[59]

It was this media landscape that the New Right sought to overturn. Conservative governments, elected at a time when developments in information technology were already leading many to foretell the digital age, saw market forces as better suited to cope with the rapidly changing telecommunications industry than publicly controlled monopolies.[60] New Right policy had a number of political aims that were intellectually underpinned by, on the one hand, a political philosophy of markets and, on the other, a techno-determinist belief in the inevitability of the 'information society'.

The political aim was to change the balance of power between public institutions and the interests of business. This political aim stemmed from the right's analysis of what had led to the demise of the post-war boom in the early 1970s. During this period, roughly from 1945 to the oil crisis of 1973, there had been a political consensus in favour of state intervention in the economy. The era had seen a transfer of power away from business to state and public collectivist organisations that were designed to counteract the anti-social effects of the market. When the boom ended in the early 1970s the right felt intellectually vindicated, seeing the resultant economic and political crisis as the inevitable result of ignoring market forces. For them the crisis was due to the stifling of enterprise by high taxation and the overbearing power of the state and its agencies. Public organisations like the BBC became a particular target for New Right radicals, and the restructuring of communications and broadcasting became an early policy objective of newly elected conservative governments. The intellectual foundations of these policies lay in a fervent belief in market forces untrammelled by state intervention and an acceptance that digital communications technologies were the new engines of economic advance (just as steam power and electricity had been in previous ages).

The power of the market

The most important aspect of New Right policy was a faith in 'market forces'. Charles Jonscher, a media adviser to the Thatcher government, outlined this faith in the market in 1988. In an article for the *Sunday Times* he challenged 'the myths of broadcasting' that, used to shape the thinking of governments on all public services from the railways to the national health, and which still survives in this field of broadcasting. The chief myth is that because an activity fulfils a public service it is not subject to basic laws of economics . . . the principles of supply and demand.[61]

The classic free-market model is based on the assumption of many buyers and many sellers, such that no single buyer or seller is able to dominate the market. Each market participant is assumed to have perfect knowledge of what goods are being offered for sale and at what price. It is also assumed that there are no barriers to any new seller entering the market, and that all sellers are faced with identical costs. Each buyer and seller will behave in a rational way to maximise their satisfaction by comparing prices and quality and buying at the lowest price. Any supplier who attempted to increase profits by pushing prices above the market level or who produced less efficiently than others in the market would lose his customers to rivals. In this way, according to the eighteenth-century political economist Adam Smith, the conflicting claims of individuals for a share of the nation's wealth would be automatically reconciled as if by an 'invisible hand'.[62]

Despite being an inappropriate model for the telecommunications and media industries as they actually existed at the beginning of the 1980s, this was to become the ideal for New Right media policy, as it was for many other aspects of the economy. Indeed it was believed that the new technologies with their promise of unlimited spectrum and multiple channels would offer a means of creating a market where before there had been only monopolistic centralised provision. In broadcasting this commitment to the market was helped by the arrival of satellite and cable channels, which removed technical barriers to an expansion of the television marketplace. In telecommunications the market was enhanced by breaking up the monopolies of AT&T, BT, Deutsche Bundepost and many others.

In broadcasting, the public service ethos prevalent in the UK and much of western Europe was based on one form of distribution (terrestrial broadcasting), and the belief that the airwaves were a common property whose use needed to be subject to public regulation and accountability. In contrast in the new age of spectrum abundance, the market view came to see communications networks as 'private clubs, with exclusive entry and separated and segmented entertainments for each class or each lifestyle'.[63] According to the market model the public good would be optimised by allowing each individual to make choices from a range of diverse and competing electronic media. In the UK the elements of this new model of broadcasting had been articulated in the 1970s and 1980s by writers associated with right-wing 'think-tanks' such as the Institute of Economic Affairs.[64] This free-market view of communications was stated with characteristic robustness by the media tycoon Rupert Murdoch, in a speech to media professionals at the 1989 Edinburgh International Television Festival. Here he spoke of British television, 'reaching maturity . . . and entering a time when independence and choice, rather than regulation and scarcity, will be its hallmarks'.[65]

Drawing heavily on the rhetoric of this ideology, the overriding assumption behind US and UK government policy in the 1980s was that the public interest would best be served by allowing the individual to have a free choice in a competitive, lightly regulated media market. This free-market model of communications was exemplified in the views of Mark Fowler, the chairman of the Federal Communications Commission (FCC) from 1981 to 1987, and the architect of the Reagan administration's deregulatory policies. Fowler rejected previous notions of public service obligations for broadcasting content, believing that communications and media were like any other market, subject to the laws of supply and demand. He went on to describe television as 'a toaster with pictures'.[66] According to Fowler the public interest could be adequately expressed through 'consumer sovereignty' rather than by state regulation, and in 1981 he announced to a gathering of media professionals that 'from here onward, the public's interests must determine the public interest'.[67]

The inevitability of information technology

The other intellectual foundation of New Right policy was a determinist faith in the commercial, economic and social potential of the 'micro'. This belief in the revolutionary potential of microelectronics was not confined to the right. It had become the conventional wisdom of all shades of political opinion since the late 1970s when the potential of the microchip first entered the popular consciousness through the media. A programme/broadcast in 1978 by the BBC, titled *Now the Chips are Down* (part of the *Horizon* documentary strand), so impressed the British Labour Party Prime Minister, James Callaghan, that he instructed the Cabinet's Central Policy Review Staff (CPRS) to look into the implications of this technology for the British economy.[68] Shortly afterwards Margaret Thatcher's Conservative government underlined the importance it placed on new technology by declaring 1982 'Information Technology (IT) Year', complete with a special set of postage stamps. As part of this initiative a minister was appointed with responsibility for the promotion of IT. In 1982 the first holder of the office, Kenneth Baker, proclaimed:

> We need IT for the stimulus it gives to innovation. We need it for the greater efficiency and productivity it brings to industry, commerce and education. As an exporting nation we need it in order to carve ourselves a share of what is already a world market of £50 billion a year.[69]

Typical of this belief in the inexorable power of information technology at this time was a 1982 speech by Peter Jay, then Chairman and Chief Executive of the British TV company TV-AM. In his speech to the Edinburgh Television Festival in 1982, Jay compared those who doubted the new technology to 'medieval monks and barons – the vested interests of the age – debating whether or not to permit the Renaissance'.[70]

In the US such ideas have also had a great impact. Alvin Toffler has been one of the most influential gurus of the revitalising effects of new technology through his book *The Third Wave*.[71] Toffler has argued that the new information technologies are radically changing our civilisation's 'info-sphere',[72] leading to a new phase in human history, the 'Third Wave'. He asserts that:

> as we construct a new info-sphere for a Third Wave civilization, we are imparting to the 'dead' environment around us, not life, but intelligence.[73]

Toffler's writings have had a great influence on American politicians, most notably the Republican Speaker of the House of Representatives and a passionate advocate of the free market, Newt Gingrich. Gingrich has frequently consulted Toffler and acknowledged his influence.[74]

New Right policy agenda: deregulation and privatisation

Thus at the heart of New Right policy was the belief that it was the dynamic of the free market that would most effectively transform the existing telecom and broadcasting monopolies into a market for many diverse digital telecommunication services including, eventually, multimedia. For the Thatcher and Reagan governments 'technology and private enterprise were seen as the foundations of the new information economy'.[75] In terms of policy this meant the deregulation and privatisation of the existing broadcasting and telecommunications monopolies in order both to provide financial incentives for innovation and to benefit consumers by encouraging competition between media and telecommunications providers. This free-market approach, characterised by Mansell as the 'idealist model', saw new media technologies as:

> harbingers of the new wave of ubiquitous communication services that will be accessible to all . . . a vision of a fully interactive service environment in which access, via the public service network, to all conceivable electronic services is available to customers at ever decreasing prices.[76]

This vision was echoed in 1998 by OFTEL, the regulatory authority for telecommunications in the UK, which saw the telecommunications system evolving into an eventual 'Open State' which it described as a:

> mature multi-channel market, characterised by the absence of significant capacity constraints and the near universal availability of control access systems [and] where there are no material capacity constraints on businesses setting up to offer these new services, provided they stick within a simple set of rules. In this 'Open State' all consumers must be able to pass smoothly and at an affordable price through the electronic turnstile which gives them access to the new education, information and entertainment services.[77]

When New Democrat and New Labour administrations replaced New Right conservative governments in the US and the UK in 1992 and 1997 respectively, the basic premises of communications policy did not change. There was still the same techno-revolutionary zeal allied to an unerring faith in market forces.

In the US this faith in technological progress was represented by Vice-President Al Gore. In fact, before becoming Bill Clinton's running mate in 1992, Gore had established impeccable counter-culture credentials, publishing a book called *Earth in the Balance: Ecology and the Human Spirit* in 1992.[78] Gore was a force behind the launch of the National Information Infrastructure Initiative in 1993. Here the US government committed itself to building a National Information Infrastructure (NII), a 'seamless web of communications networks, computer databases, consumer electronics capable of transmitting, storing, processing and displaying voice, data and images'.[79]

The construction of the NII was to be achieved through co-operation between government and business, but it was clear that this co-operation would take place more or less on business's terms. The Clinton administration agreed with the preceding Reagan–Bush administration that investment should come from the private not the public sector. This was acknowledged by Vice-President Gore in 1993 when he stated:

> [The] communication industries are moving to the unified information market-place of the future. [To meet] this development, we must move from the traditional adversarial relationship between business and government to a more productive relationship based on consensus. We must build a new model of public-private cooperation.[80]

Gore reaffirmed the new administration's allegiance to market forces with a certainty no less than the previous Republican administration, declaring that,

We begin with two of our basic principles – the need for private investment and fair competition. The nation needs private investment to
complete the construction of the National Information Infrastructure.
And competition is the single most critical means of encouraging that
private investment.[81]

The Gore initiative promised such incentives as tax concessions and research
funding to private firms in return for an obligation on the part of the
companies to facilitate a universal service to avoid the creation of 'information
have-nots'. In return the government also acknowledged the industry's case
for changes in the rules concerning companies operating in each other's
transmission domains, and promised to let telephone companies operate cable
services, and local telephone companies provide long-distance services,
promises which were implemented in the 1996 Telecommunications Act.

However, a problem with the free-market model advanced by many
policy-makers was that the media and communications 'market' as it
existed at the end of the 1970s, was very different from the collection of small
traders described by Adam Smith two centuries earlier. As we have seen,
policy from the 1920s to the 1970s had been based on the assumption that
telecommunications and broadcasting constitute 'natural monopolies' and
their institutional structure, history and culture reflected this. However, there
were also basic contradictions at the heart of New Right policy arising from
conflicts between some of its policy aims.

On the one hand the market theorists wanted to encourage competition
in order to prevent the 'market distortions' caused by monopoly (i.e. loss
of consumer choice and inefficient use of resources). However, this had to be
balanced against another policy aim of encouraging the heavy investment
required to install the new technology. Companies would only be encouraged
to invest if they could be assured of a flow of high and stable profits, and too
much competition posed a threat to profits.

The other contradiction lay in the tension between the New Right's
desire to remove state regulation and its commitment to 'family values' and
'back to basics'. The New Right's economic instincts were to have as little
state intervention as possible while its social authoritarianism led it to want
to prohibit the airing of explicit sexual and violent material. In the US
Telecommunications Act of 1996 these contradictions were addressed by
putting faith in 'v-chip' technology. This would enable parents to screen out
undesirable material. Broadcasters would have the responsibility of grading
and coding adult material and set manufacturers would have the responsibility
of installing the v-chip.[82]

Encouraging competition

The first moves towards liberalisation in the US and UK came in the telecommunications sector with the aim of ending the monopoly or near monopoly status of the dominant telephone companies: the state-owned British Telecom (BT) in the UK, and, the privately-owned, but state regulated AT&T in the US. However, as the 1980s wore on the cable and broadcasting sectors were also subjected to deregulation.

Telecommunications deregulation

In the UK the process began with the Telecommunications Act of 1981 which ended BT's monopoly of long-distance business communications carriage. In the following year Mercury Communications was awarded a licence to compete with BT in long-distance telecommunications services. In 1984 BT was privatised. In order to ensure that BT did not abuse its economic dominance the government, following the American model of the FCC, established the Office of Telecommunications (OFTEL) in 1982 as an independent regulatory body to 'ensure fair competition and fair prices'.[83] The BT/Mercury duopoly in telephony was itself ended in 1991 with the entry of cable companies into the British telephony market following the publication of the government White Paper, *Competition and Choice: Telecommunications Policy for the 1990s*, by the Department of Trade and Industry.[84] The process of opening telephony to competition was also furthered during the 1990s by the proliferation of mobile phone networks.

In the US the most significant moment in the development of New Right policy towards telecommunications occurred when the judiciary intervened to break up the AT&T monopoly in telephony in 1984. In the 1960s AT&T's long-distance monopoly was challenged by companies using microwave transmissions, most significantly in 1969 when MCI established a microwave link between Chicago and St. Louis. However, AT&T's control of local telephone companies gave them the power to keep the new long-distance operators off most of the US telephone network. Two of these long distance operators, Sprint and MCI, challenged AT&T in the courts claiming that it was abusing its dominant power through its pricing policies and technical connection restrictions. In 1984, as a result of these legal actions, AT&T agreed to divest itself of its local operators known as Regional Bell Operating Companies (RBOCS). The RBOCS became independent, private, local telephone operators while the new AT&T became an exclusively long-distance carrier, unable to restrict access to the local 'Baby Bells' by other carriers.

Cable deregulation

The deregulation of cable in the US began in 1980 when the FCC abolished the rules that limited the ability of local cable operators to import transmissions from outside their franchise area.[85] The process of deregulation continued in 1984 with the Cable Communications Policy Act that prevented local authorities regulating the rates cable operators charged their customers.[86] However, the operators abused their power and raised prices to such an extent that the industry had to be re-regulated in 1992, with the FCC being given the power to force cable operators to lower their prices in the public interest.[87]

In the UK, meanwhile, the Conservative government saw the cable industry as the vanguard of the information revolution. As we have seen cable television was not new to the UK and by the early 1980s about 12.8 per cent of households were connected to cable systems, mainly in areas where broadcast reception was poor.[88] Until the 1980s the industry had been in decline, unable by law to generate its own programming, and with improvements in the quality of broadcast transmissions it was losing its principal market attraction.[89] Indeed, in 1977 the Annan Committee of Enquiry into Broadcasting had dismissed the benefits of the further development of commercial cable systems calling cable 'a parasite'.[90] Yet by the early 1980s, the Thatcher government was promoting privately-owned cable systems as the main route to the establishment of more technologically advanced cable broadband services. The process began in 1980 when William Whitelaw, the Conservative Home Secretary, ended the previous policy of prohibiting cable operators from originating their own programmes and licensed thirteen pilot cable projects.[91] In 1981 Prime Minister Thatcher was presented with a Cabinet Office report commissioned by the previous Labour administration. The Advisory Council for Applied Research and Development (ACARD) report took a strongly economic line stressing the urgency of Britain gaining commercial benefit from this revolutionary new technology. Mrs Thatcher took the issue so seriously that she set up a special unit within the Cabinet Office to deal with the challenge. Essentially the role of the unit was to encourage the spirit of free enterprise in the emerging information technology sector, thereby ensuring that the UK got an early foothold in the new 'information age'.

In 1981 the UK government established ITAP (the Information Technology Advisory Panel), a panel of leading executives from the computing and electronics industries.[92] ITAP's *Cable Systems* report[93] in 1982 recognised that the growth of a market required a rise in consumer demand and this was most likely to occur if subscribers were offered entertainment channels. The report pointed out that, cable systems, based on co-axial cables or optical fibres, can provide many new telecommunications-based services to homes and businesses. The initial attraction for home subscribers could be the extra television entertainment channels. However the main role of cable systems eventually will be the delivery of many information, financial and other services to the home and the joining of businesses and homes by high capacity data links.[94]

The ITAP report was particularly significant for broadcasting policy because for the first time economic and industrial issues were considered as equally if not more important than social and political concerns, an unsurprising outcome given the overwhelming preponderance of businessmen on the committee.[95] Entertainment services were seen as the driver for the implementation of business and interactive services. In the same year as the publication of the ITAP report, the government-appointed Hunt Committee produced a report on the cable industry which recommended the establishment of a Cable Authority, to license and oversee privately-owned broadband cable franchises.[96] The Hunt Committee's findings were implemented in the Cable and Broadcasting Act of 1984. The 1984 Act allowed the granting of cable franchises to operate local cable monopolies under the control of a statutory Cable Authority. The first eleven franchises were allocated to local cable companies in 1984. However, throughout the 1980s the growth of the cable industry was very slow. A number of companies pulled out including BT, who sold all but one of the franchises it had acquired in 1984. This situation did not change until 1991 when the government relaxed the rules and allowed cable companies to offer telephone services as well as television. The government sought to favour the cable companies further by the so-called 'asymmetry' rule whereby BT was prohibited from transmitting video services that competed with cable to ensure that these fledgling services were not crushed by the former monopolist's market dominance and financial strength. Another significant fact which sustained the cable industry in the 1990s was a consolidation of ownership under North American companies. They were attracted by the ability to offer entertainment and telephony together, something which did not occur in the US until 1996.

Broadcasting deregulation

While American broadcasting has always been subject to strong market forces, the British system of regulating broadcasting up to the 1980s sought to strike a balance between commercial priorities and the principles of public service broadcasting. It did this by ensuring that no broadcasting organisation competed for the same source of revenue, and that therefore there was an incentive to compete in terms of balanced programming rather than simply audience size and ultimately revenues.[97] For example, when Channel Four was established in 1982, it was funded by a subscription from the ITV companies; they in turn sold Channel Four's airtime.[98] This was the 'delicate television ecology'[99] which was challenged in the mid-1980s by the free-market policies of the Conservative government, supported by the increased possibilities of cable and satellite transmission.

At a policy level, a marked change was achieved with the passage of the 1990 Broadcasting Act,[100] which combined increased commercialisation, weakened regulation and easier access to the broadcast media for other commercial interests. The passage of the Act also marked a change in the relationship between television and its audience, with greater emphasis placed on the audience as consumers, rather than on their role as citizens to be informed and entertained.[101]

The 1990 Act was based on the assumption that there would always be access to quality public service broadcasting through the BBC and Channel Four. Within this context the 1990 Act loosened the requirements for balance on the commercial terrestrial network, ITV. Prior to the 1990 Act commercial terrestrial television and local radio were regulated by the Independent Broadcasting Authority (IBA), which functioned as both a broadcaster and regulator. The IBA had a contractual arrangement with each regional ITV company and had the right to preview programmes and approve schedules in accordance with public service criteria. It was also responsible for providing the service on Channel Four, an IBA subsidiary. The 1990 Act provided a new regulatory framework. Two new regulatory bodies, the Independent Television Commission (ITC) and the Radio Authority, replaced the IBA and the Cable Authority that had licensed the cable industry. The ITC was made responsible for licensing and regulating (but not broadcasting) all commercial television services.[102] Where the IBA had been both publisher and broadcaster of ITV, as well as its regulator, the ITV licensees are now responsible for programme content within the framework of their licences and the existing ITC regulatory codes. The IBA's previewing powers were removed, and programming and scheduling powers were allocated to the ITV Network Centre, run by the ITV companies. The ITC's main task after the award of licences is to ensure that the licensees' programming policies are delivered and that licence and code requirements are adhered to.

Crucially the Broadcasting Act of 1990 introduced a system whereby ITV franchises would be put up for sale by competitive tender and awarded to the highest bidder, after a 'quality threshold' and financial sustainability test had been passed.[103] Cable and satellite programme licences were to be issued virtually on demand for services complying with the consumer protection requirements in ITC Codes.[104]

Market consolidation

By the 1990s, despite the free market rhetoric, New Right policy in both the UK and the US had become preoccupied with encouraging the formation of monopolistic media and communications conglomerates rather than encouraging competition. Ownership and cross-ownership restrictions were relaxed with the aim of creating 'enterprise friendly' regimes which encouraged risk-taking and investment. The prospect of convergence between different delivery platforms and the high cost of introducing digital technologies played a role in the drive to consolidate ownership as it was believed that companies should have sufficient financial resources to undertake the necessary investment. The anti-monopolistic nature of previous telecommunications and broadcasting legislation was seen as limiting conglomerates' global competitiveness. In this context market dominance was seen as a price well worth paying in order to encourage the establishment of the new media order. This led New Right governments to prioritise media investment over other goals, such as restricting media concentration to ensure diversity and pluralism in media and communications.[105]

Telecommunications – the case of the United States

In the US the process of telecoms deregulation and privatisation culminated in the 1996 Telecommunications Reform Act which removed barriers to entry, allowing extensive cross-ownership including network control and service provision. This resulted in consolidation both within the telecommunications industry and in its relationship with the media and information industries.[106] Essentially the Act tried to reconcile the contradiction implicit in giving private capital the risky task of building a fibre-optic national broadband network while submitting its activities to the harsh forces of competition. The uncertainties and low profit margins inherent in increased competition were reduced by lifting most restrictions on cross-media ownership. At the same time, price controls on cable television rates were removed to encourage cable companies to generate the profits needed to invest in a fibre-optic infrastructure. The Act deregulated telephone services (local, long-distance, cable television, cellular phone and on-line computer services) thereby enabling the companies that provided these services to enter each other's business. The intention of the Act, according to the rhetoric of those who supported it, was to unleash an era of vigorous competition between cable operators and long- and short-distance telephone companies.[107] The Act aimed to do this by encouraging cross-ownership as an incentive to invest. In reality, however, it simply accelerated the trend towards mergers, acquisitions and strategic alliances as telephone companies geared up to offer all-in-one home and communications packages to business users and domestic consumers.[108] Ironically the consequence of the 1996 Telecommunications Reform Act was not an increase in competition, but a reconstitution, through mergers and alliances, of a monopolistic regime similar to the one that had apparently been broken up by the divestiture of AT&T in 1984. The companies which emerged from the restructuring of the industry actually shrank from competing in each other's markets, largely due to the high capital costs of entry. For example, telephone companies baulked at competing in the cable market because high capital costs included not just those of laying cable, but also the cost of installing expensive untried multimedia technologies such as those required for interactivity and video-on-demand.

Broadcasting – the case of the United Kingdom

An early example of the contradiction, between free-market rhetoric and the high capital cost of establishing new media technologies can be seen in the way that direct broadcast satellite (DBS) was introduced to the UK in the 1980s. The Conservative government understood that DBS was likely to play a crucial role in the emerging new media environment, and as early as 1980 it initiated a study of 'the implications of establishing a United Kingdom direct broadcasting satellite service by about 1985'.[109] The policy that emerged was to grant a monopoly licence through the commercial television regulatory body, the Independent Broadcasting Authority (IBA), to just one satellite broadcaster, British Satellite Broadcasting (BSB). However, the establishment of BSB was pre-empted by News Corporation's Sky television, using transponders on the Luxembourg-owned Astra satellite to broadcast to the British Isles. Sky were able to take advantage of BSB's technical problems with both their Marco Polo satellite and receiving equipment to establish a four channel service in February 1989[110] before BSB even began transmitting. Eventually, in November 1990,[111] Sky and BSB merged to form BSkyB, with BSkyB effectively absorbing BSB.

The 1996 Broadcasting Act further reflected this belief that relaxed cross-ownership rules represented a necessary prerequisite for investment in new technologies. The Act adopted a new approach to the definition of monopoly power based on a complicated calculation of 'market share' rather than ownership.[112] The effect of the Act was to reduce restrictions on cross-media ownership with the aim of encouraging the creation of media conglomerates which could both undertake investment in the new digital technologies and compete in global markets.[113] This change in policy came about in no small measure because of intensive lobbying by the industry for the government to relax the rules. As a result of the greater competitive atmosphere and financial instability following the 1990 Broadcasting Act, the major ITV companies lobbied for a relaxation of ownership rules in order to allow them to consolidate and compete in the international marketplace.[114]

The British Media Industry Group, established in 1993 by the UK's leading newspaper groups, was also highly influential in calling for a relaxation of cross-ownership rules.[115]

Facing the digital challenge

It has already been argued that the transformation of media and communications in recent years is more closely connected to deregulatory policies and commercialisation than technological advances, but digitalisation does complicate the policy-making process. What is noticeable about previous state intervention is that it has tended to focus on access to separate delivery platforms with different degrees of regulation, depending on the nature of the services provided and the degree of public access to these services. For example, broadcasting has always been strictly regulated in terms of content, because it is aimed at a mass audience, whereas the one-to-one nature of telecommunications, and later computing, has traditionally involved only limited content regulation.

The challenge for regulators now is to cope with the converging nature of networks and what they provide, as telecommunications, broadcasting and computing networks start to deliver similar types of services both on a one-to-one (e.g., video-on-demand) and one-to-many basis (e.g., Internet radio). However, many new services do not fit into existing regulatory and institutional structures, reinforcing uncertainty over the justification for regulation and whether it can be realistically implemented, particularly given the huge increase of services on distribution systems like the Internet.[116] In regulating for a digital future, policy-makers need to strike a fine balance between the political, social and cultural values traditionally associated with media policy (i.e. universal access, diverse content, etc.), and the predominantly commercial and economic priorities associated with tele-communications policy (i.e. avoiding abuse of a dominant market position, promoting industrial growth).

Policy-makers also face other difficulties in constructing a policy framework for digital media, not the least because legislative activity lags substantially behind developments in the market-place. The situation is exacerbated further still by the increasing internationalisation of broadcasting, telecommunications and computing, with the emergence of multinational multimedia groupings involved in several territories, and within and across several related industries. This convergence of ownership, particularly at an international level, serves to diminish the importance and effectiveness of national and sector specific legislation, and underlines the continued lack of co-ordination between media, telecommunications and information technology policy.[117] This new situation has led Wolfgang Hoffmann-Riem to conclude that:

The regulatory philosophy of media laws to date will certainly come unstuck when faced by the globally structured multimedia and information society of the future. The actors in this environment can move with relative ease from one level and sphere of action to another, disguise themselves through structural interlocking, submerge in international networks or openly risk power struggles with supervisory bodies – and usually win on account of the numerous dependencies.[118]

In the UK this perceived lack of co-ordination and ineffectiveness of sectoral control led to recommendations in May 1998 from the House of Commons Select Committee for Culture, Media and Sport for a separate government Department of Communications to assume the broadcasting and media responsibilities of the Department of Culture, Media and Sport (DCMS), and the telecommunications responsibilities of the Department of Trade and Industry (DTI).[119] Such a reorganisation would have removed the division between economic regulation (traditionally the preserve of the DTI) and content regulation (traditionally the preserve of the DCMS). The Committee went on to recommend one Communications Regulation Commission to supervise every aspect of the emerging communications infrastructure including access, ownership, competition issues and content regulation.[120] However, this approach is not supported by those who believe that there should continue to be a distinction between, on the one hand, regulation in pursuit of economic aims and consumer protection, and on the other content regulation to preserve and promote cultural goals and the public interest.[121] A British government Green Paper, while acknowledging a need for greater co-ordination, stated that commitment to a particular institutional model would be premature at this stage, and invited views on a number of different models for the regulation of a converged market.[122]

While ownership and control have emerged as key issues in the debate concerning the introduction of digital media, control of consumer access through ownership of distribution networks, conditional access systems and electronic programme guides has also emerged as a major area of concern in relation to market dominance. Conditional access systems based on the gateway of set-top boxes are important because they form the basis of subscription management and encryption which restricts reception to those who have subscribed to a particular service. However, there is mounting concern about the risk of anti-competitive or exploitative behaviour in situations where the main gatekeeper to the distribution system for other programme providers should also be a major provider of rival programme services and rights for that market both directly as a retailer and indirectly as a wholesaler to rival distribution systems.[123] For consumers the best system would involve a common interface, where decoders are not linked to a particular conditional access system, but this seems unlikely given the amount of investment by operators in proprietary conditional access systems.[124] Common wisdom supports the view that consumers will only buy one set-top box, which means that a small number of companies may well end up dominating the digital market just as a limited number of operators now dominate the analogue market for subscription television through their proprietary conditional access systems.[125] Legislators are not entirely unaware of the dangers of monopolistic abuse which might deter new service providers, and reduce choice, competition and innovation, but their responses have tended to be slow and piecemeal, with legislative efforts lagging behind developments in the real world where battles are already being fought and won between rival and incompatible systems.[126]

In addition to the debate about access in the digital era, the prospect of digital plenty has prompted further deliberations about supervision of content. While supervision of content has played a prominent role in broadcasting regulation, content regulation in the telecommunications and computing sectors has traditionally been limited. With the ascendancy of the New Right more regulatory emphasis was placed on economic regulation to strengthen market forces and enhance consumer choice. However, economic diversity should not be confused with content issues, particularly where they relate to the media's role in contributing to the formation of public opinion. Emphasis on economic regulation also fails to take account of the public's desire for continued supervision of undesirable content. The expansion in transmission capacity through digital technology does not remove the need for regulation, although detailed supervision of content has become less effective with the large increase in content in recent years, particularly on the Internet. However, the special nature of the right to communicate and the cultural and political role of universally available services like broadcast television, suggests that these cannot always be left simply to regulation by the market or competition law, even in the digital era. The principles of diversity, pluralism, independence and equality of access that have traditionally underpinned the media's important role in shaping and informing public opinion suggest that in spite of the promise of bountiful services in future, there are still strong grounds for persisting with some form of content regulation which emphasises the importance of these principles.[127] Content regulation in this instance can act as a counterweight to risks to diversity from ownership concentration which may undermine choice. It is also likely to remain important for conventional broadcasting which will continue to be the most widely accessible form of television for several years until widespread access to digital media allows television to operate more like publishing.

This distinction between different types of content, with different degrees of impact on public opinion, has reinforced calls for different levels of content regulation depending on the nature of the service and its importance to public debate. However, this approach then needs policy decisions about what these levels of content should be, to what degree different forms of content influence public opinion, and to what extent the supply of certain types of content should be allowed to be dominated by a few concerns.[128]

An approach which distinguishes between different levels of content regulation in line with the public accessibility to services was proposed by a UK House of Commons Select Committee Report in May 1998.[129] This tentatively suggested that content regulation might fall into four tiers subject to a basic framework of standards and decency, although it admitted that free-to-air services on digital platforms will eventually blur the distinction between terrestrial and non-terrestrial distribution. The committee proposed the following four tiers:

(a)   Limited content regulation for transaction or non-scheduled services which comply with ratings and filtering standards.
(b)   Minimal positive programming requirements for scheduled non-terrestrial services like subscription television.
(c)   Broad programming requirements for scheduled free-to-air commercial services.
(d)   Detailed programming requirements for scheduled free-to-air services of a public service nature.

This approach is in line with current trends where public service broadcasting is expected to meet higher programme standards to make up for the programme shortfalls of commercial operators who are subject to 'lighter' touch regulation.[130]

A further challenge facing the state is when the final transition to digital transmission should take place. Switching off analogue transmissions is a risky decision as it could disenfranchise those who do not have adequate access to digital media. The US government has announced a target of 2006 for the switch-off of all analogue television transmissions (provided there is an 85 per cent penetration of digital receivers or set-top boxes prior to switch-off in a particular market).[131] A recent report by the UK's House of Commons Select Committee on Culture, Media and Sport suggested a less ambitious target of 2010.[132] The UK government has decided to defer a switch-off 'until the overwhelming majority of the United Kingdom population have access to digital reception via one delivery platform or another'.[133] An early digital switch-off will encourage industry investment, but it also has attractions for governments who could raise funds by privatising the radio spectrum.[134]

Conclusion

The regulatory regimes for telecommunications and broadcasting evolved during the first seven decades of the twentieth century in order to impose a certain set of values upon communications technologies. In these pre-digital days 'each chunk of spectrum was a specific communications or broadcast medium with its own transmission characteristics and anomalies, and with a very specific purpose in mind'.[135] However, more importantly, the basic assumption upon which regulation had been based was that spectrum was scarce and consequently telephone and broadcasting systems were 'natural' monopolies for which competition on the classical model was inappropriate.

The coming of digital transmission technologies challenges these assumptions based on scarcity. However, the radical right shift in state policies has not been solely dependent on changes in communications technology. The advent of new digital technologies was, in fact, preceded by the politics of free markets, and although changes in technology have provided the pretext and rationale for policy changes there is no necessary connection. The origins of deregulation and privatisation are not to be found solely in digitisation and technological advance, but rather a resurgence in the power and influence of large capitalist corporations. These conglomerates have been supported by national governments who are prepared to enact policies that are market-friendly in the interest of promoting industry investment and global competitiveness. These policies, however, may conflict with traditional public interest concerns connected with diversity and pluralism.

In the next chapter we shall examine how the new paradigm has led to a dramatic restructuring of media industries both nationally and globally. We shall also examine how these changes have helped or hindered the bringing of putative benefits of new media technologies to the population at large.

Notes

1 P. Young, *Person to Person. The International Impact of the Telephone*, Cambridge, Granta Editions, 1991, p. 17.
2 Ibid., p. 58.
3 J. Browning, 'Universal Service (An Idea Whose Time is Past)', *Wired*, April 1994. Available on-line at
   http://www.wired.com/wired/2.09/features/universal.access.html (4 June 1998).
4 Ibid.
5 Ibid.
6 Ibid.
7 G.R.M. Garratt, *The Communications Explosion in the Nineteenth Century: Some Contributions of Electrical Engineering*, Milton Keynes, Open University Press, 1973, p. 36.
8 No named author, 'Telecommunications History Timeline', Webb & Associates website. Available on-line at http://www.webbconsult.com/timeline.html#1800 (4 August 1998).
9 Ibid.
10 B. Sterling, *The Hacker Crackdown*, London, Penguin, 1992, p. 10.

11 Ibid.
12 'Telecommunications History Timeline', op. cit.
13 Sterling, op. cit., p. 11.
14 A. Crisell, *Understanding Radio*, London, Routledge, 1994, p. 17.
15 Ibid.
16 A. Briggs, *The Birth of Broadcasting*, London, Oxford University Press, 1961, p. 29.
17 Garrett, op. cit., p. 45.
18 L.S. Gross, *Telecommunications. An Introduction to Electronic Media*, Madison, Wisconsin, Brown and Benchmark, 1995, pp. 49–50.
19 C. Heller, *Broadcasting and Accountability*, London, BFI Publishing, 1978, p. 12.
20 Gross, op. cit, pp. 53–6.
21 Ibid.
22 Ibid.
23 The third network, the American Broadcasting Company (ABC), was formed in 1943 as a result of the FCC's (Federal Communications Commission) efforts to reduce the monopoly power of NBC and CBS.
24 Heller, op. cit., p. 12. Similar concerns about 'Wellenchaos' (chaos of the airwaves) were evident in Germany. See W. Lerg, *Die Entstehung des Rundfunks in Deutschland*, Frankfurt am Main, Josef Knecht, 1965, p. 123.
25 J. Cain, *The BBC: 70 Years of Broadcasting*, London, BBC, 1992, p. 9.
26 Crisell, op. cit., p. 18.
27 Cain, op. cit, p. 9.
28 Crisell, op. cit., p. 20.
29 Ibid.
30 R. Williams, *Communications*, London, Penguin, 1962, p. 29.
31 Cited in E.S. Herman and R.W. McChesney, *The Global Media*, London, Cassell, London, 1997, p. 138.
32 Gross, op. cit., p. 58.
33 Cited in Cain, op. cit., p. 12.
34 Ibid., p. 18.
35 Ibid., p. 22.
36 N. Garnham, 'Public Service versus the Market', *Screen*, Jan–Feb 1983, p. 13; J-C. Burgelman, 'The Future of Public Service Broadcasting: A Case Study for a "New" Communications Policy', *European Journal of Communication*, vol.1, 1986, p. 186.
37 Broadcasting Research Unit, *The Public Service Idea in British Broadcasting – Main Principles*, London, Broadcasting Research Unit, 1985.
38 J. Peasey, *Public Service Broadcasting in Transition*, unpublished PhD Thesis, University of Bath, 1990, p. 17.
39 M. Tracey, *The Decline and Fall of Public Service Broadcasting*, Oxford, Oxford University Press, 1998, pp. 100–1.
40 Ibid., pp. 104–20.
41 Gross, op. cit., pp. 49–52.
42 Cain, op. cit., p. 12.
43 Herman and McChesney, op. cit., pp. 138–9.
44 Ibid., p. 138.
45 Cited in Gross, op. cit., p. 100.
46 Ibid., p. 114.
47 Ibid., p. 114.

48 Herman and McChesney, op. cit., p. 148.
49 Ibid., p. 139.
50 Ibid.
51 Ibid.
52 Gross, op. cit., p. 124.
53 Crisell, op. cit., p. 22.
54 T. Hollins, *Beyond Broadcasting: Into the Cable Age*, London, BFI Publishing, 1984, p. 39.
55 Gross, op. cit., p. 134.
56 Ibid., p. 135.
57 Ibid., p. 136.
58 Ibid.
59 G.J. Mulgan, *Communication and Control: Networks and the New Economies of Communication*, Cambridge, Polity Press, 1991, p. 253.
60 Hollins, op. cit., p. 53.
61 C. Jonscher, *Sunday Times*, 1 May 1988. Quoted in M. Tracey, op. cit., pp. 47–8.
62 R.L. Heilbroner, *The Worldly Philosophers. The Lives, Times, and Ideas of the Great Economic Thinkers*, New York, Simon & Schuster, 1953, p. 45.
63 G. Mulgan, op. cit., p. 244.
64 See, for example, C. Veljanovski and W. Bishop, *Choice by Cable*, London, Institute of Economic Affairs, 1983; C. Veljanovski, *Commercial Broadcasting in the UK: Over-regulation and Misregulation*, London, Centre for Economic Policy Research, 1987; S. Brittan, 'The Fight for Freedom in Broadcasting', *Political Quarterly*, vol.58, no.1, 1987, pp. 3–23.
65 Quoted in R. Collins and C. Murroni, *New Media, New Policies*, Cambridge, Polity Press, 1996, p. 6.
66 Quoted in Tracey, op. cit., p. vii.
67 Quoted in Tracey, op. cit., p. 48.
68 Hollins, op. cit., p. 51.
69 K. Baker, Minister for IT, *Fibre Optics and Opto-Electronics*, London, HMSO, 1982, Introduction.
70 Quoted in Hollins, op. cit., p. 78.
71 A. Toffler, *The Third Wave*, London, Collins, 1980.
72 Ibid., p. 48.
73 Ibid., p. 184.
74 S. Krempl, 'Newt Gingrich's Vision: An Interview with Mr. Speaker During his "house visit" at Oracle in Silicon Valley', 15 January 1998, Telepolis website. Available on-line at http://www.heise.de/tp/english/inhalt/te/1417/1.html (1 September 1998).
75 Hollins, op. cit., p. 53.
76 R. Mansell, *New Telecommunications: A Political Economy of Network Evolution*, London, Sage, 1993, p. 192.
77 Oftel, *Beyond the Telephone, the Television and the PC. Second Submission to Commons Culture, Media and Sport Committee Inquiry Into Audio-Visual Communications and the Regulation of Broadcasting*, March 1998, Annex A.
78 A. Gore, *Earth In the Balance: Ecology and the Human Spirit*, Boston, Houghton Mifflin, 1992.
79 US Government, *Realizing the Information Future: The Internet and Beyond*, 1993. Available on-line at http://nii.nist.gov/nii/niiinfo.html (6 July 1996).
80 Quoted in H.I. Schiller, *Information Equality*, London, Routledge, 1996, p. 83.

81 Quoted in Schiller, ibid., p. 81.
82 Telecommunications Act of 1996, Section 502. Available on-line at
    http://thomas.loc.gov/cgi-bin/query/z?c104:s.652.enr (4 September 1998).
83 Collins and Murroni, op. cit., p. 18.
84 Oftel, *A Brief History of Recent UK Telecoms Developments*. Available on-line at
    http://www.oftel.gov.uk/history.htm (11 August 1998).
85 Gross, op. cit., p. 151.
86 Ibid., pp. 151–2.
87 Ibid., p. 152.
88 Hollins, op. cit., p. 43.
89 S. Metcalfe, 'Information and Some Economics of the Information Revolution',
    in M. Ferguson (ed.), *New Communications Technologies and the Public Interest*,
    London, Sage, 1986, p. 46.
90 In Tracey, op. cit., p. 203.
91 Ibid., p. 203.
92 Hollins, op. cit., p. 54.
93 Information Technology Advisory Panel (ITAP), *Cable Systems: A Report by the
    ITAP*, London, HMSO, 1982, p. 7.
94 ITAP, op. cit., p. 7.
95 Hollins, op. cit., p. 55.
96 Home Office, *Report of the Inquiry into Cable Expansion and Broadcasting Policy (the
    Hunt Report)*, London, HMSO, 1982, Cmnd 8679.
97 See Broadcasting Research Unit (BRU), op. cit.
98 This changed with the passage of the 1990 Broadcasting Act when Channel
    Four was allowed to sell its own advertising airtime.
99 ITV, *Television and the Role of ITV*, London, Spectrum Strategy Consultants,
    1995, p. 2.
100 *Broadcasting Act 1990*, London, HMSO, 1990, Chapter 42.
101 J. Steemers, 'Die terrestrische Fernsehsektor in Grossbritannien', *Media
    Perspektiven*, June 1998, p. 287.
102 The IBA's transmitters have since been transferred to a separate company,
    National Transcommunications Ltd (NTL), which has been privatised.
103 *Broadcasting Act 1990*, op. cit., ss. 15, 16, 17.
104 Ibid., ss. 44, 45, 6, 7.
105 P. Humphreys and M. Lang, 'Digital Television Between the Economy and
    Pluralism', in J. Steemers (ed.), *Changing Channels: The Prospects for Television in
    a Digital World*, Luton, John Libbey, 1998, p. 16.
106 Herman and McChesney, op. cit., pp. 109–10.
107 C. Woodyard, 'Bill Will Decide Industry's Future', *Houston Chronicle*, 5
    December 1995. Available on-line at http://www.chron.com/ (12 August 1996).
108 M. Tran, 'Telecom Firms Ring No Changes', *Guardian*, 2 June 1997.
109 *Direct Broadcasting by Satellite: Report of a Home Office Study*, London, HMSO,
    1981.
110 Tracey, op. cit., p. 217.
111 Cain, op. cit., p. 124.
112 For a more detailed analysis see J. Steemers, 'Die terrestrische Fernsehsektor
    in Grossbritannien', op. cit., p. 291.
113 T. Gibbons, 'De/Re-regulating the System: The British Experience', in
    J. Steemers (ed.), *Changing Channels*, op. cit., pp. 85–6.
114 Humphreys and Lang, op. cit., pp. 17–18.

115 Ibid., p. 17.

116 J. Steemers, 'Broadcasting is Dead. Long Live Digital Choice', *Convergence*, vol.3, 1997, pp. 54–5.

117 Ibid., p. 64. For example, the UK's 1996 Broadcasting Act was more concerned with the establishment of the conditions to introduce digital terrestrial television, than with its interaction with other digital media.

118 W. Hoffmann-Riem, 'New Challenges for European Multimedia Policy', *European Journal of Communications*, vol.11, 1996, p. 330.

119 Select Committee on Culture, Media and Sport, *The Multi-Media Revolution (Fourth Report)*, 6 May 1998, HC520-I, Para. 140. Available on-line at http://www.parliament.the-stationery-office.co.uk/pa199798/cmselect/cmcumeds/520-V139-140 (6 August 1998).

120 Ibid., Para. 158.

121 See Oftel, *Digital Television and Interactive Services: Ensuring Access On Fair, Reasonable and Non-Discriminatory Terms Consultative Document*, March 1998, Para. 3.3. Available on-line at http://www.oftel.gov.uk/broadcast/dig398.htm, (6 March 1998); see also Gibbons, op. cit., pp. 90–4.

122 Department for Culture, Media and Sport and Department for Trade and Industry, *Regulating Communications: Approaching Convergence in the Information Age*, July 1998, CM4022, Chapter 5. In the short term the present structure of regulation involving the ITC, OFT (Office of Fair Trading) and OFTEL is likely to remain in place with greater co-ordination and collaboration.

123 Steemers, 'Broadcasting is Dead', op. cit., p. 58.

124 Ibid., p. 59.

125 For example, BSkyB's dominance of the UK analogue satellite TV market is reinforced by its ownership of Videocrypt, the only satellite encryption system to have established itself in the UK.

126 Steemers, 'Broadcasting is Dead', op. cit., p. 59.

127 Ibid., p. 64.

128 Ibid., p. 55.

129 Select Committee on Culture, Media and Sport, op. cit., Para. 116.

130 J. Steemers, 'On the Threshold of the "Digital Age": Prospects for Public Service Broadcasting' in J. Steemers (ed.), *Changing Channels*, op. cit., pp. 97–124. See also, *Regulating Communications: Approaching Convergence in the Information Age*, op. cit., p. 4, Para. 4.33.

131 See Select Committee on Culture, Media and Sport, op. cit., Para. 126.

132 Ibid., Para. 137.

133 Ibid., Para. 124.

134 For example, the US government privatised portions of the radio spectrum in 1993. H. Schiller, op. cit., p. 83.

135 N. Negroponte, *Being Digital*, London, Hodder & Stoughton, 1996, p. 54.

Chapter 6

Capital and multimedia

Introduction

The premise upon which state media and communications policy was based during the 1980s and 1990s was that a combination of digital technology and free markets would bring rich and diverse media offerings to consumers and a boost to the general economy. Although the two are sometimes conflated, the technical benefits of digitisation and the economic benefits of free markets are logically independent. Indeed, as we have seen in the previous chapter, deregulation and privatisation, which began in the early 1980s, preceded the introduction of digital technologies in the 1990s. The rhetoric associated with these changes was that they would allow the fresh wind of competition to blow through the formerly monopolistic broadcasting and telecommunications industries. This view is also shared by a number of commentators such as Alvin Toffler and Nicholas Negroponte who believe that digital media technologies (and particularly the Internet) will spell the demise of the large monopolistic mass-media corporation. According to them a competitive market in multimedia products will take the place of monopoly, precipitating 'de-massification of the media'[1] in which 'the monolithic empires of mass media ... dissolve into an array of cottage industries'.[2] Typical of this optimistic belief that new media technologies will result in ever widening choices and a consequent empowerment of media 'consumers', is the

FIGURE 6.1 Leading players in the deregulated global media market: (left) Rupert Murdoch, the head of News Corporation; (right) Bill Gates, the head of Microsoft
Copyright © 1997, 1998 John Spelman/Retna

introduction to the US government's *The National Information Infrastructure: The Administration's Agenda for Action*, published in 1993, which asks its readers to:

> Imagine you had a device that combined a telephone, a TV, a camcorder, and a personal computer. No matter where you went or what time it was, your child could see you and talk to you, you could watch a replay of your team's last game, you could browse the latest editions to the library, or you could find the best prices in town on groceries, furniture, clothes –whatever you needed [. . .] you could see the latest movies, play the hottest video games, or bank and shop from the comfort of your home whenever you chose.[3]

The argument put forward in this chapter is that the New Right policies of deregulation and privatisation which were designed to increase competition have, in fact, led to an increase in monopoly power. While the pretext for these policies was based on technological change, including digital transmission, the post-1980 regulatory regime in the US, UK and much of the developed world preceded and has no necessary connection with digital technology. The main purpose of these policies was to encourage profit-making media enterprises and to create an environment in which they could thrive. Furthermore, far from fostering innovation, it is argued here that the new political and regulatory order has created an environment in which the main players have actually become reluctant to exploit the full potential of the new digital technologies.

Convergence: technological and institutional

'Convergence' has become a cliché of the information age. In its current usage it refers to two distinct though related phenomena: (i) the way that all transmission media become bit-carriers so that different 'network platforms'[4] can carry similar kinds of services; and (ii) the tendency of the previously separate worlds of broadcasting, film, telecommunications, publishing and computing to become involved in each other's businesses.

Technological convergence

At the technical level, as we have seen, digital transmission has the potential to deliver integrated interactive text, video, voice and data to a mass audience – what we might call 'real multimedia'. However, historically each part of the spectrum and mode of transmission became associated with a different form of communication: point-to-point communication became the province of the telephone, and wireless transmission became associated with broadcast news and entertainment. This is now changing. With digital compression techniques the limited transmission capacity of existing telephone and cable infrastructures can be expanded to deliver a range of multimedia services that previously could only be carried on expensive broadband networks. Similarly digital compression allows point-to-point communications to be conducted increasingly by advanced forms of radio transmission.

Institutional convergence

By the 1990s government media and communications policy, although dressed up in free-market rhetoric, was much more concerned with making it easier for media companies to become involved in each other's businesses than in fostering competition. Governments justified this policy of encouraging business mergers and alliances by the need to encourage national players to innovate and compete globally. This view was endorsed by the Select Committee on Culture, Media and Sport Report in May 1998 which warned that,

> excessive concern over ownership and size in a domestic context might create a market so fragmented that the United Kingdom lacks

organisations with the range of skills and the investment capital to compete effectively in increasingly global markets.[5]

The committee further argued that,

dominant positions are often beneficial viewed in an international context; they are also often a legitimate reward for risk and innovation.[6]

Even before the advent of digital technology governments in the UK and the US began to consider allowing cable, telephone and broadcasting companies to enter each other's markets. In the UK an 'asymmetrical' approach was adopted at first which allowed cable companies to provide telephony, but prevented British Telecom from offering broadcast entertainment. In the US the 1996 Telecommunications Act permitted telephone companies to provide video, creating a new entity, the 'open video system'.[7] In this new competitive environment, the prospect of digital technology has resulted in a flurry of mergers and acquisitions as companies involved in film, broadcasting, publishing, cable and computer software try to keep all their options open. This has been reflected in the growth of the communications sector – in the 1990s the information-communications sector worldwide grew at twice the rate of all other industry sectors,[8] and by 1996 the value of worldwide mergers and acquisitions in the information and communications sector totalled US$1 trillion.[9]

The institutional effect of communications privatisation and deregulation has been to initiate a process by which an industry which once consisted of a few large state regulated and/or owned institutions has been transformed into a market controlled by a few large private companies. This is a situation which economic theory defines as an oligopoly. Oligopoly can be contrasted with both free markets and monopoly. In the classic free-market model there are many firms so that no one company can control prices, and profits are not excessive – over-pricing or inefficient production is punished by bankruptcy and so it is in a firm's interest to keep the customer satisfied. By contrast in a pure monopoly, where one company controls a market, it is in the monopolist's best interest to keep prices and profits as high as possible as the customer cannot take their business elsewhere. For firms operating in an oligopolistic market the most rational form of behaviour is either to absorb rivals or to co-operate with them. This describes the behaviour of the main players in the global media and communications system.

Mergers and acquisitions

Industry integration

The privatising legislation of the 1980s threw open the domain of public communications to large global media corporations even before the introduction of digital technologies. These corporations, involved mainly in broadcasting, telephony and computing, had their power and scope of action greatly increased, and this led to a process of institutional convergence as enterprises that previously operated in different domains came together in a series of mergers, acquisitions and alliances. This trend was motivated not only by a desire to exploit the new technologies, but also to protect existing investments and market share.

The process of absorbing other companies is called 'integration' by economists and can be either 'horizontal' or 'vertical'. The acquisition by a firm of a direct competitor producing the same product or service is described as 'horizontal integration'. A cable company buying a chain of video stores (for example when Viacom acquired the Blockbuster video rental chain) would be a case of horizontal integration since both are forms of distribution. Where a firm takes over another company at a different stage in the production/distribution chain, the acquisition is known as 'vertical integration'. 'Backward vertical integration' involves a company taking over or merging with a supplier of the goods or services that it needs to trade. For example, a cable company taking over a film studio would be a case of backward vertical integration. 'Forward vertical integration' is where a company acquires a distributor of the goods or services it produces.

The response of media, communications and computer corporations to deregulation and the prospect of digital transmission has been to engage in both horizontal and vertical mergers and alliances. This process of integration has been prompted by a number of considerations as demonstrated by a study undertaken on behalf of the European Commission.[10] The study discerned two main trends in the responses to liberalisation and technological convergence: on the one hand firms attempt horizontal consolidation to protect their current activities and on the other they seek to diversify vertically into different stages of the value chain.[11] Motives for horizontal integration, according to the study, include: increasing market power; gaining economies of scale; raising capital for investment in digital technologies; insuring against uncertain demand for new services; and gaining access to wider, especially international markets.[12] Motives for vertical integration include countering uncertainty of demand; acquiring ownership of new skills; gaining distribution channels; moving into more profitable parts of the value chain and countering competition from rivals.[13]

Telephone and cable companies

Digital convergence has had important implications for those involved in wired transmission because compression techniques permit the cable and telephone companies to transmit multimedia over their existing copper infrastructure. During the twentieth century, telephone companies accumulated considerable market power as state-owned (or, in the case of the US, state-approved) monopolies. As unrivalled monopolists the telephone companies did not have to be concerned with the content of the signals that travelled down their wires, but with increased competition, they ran the risk of being relegated to mere 'bit transporters'. When all distributors are delivering flows of bits, the content of these flows becomes a crucial factor. The most successful companies will be those who offer what customers most want to pay for. This represents a significant shift in the value chain with value 'migrating from simple delivery to the production of and packaging of content or the offer of on-line services and transactions'.[14] This represented the real challenge for the telephone companies. Despite being the oldest of the technologies on offer, telephony still remained the most profitable sector of the telecommunications business in the 1990s.[15] But the telephone companies recognised that there was great scope for expanding telephone use since the telephone system, the most ubiquitous and pervasive network on earth, is under-used. For example, it has been estimated that the average daily usage for each telephone in the UK is about thirty minutes. To counter this under-use, they needed to offer additional services and content.

One response of the telephone companies to seeing their core business becoming a low-margin high-volume operation has been to try to increase volume and geographical reach through a process of horizontal global alliances and mergers. This process started in 1994 when the cable operator Tele-Communications Incorporated (TCI) bid for the telephone company Bell Atlantic. In the event the US Federal Communications Commission (FCC) thwarted the attempt as being anti-competitive. The merged companies would have reached 40 per cent of homes in the US.[16] However, this intervention proved to be only a minor hiccup in a process that has seen a complex web of mergers, acquisitions and alliances between telephone companies and cable operators on both sides of the Atlantic.

In Europe the process began with the European Commission's framework directive on open network provision, published in 1990, which called for the complete liberalisation of Europe's telecommunications industry by 1998.[17] Liberalisation of the industry in Europe began in the UK when cable companies began offering telephony, and this led to a rush of US telecommunications companies trying to enter the UK and subsequently the European market. These companies believed that there were high profits to be made in Europe, where lack of competition had stifled innovation and kept prices high. One of the main objectives of these US companies was to seek alliances with newly or soon-to-be privatised European telecom networks. The aim was to become one of a few global 'supercarriers' in a fast-growing market for international corporate network services, that could offer business customers seamless cross-border services.[18]

These ambitions were not just confined to American telephone companies. In 1996 British Telecom (BT) announced a joint venture with the American long-distance telephone company MCI (in which it already had a 20 per cent share) to form Concert Communications, a global communications and high-speed data transmission network for multinational corporations.[19] BT's bid to merge with MCI was thwarted, however, when it was outbid by its smaller rival WorldCom in November 1997.[20] Other global telecommunications realignments have included AT&T's alliance with Singapore Telecom to form World Partners in 1995, and the formation of Global One by an alliance between the American long-distance telephone company Sprint, Deutsche Telecom and France Telecom in 1996.[21] The largest of these horizontal mergers was between two US former RBOCs or Baby Bells. This involved a US$23 billion (£15.2 billion) deal announced in April 1996 between Nynex, the regional telephone company for the New York area, and its rival Bell Atlantic.[22]

Telecoms/broadcasting integration

Telecommunications corporations have also sought to enter the domain of 'traditional' broadcasting both in order to exploit digital transmission of television over their wires and to defend themselves from cable broadcasters challenging them in telephony.[23] Not all of these attempts to move into content creation have proved successful. In 1994 three of the US Baby Bells (Bell Atlantic, Nynex and Pacific Telesis)[24] agreed to invest US$300 million in an interactive television company, Tele-TV. However, Tele-TV was not successful and was wound up in 1997.[25] The big opportunity for telecommunications operators to move into broadcast media came with the liberalisation of the British cable industry in 1991, although ironically, because of the 'asymmetry rule', British Telecom was unable to participate in this at first. US telecommunications companies made their first international forays into the British cable industry in the early 1990s. As we saw in Chapter 5, cable was a crucial element in the UK Conservative government's strategy for encouraging media technologies by allowing new players to challenge the incumbent broadcasting and telecommunications monopolies. But in spite of the 'hype' surrounding these developments, cable failed to take off as quickly as hoped. This was due to a number of factors. Cable was under-capitalised from the start, a situation that was made worse when the government removed capital allowances in the 1984 budget.[26] The cable industry was only revived by the government's agreement in 1991 to let the cable companies provide telephony services in competition with BT, and also by the success of satellite television in the 1990s which provided programming to attract consumers. However, one of the most significant factors in sustaining the British cable industry was a consolidation of ownership principally under American companies. The Regional Bell Operating Companies (RBOCs or Baby Bells) and American cable operators such as TCI were attracted by the British government's policy of allowing cable companies to offer both entertainment and telephony services at a time when this was not permitted in the US. The value of this to the American companies was starkly put by the head of the US's biggest cable company TCI, John Malone, when he told a US trade conference that the UK was a laboratory rather like Spain during the Civil War in 1938, 'a place where they were able to test their heavy weapons for the real and coming struggle'.[27]

However, the cost of laying cables proved too expensive for the original British cable franchisees who also suffered public relations problems as a result of the disruption and damage caused by cable laying as well as complaints of bad service. By 1997, having invested some £8 billion to build their networks, the UK cable companies had not increased their penetration beyond about 22 per cent of UK homes passed by their cables and were still not making the profits necessary to finance the move from analogue to digital transmission.[28] They were consequently obliged to embark on a series of horizontal mergers which resulted by 1998 in the market being split between three dominant players: Cable and Wireless Communications (C&WC) and two smaller American controlled operators, Telewest and NTL. The high costs of the new technologies also led Cable and Wireless Communications to decide not to compete directly in the emerging UK digital television market, but rather to enter into a partnership with BSkyB to carry the satellite company's programming on the C&WC network.[29]

In the US the restructuring of the cable and telecoms industries has involved both vertical and horizontal integration. An example of vertical integration can be seen in Time-Warner's 1995 acquisition of two cable operations: Houston Industries (for US$2.2 billion) and Cablevision (for US$2.6 billion), acquisitions which increased its subscriber base to 11.5 million.[30] The trend towards horizontal integration is exemplified by the merger between the telephone company AT&T and the cable operator Tele-Communications Incorporated (TCI) announced in June 1998. The rationale behind the proposed US$48 billion AT&T–TCI deal was that the resulting merged entity, AT&T Consumer Services, would be able to generate the capital necessary for investment in digital infrastructure.[31]

Digital satellite

It was not until 1995 that digital services, including TV, programme-related content and Internet access, actually arrived with the launch in the US of the first digital direct broadcast satellite, DirecTV. As with other new technology enterprises the investment costs and market uncertainties involved meant that digital satellite operation could only be undertaken by industry alliances. Two separate companies own DirecTV: Hughes Communications, a division of General Motors, and the United States Satellite Broadcasting Company (USSB). DirecTV had 2.9 million US subscribers by 1997(compared with approximately 65 million for cable).[32] Also involved in the venture with Hughes were the US telecommunications company AT&T and Microsoft. AT&T, which has an equity holding in DirecTV, provides its marketing expertise to market and distribute DirecTV television services as well as the dishes and other receiving equipment.[33] DirecTV also signed an agreement with Microsoft in April 1996 to allow DirecTV viewers to receive data services from the DirecTV satellites on specially modified PCs. The services include programme-related content, Internet services and data and multi-media feeds.[34]

US cable operators responded to DirecTV by forming a consortium, including cable giants TCI and Time-Warner, to defend their market share by launching their own rival digital satellite, PrimeStar. The potential of digital DBS to eat into cable audience share also attracted Rupert Murdoch's News Corporation which already had considerable experience of satellite operations around the world with BSkyB in the UK, STAR in South Asia, JSkyB in Japan and Sky-Latin America (which operates primarily in Mexico and Brazil). In partnership with US long-distance telecom operator MCI, News Corporation developed ASkyB and aimed to launch in 1997. News Corporation tried to further this strategy by buying into an existing satellite operation, attempting a deal first with EchoStar and then with PrimeStar in 1997. However, both these deals collapsed in acrimony in June 1997 with News Corporation agreeing to sell its ASkyB operation to PrimeStar.[35]

Policy in the UK was aimed at preventing one company dominating digital transmission while at the same time permitting, indeed encouraging, the formation of alliances between different companies. The regulatory regime that emerged for digital transmission was one that envisaged competition between satellite, terrestrial and cable monopolists for the provision of digital television and other interactive services.

In the case of satellite the licence to provide digital services was given to British Interactive Broadcasting (BIB). British Interactive Broadcasting is a consortium consisting of BSkyB, British Telecom, the Midland Bank and the Japanese electronics firm Matsushita.[36] BIB's system is based on an enhanced set-top box, produced by Matsushita, connecting to both a satellite dish and BT's network. This set-up enables BSkyB's digital TV viewers to access interactive services such as shopping, public services, banking and internet services over the public telephone system.[37] BSkyB's digital TV service started in October 1998 although the interactive services were delayed by technical problems and were not due to launch until some months later.[38]

Digital terrestrial TV

By 1998 the UK was in advance of all other countries in preparing for the introduction of digital terrestrial television (DTT). The 1996 UK Broadcasting Act created a statutory framework based on entities known as multiplexes which were licensed to co-ordinate and manage digital terrestrial television broadcasting. Of the six available terrestrial digital 'multiplexes', each capable of carrying between three and six television channels, three were awarded to the existing terrestrial broadcasters (BBC, ITV, Channel Four, Channel 5, S4C). The BBC was awarded its own digital terrestrial multiplex for the distribution of its existing enhanced and new free-to-air services. ITV and Channel Four were to share one multiplex between them. The Independent Television Commission (ITC) awarded the licence to run the remaining multiplexes to British Digital Broadcasting (BDB), later renamed ONdigital, a consortium in which the ITV television companies Carlton and Granada held equal shares with the satellite broadcaster BSkyB. However, the licence was only awarded by the ITC on condition that BSkyB withdrew as a shareholder because of competition concerns, although BSkyB remained as a programme supplier.[39] ONDigital was launched in 1999.

With the launch of these services there have been concerns and uncertainties about how competition between the different forms of digital transmission will evolve. Particular concern has centred on the compatibility of the rival set-top boxes needed to convert digital signals for display on analogue TVs. Evidence to the House of Commons Select Committee on Culture, Media and Sport suggested that BIB's and ONdigital's boxes should be 'inter-operable' so that a consumer who had purchased a set-top box for digital satellite television, but wished to change to digital terrestrial, or vice versa, could do so.[40] However, the digital cable service planned by Cable & Wireless Communications for launch in late 1998[41] was to have a set-top box that would not be compatible with the other digital services, and subscribers wishing to switch would be obliged to cease renting the cable box and purchase another box.[42]

The scramble for content

The process of vertical integration was described by the 1997 European Commission Green Paper as the most significant indicator of the media and communication industry's response to digital convergence. It states that:

> Few, if any of today's market players will have the skills or resources to straddle the whole of the value chain within a converged environment, so that the emergence of major players in the sectors affected by convergence will inevitably rely on partnering to varying degrees.[43]

Regulatory constraints, market saturation and competition from new market entrants have rendered signal delivery less profitable to companies than the provision of content. On the other hand profits from the ownership of content including feature films and sports rights, which can be delivered digitally into the home, are seen to be potentially very high, especially if skilful marketing can be used to raise demand. The ownership of content and a clear brand identity are now acknowledged as a primary business asset, and as a result there has been a scramble by media and communications corporations to acquire 'premium' content, particularly films and sports rights. With the growing importance of digital images in publishing, the ownership of these rights has also become extremely lucrative.

This scramble for content has become particularly evident in a number of corporate mergers and acquisitions, mainly in the US. In 1985 the Turner Broadcasting System's cable 'superstation' (TBS) acquired the MGM film library. In the same year the Hollywood studio, 20th Century Fox, was acquired by Rupert Murdoch's News Corporation as a prelude to the establishment of a fourth US TV network, Fox, in 1987.[44] In 1988 the Japanese electronics giant Sony bought CBS Records, and in the following year it acquired Columbia Pictures and its feature film back catalogue. In 1990 the Japanese electronics company Matsushita acquired Hollywood's largest film library, MCA/Universal. In 1990 Time Inc. bought Warner Communications to form Time-Warner Inc. making it the world's largest media and entertainment conglomerate with a leading position in publishing, music, television and films.[45] And, in October 1996, Time-Warner bought Turner Broadcasting, owner of Cable News Network (CNN) and other globally distributed satellite channels, for US$7 billion and integrated it into Warner Studios.[46]

The acquisition of sports rights has been especially important for the profitability of television networks. In the UK, BSkyB's analogue satellite television service only became profitable after it obtained the exclusive right to show the English premier football league on its subscription sports channels. With the prospect of many digital channels, individual sports clubs are now in a position to market their own games as pay-per-view. As a hedge against this a number of media owners have been buying clubs. In the US Time-Warner owns the Atlanta Braves baseball team and News Corporation's Fox Network owns the Los Angeles Dodgers baseball club as well as having a stake in the New York Knicks Basketball club.[47] In September 1998 News Corporation's BSkyB made a £625 million take-over bid for Britain's largest football club, Manchester United.[48] This bid, however, was blocked by the British government in April 1999 after an investigation by the Competition Commission.

The Internet

While the cable companies and telephone companies continue to restructure into an oligopoly of vertically and horizontally integrated media conglomerates, the anarchic phenomenon of the Internet did not at first prove amenable to commercial exploitation by established media corporations. In its early days the Internet was the province of academics and computer enthusiasts. What changed the situation was the development of the World Wide Web and easy-to-use hypertext-based 'browsers'. Also crucial in the transformation of the Internet into a popular medium was the US government's decision in 1995 to withdraw from its involvement in the running of the Internet's 'backbone' – the high capacity fibre-optic links on which the Internet depends. The US government's share was handed over to five major telecommunications companies: MCI, Sprint, WorldCom, PSINet and GTE.[49]

The rapid growth of the graphically interfaced World Wide Web on the Internet from the mid-1990s took Microsoft, the dominant player in PC operating systems and software, by surprise. By the beginning of the 1990s it was becoming clear that the PC market, if not saturated, was at least unlikely to show the growth rates of the 1980s. During this period the PC in the office went from being rare to being ubiquitous. Microsoft and Intel had tried to consolidate their market dominance through branding and advertising: for example, the 'Intel Inside' campaign and Microsoft's huge launch campaign for Windows 95. Microsoft had built up its power as the supplier of the operating system for 90 per cent of all PCs sold. The royalty it receives every time a PC is sold in effect amounts to a tax and, coupled with the low marginal costs of software production, has made Microsoft cash-rich. As we saw in Chapter 3, the focus of attention at Microsoft in the late 1980s and early 1990s was the development of stand-alone multimedia PCs that could run CD-ROMs. Part of this strategy involved the acquisition of content through buy-outs, mergers and alliances with content owners including print publishers. Additionally, Microsoft chief executive Bill Gates' private company, Corbis, has acquired the digital image rights to thousands of paintings and photographs, including photographic images from the collections of the National Gallery in London and the Smithsonian Institute in Washington, making it the largest collection of its kind in the world.[50]

Web browsers

By the early 1990s Microsoft had failed to anticipate the speed and scale of the migration of computing from stand-alone PCs to networks. In the new networked environment personal computers could make use of software that no longer belonged to Microsoft, thus threatening Microsoft's domination of the software industry.

The first indication of this threat came with Netscape's web browser, Navigator. Navigator was launched in 1994 and was given away free to non-commercial users on the Internet.[51] As a consequence of the launch of Navigator, the number of users of the Internet began to increase by about 10 per cent a month and the number of commercial sites increased from fifty in January 1993 to 10,000 in October 1997.[52] Navigator had 80 per cent of the browser market in 1997,[53] and it became clear that an important new personal computing market was developing in which for the first time Microsoft was not a major player.

Microsoft's initial response to the Internet phenomenon was to establish its own proprietary Microsoft Network (MSN) and attract PC users by incorporating it into the Windows 95 operating system. In this enterprise, in partnership with TCI, Microsoft was following the model of existing proprietary on-line providers such as America Online (AOL), Prodigy and CompuServe. Like these operations MSN was independent of the Internet. PC users gained access to MSN by clicking an icon on the Windows 95 interface.

By 1996, with the success of Netscape and Internet providers who gave customers Internet access at a lower cost than the proprietary providers, it became clear that Microsoft could no longer sustain its strategy of main-taining MSN as a 'walled garden' separate from the rest of the Internet. Consequently in November 1996 Microsoft ended its partnership with TCI and changed MSN from being a subscriber-only service to one accessible to any user logged on to the Internet.[54] Parallel with this move, Microsoft responded to the Netscape challenge by introducing its own Internet browser, Internet Explorer, based on one of Navigator's rival browsers, Mosaic, which Microsoft in typical fashion had purchased from its owner, Spyglass.[55] Microsoft then proceeded to market Internet Explorer aggress-ively by bundling it with its Windows software, a strategy which has brought it into conflict with the US Department of Justice which has claimed that this is an abuse of its PC operating system monopoly.

Communications, Microsoft invested US$10 million in the Teledesic system to provide wireless Internet access to PC users using cellular telephone technology. The system will consist of 288 satellites, creating a global 'Internet in the sky' in a low earth orbit (LEO) of 1,375 kilometres above the Earth.[72] At a capacity equivalent to 20,000 simultaneous T1[73] lines, the Teledesic network is designed to offer voice channels, videoconferencing and interactive multimedia channels by 2002. The system would, in the words of one of its promoters, 'seamlessly link people and businesses anywhere on the planet'.[74]

Computer/broadcasting integration

The Internet as it now exists in 1998 is not suitable for the transmission of broadband video-quality interactive multimedia. The Internet runs on the established telecommunications system which does not have sufficient bandwidth to compete with 'traditional' broadcasting for the transmission of digital television. Certainly BT in its evidence to the UK Parliament's Select Committee on Culture Media and Sport in 1997 did not believe that telecommunication networks would compete with digital satellite and terrestrial broadcasting for the 'foreseeable future'.[75] However, the committee did believe that a digitised copper network could compete with Internet services and video-on-demand.[76] For the Select Committee the set-top box which allows an analogue television to receive digital TV 'is a first step along a path which . . . would lead to a convergence in the capacity of the TV and the PC'.[77] The committee saw the distinction between the TV and the PC disappearing with the two devices merging to become 'the screen'.[78]

With the functions of television (and radio), telephone and personal computers converging there have been clear opportunities for computer hardware and software companies to expand their markets. Not surprisingly Microsoft has been particularly active in this respect. Microsoft's strategy to be at the heart of 'the screen' has involved acquiring PC-TV technologies as well as making alliances with broadcasters and the owners of transmission infrastructure.[79] Microsoft made a start on this strategy in 1994 when it invested in Internet content through an alliance with the NBC television network to set up the MSNBC 24-hour cable television news channel. In addition, the company also runs MSNBC Online, an interactive, web-based news service.

In June 1997 Microsoft acquired a US$1 billion stake in the US's fourth largest cable company, Comcast.[80] This was a reversal of Microsoft's previous policy of not getting involved in infrastructure.[81] Bill Gates now saw that the deal would give Microsoft not only a foothold in the cable industry, but more important, a chance to establish its proprietary operating system Windows CE (for Consumer Electronics) on television sets.[82] However, attempts to establish its technologies as digital broadcast standards have not been completely successful. In January 1998 the cable company Tele-Communications Incorporated (TCI) signed an agreement with Microsoft to use Microsoft's Windows CE operating system in its next generation of interactive TV set-top boxes. But, in an indication that other players might not be willing to accede to Microsoft dominance, TCI refused to commit itself exclusively to Windows CE and announced that it would also be using systems from Sun Microsystems and possibly Sony.[83]

As a means of gaining some control over the development of the converging worlds of computing and television Microsoft also embarked on a policy of buying out companies which have developed technologies in this area. In 1997 Microsoft acquired WebTV Networks and established WebTV as a wholly owned subsidiary. WebTV had developed a set-top box which enables broadcasters to embed information into their TV signal so that viewers can watch television while browsing the Internet. This technology became a key element in Microsoft's move into the UK market. In 1998 Microsoft entered into alliances with both British Telecom and the BBC, offering WebTV as a solution to both organisations' digital convergence strategies. The BBC was keen to be associated with Microsoft. Since the 1980s the Corporation had been obliged by the British government to both seek outside business partners and become involved in commercial activities itself. Among the fruits of this policy was beeb.com – a jointly owned commercial venture with ICL to establish a presence on the Internet for the BBC brand name. However, it was not successful because beeb.com was increasingly sidelined by the BBC's own free website which progressively became bigger and more popular as it added news and sports coverage to its on-line content.[84] It was against this background that BBC management embraced Microsoft's WebTV technology, seeing it as a crucial element in its digital broadcasting strategy of 'delivering enhanced, interactive services to the home'.[85] In a similar alliance the dominant UK telephone company British Telecom signed an agreement in 1998 with WebTV to run a trial in which the BT Internet service will combine with the WebTV set-top box to provide enhanced television to households.[86] These activities led to rumours in early 1998 that Microsoft was planning a merger with BT[87] although these later proved to be unfounded.[88]

Webcasting and web advertising

One of the strategies currently employed by the major media conglomerates is to become involved in 'webcasting' using the Internet, and the World Wide Web in particular, to broadcast specific information 'channels' which subscribers can receive on their personal computers. Unlike typical Internet surfing, which relies on a 'pull' method of transferring web pages, webcasting uses 'push' technologies like WebTV.[89] Push technologies broadcast to a client without the client requesting it. E-mail is the oldest and most widely used example of push technology. E-mail is a push technology because you receive mail whether you ask for it or not – the sender pushes the message to the receiver.[90] One of the first and most successful companies to use webcasting was PointCast, which delivers customised news to users' desktops.[91] Major media players have been keen to take up the concept of push technologies by establishing themselves on the Internet and webcasting content that they already own. By 1997 on-line sports services had been established by CBS and Disney and 24-hour live news webcasting sites had been established by MSNBC, CNN and News Corporation.[92] Revenues for these sites come from subscriptions and from selling highly targeted advertising space. This has been of great interest to advertisers who have established partnerships to obtain a presence on the web. An example of this type of collaboration is that between Time-Warner and Procter & Gamble in 1996 to establish the interactive website *Parent Time* aimed at parents of young children.[93]

Supply and demand

A singular feature of the restructuring of the media and computer industries described above has been the degree of uncertainty about the future shared by all players. This uncertainty has applied to both the costs of supplying the necessary infrastructure and the likely level of demand for new digital media services. In the face of this uncertainty companies have not been too keen to take risks and, despite the deregulating zeal and rhetoric of politicians, change has not been as rapid as some had hoped or predicted. It is true that large amounts of capital were raised in the late 1980s, and that some of this was spent on developing and introducing new technology. However, this was largely through the issuing of junk-bonds – IOUs secured on future income.[94] For example, the long-distance telephone company MCI financed the US's first nationwide fibre-optic network to carry its long-distance traffic by issuing US$3 billion of junk bonds over a four-year period.[95] However, much of this went, not into infrastructure investment, but into the financing of acquisitions and mergers. This left companies with high levels of debt and the need to generate high profits to pay them off. In a deregulated multimedia market profitability depends on reducing the uncertainty created by competition and achieving economies of scale and, as we have seen, this has been a primary motive for the mergers, acquisitions and alliances of the 1990s. The problem for both old and new multimedia players has been twofold: the cost of installing the new multimedia infrastructure to supply services to the public and uncertainty as to whether demand will be strong enough to justify the investment.

Supply

The telephone and cable companies soon realised that creating the 'wired' society would cost a lot of money. In particular, companies were beginning to balk at the expense of introducing fibre-optic networks. The large-scale provision of network multimedia to the home would inevitably require large capital investment programmes. In 1994 British Telecom had estimated that the cost of putting an optical fibre cable into every home and business would be approximately £20 billion over 10 to 15 years.[96] Similarly, the US telephone company US West estimated in 1994 that to offer video-on-demand, home shopping and games to 500,000 homes in five cities would require an investment of US$750 million over two years.[97]

By the late 1990s the plans of the cable and telephone companies to provide multimedia services were being scaled down. The high cost of installing an all-fibre integrated services digital network led to the Japanese telephone company Nippon TT abandoning its US$360 billion plan to connect every Japanese home with fibre by 2015. The world's biggest cable company TCI also had to cut back its operations in 1996, most notably reducing an ambitious plan to lay a fibre-optic network in Houston, Texas.[98] Furthermore, the slow take-up of fibre-optic cable generally has meant that prices have not dropped as expected, and the cost of connecting a home had risen to US$2,000 by 1997.[99] An indication of the disappointing pace of the installation of cable was given in September 1997 when the US manufacturer Cornin reported losses due to slower than expected growth in the sales of its fibre-optic cables.[100]

In early 1998, on the threshold of the introduction of full-scale digital services into the UK, BT decided it was not economic to go ahead with a £15 billion programme to replace its copper cables with optical fibre for the domestic market.[101] BT also decided that there was no profit to be had in competing with established players by providing digital television or video-on-demand through its network. This was a surprising decision given BT's vehement objection to the Conservative government's earlier 'asymmetry' rule, which forbade it from competing with cable operators for just such services. In a change of strategy BT entered into an alliance with Microsoft, and announced that in future it would concentrate on Internet-based interactive services rather than the provision of video services to the home.[102]

There have also been some technical problems in using existing copper infrastructure for high bandwidth transmission. Asymmetric subscriber line (ADSL) technology which permits broadband transmission over telephone lines has proved difficult to implement. The length of telephone line over which an ADSL connection can be established is limited to three to eight kilometres depending on the quality of the line and the desired data rate because the signal degrades as it travels over copper wires.[103] It is estimated that these technical limitations are likely to exclude 40 per cent of US homes from being connected to ADSL lines.[104]

There have also been problems in using cable to connect to the Internet. Whereas telephone modems provide a single link to the Internet, the design of cable networks means that users share Internet access with everyone else on the same hub, and this includes demands for cable television and telephone services.[105] As the network is shared by other users, speed rates can decrease as people log on to the service. This means that cable modems will not always deliver the high speeds they promise.

Demand

Another major difficulty for companies trying to estimate the likely return from multimedia investment is that no one has any idea what demand is likely to be or what types of digital services are likely to be commercially successful. Evidence from analogue cable and satellite television, the 'first wave' of new media technologies, suggests that the most lucrative services are likely to be feature films and sports.[106] This is because, in the developed world at least, television viewing is already the single most popular leisure activity, and so no new consumer habits need to be developed. The demand for other services such as home shopping is less certain. However, the financial success of pay-per-view for sports events on analogue cable and satellite channels indicates that there is likely to be a lucrative market for narrow-casting subscription and pay-per-view services (such as being able to follow all of one football team's games) on digital channels. However, some believe that there is little scope for an expansion of demand for audio-visual services.[107] It has also been suggested that the amount of disposable income spent by consumers on media is related to the level of national income and remains constant over time.[108] In the US it is estimated that consumers spend less than US$150 per year on video rental which translates into a market of US$14 billion. Even if all of these homes switched entirely to video-on-demand, profits would not seem adequate to make the huge investment worthwhile.[109]

If these trends for the supply and demand of new media technologies hold, then the technological utopia predicted by those who have praised the liberating potential of these technologies will prove to be no more than a chimera. One indication of the possible future pattern of demand and supply has been provided by a trial carried out by the Time-Warner conglomerate in Orlando Florida.

Orlando FSN

In December 1994 Time-Warner Cable started an interactive Full Service Network (FSN) in Orlando Florida in partnership with AT&T, who developed the high-speed switches, and Silicon Graphics who supplied the software.[110] This was not the first time the company had been involved in a high-profile interactive cable experiment. Between 1979 and 1985 Warner Communication's subsidary, Warner Cable, in conjunction with Amex Cable, had established the interactive system, QUBE, in Columbus, Ohio.[111]

Although only a pilot involving 4,000 households, the Orlando FSN was widely expected to lead to the rapid implementation of broadband services and interactive hybrid-telephone systems across the US.[112] The households participating in the Orlando trial were offered a range of services including: video-on-demand with a choice of 100 feature films; distance learning; interactive games; interactive shopping; news-on-demand; on-line health-care information; and pizza delivery.[113] At its opening Gerald Levin, Time-Warner's chairman, claimed that the pilot was 'a turning point for the communications industry'.[114] At the launch Mr Levin and a colleague 'showed off the system in a mock living room dominated by a huge television screen. Using a remote . . . the on-demand technology was used to call up Warner Brothers' recent hit films . . . The films were fast-forwarded reversed or put on pause while the two executives strolled down the interactive shopping mall.'[115]

During the trial many of the problems of supply and demand outlined previously became apparent, although to what extent is not clear since Time-Warner has not made available all of the results from the trial.[116] On the supply side the technological elements of the system, the hybrid fibre-coaxial broadband network, and the graphical navigators were much more expensive and complex than expected.[117] At the time of its launch only five of the 400 households were operationally connected to the system.[118]

On the demand side one of the lessons of the Orlando Full Service Network was that consumers did not appear willing to significantly increase their expenditure on electronic entertainment and information even when they had the convenience of having it delivered digitally into their home.[119] Certainly the evidence from this pilot seems to indicate that the profits likely to be derived from digital services would not justify the enormous investment required.[120]

Time-Warner's share price languished in 1996 because of debts and expensive cable operations, and in May 1997 the company announced that the Orlando Full Service Network was to close down.[121]

Conclusion

Even with the widespread introduction of digital technologies and the deregulation of broadcasting and telecommunications, interactive multimedia have not yet arrived in the form envisaged by the techno-optimists. On the institutional side the problem has been that, from the 1980s, governments have been trying to artificially impose a free market on an existing institutional and trading environment that is very far removed from Adam Smith's world of localised markets of small tradesmen. Indeed, it could be argued that the free-market model promoted by many governments in the 1980s and 1990s has actually acted as a disincentive to corporations to build digital networks. Those players with sufficient financial strength to make these investments will only do so if they can be sure of a good return on their investment. In the face of increased competition it makes more sense to use capital in order to secure and expand markets through mergers, alliances and acquisitions than to invest in risky new interactive services.

This reluctance to invest in innovation is reinforced by the apparent lack of demand from consumers for interactive multimedia, as was demonstrated by the failure of Time-Warner's Orlando Full Service Network pilot. The promise of increased competition has not materialised. Instead the deregulation of the 1980s and 1990s has led to the creation of an oligopolistic market dominated by a small number of vertically integrated media and telecommunications conglomerates tied together by a web of strategic alliances and joint enterprises.

Notes

1 A. Toffler, *The Third Wave*, London, Collins, 1980, p. 171.
2 N. Negroponte, *Being Digital*, London, Hodder & Stoughton, 1996, p. 57.
3 *The National Information Infrastructure: The Administration's Agenda for Action*, Washington, DC, September 1993. Quoted in H.I. Schiller, *Information Inequality*, New York, Routledge, 1996, pp. 78–80.
4 European Commission, *Green Paper on the Convergence of the Telecommunications, Media and Information Technology Sectors*, I.1, Brussels, December 1997. Available on-line at http://www.ispo.cec.be/convergencegp/97623.html (11 August 1998).
5 Select Committee on Culture, Media and Sport, *The Multi-Media Revolution (Fourth Report)*, 6 May 1998, HC520-I, Para. 162 (viii). Available on-line at http://www.parliament.the-stationery-office.co.uk/pa/cm199798/cmselect/cmcumeds/520-vol1/52003.htm (25 August 1998).
6 Ibid.
7 US Government, *Telecommunications Act of 1996*, SEC. 653. *Establishment of Open Video Systems*. Available on-line at http://thomas.loc.gov/cgi-bin/query/z?c104:s.652.enr: (8 October 1998).
8 E.S. Herman and R.W. McChesney, *The Global Media*, London, Cassell, 1997, p. 108.
9 European Commission, op. cit., I.3.
10 Squire, Sanders and Dempsey LLP and Analysys Ltd., *Study on Adapting the EU Regulatory Framework to the Developing Multimedia Environment*, December 1997, quoted in European Commission, *Green Paper*, ibid., I.3.
11 Ibid.
12 Ibid.
13 Ibid.
14 European Commission, op. cit., II.2

15 This was pointed out by John Malone, TCI's (Tele-Communications Incorporated) Chief Executive Officer who built TCI into the world's biggest cable operation by means of junk-bond financed mergers, in an interview in *Wired* in 1994: '(Q) The RBOCs' [Regional Bell Operating Companies] real deal here was raiding other RBOCs?' (A) 'Ri-i-ight.' (Q) 'And the info highway was just a great flag to wave around while doing it?' (A) 'Absolutely.' Cited in D. Kline, 'Infobahn Warrior', *Wired*, 2 July 1994.

16 L.K. Grossman, 'Reflections on Life Along the Electronic Superhighway', *Media Studies Journal*, Winter 1994. Available on-line at http://www.gspa.washington.edu/Courses/Net/*grossman.html, (8 July 1998).

17 Council of the European Communities, *Council Directive on the Establishment of the Internal Market for Telecommunications Services Through Open Network Provision*, 90/387/EEC OJ L 192/10 (1990).

18 Herman and McChesney, op. cit., p. 111.

19 Ibid., p. 113.

20 C. Pretzlik, 'WorldCom Wins Battle for MCI', *Electronic Telegraph*, Issue 901, 11 November 1997. Available on-line at http://www.telegraph.co.uk, (5 January 1998).

21 Webb & Associates, *Telephone History Time Line*. Available on-line at http://www.webbconsult.com/timeline.html#1800 (8 July 1998).

22 C. Pretzlik, 'Bell Atlantic Swallows Nynex in $23bn Deal', *Electronic Telegraph*, Issue 368, 23 April 1996. Available on-line at http://www.telegraph.co.uk (5 May 1998).

23 Herman and McChesney, op. cit., p. 114.

24 K. Pilgrim, 'Merger May Create Static for Tele-TV', *Cable News Network*, 2 April 1996. Available on-line at http://www.cnnfn.com/news/9604/02/tele_tv/ (4 August 1998).

25 J. Pelline, 'The Old Guard: Telephone Companies', *CNET News*, 7 February 1997. Available on-line at http://www.news.com/SpecialFeatures/0,5,7730,00.html (5 March 1998).

26 M. Tracey, *The Decline and Fall of Public Service Broadcasting*, Oxford, Oxford University Press, 1998, p. 211.

27 Ibid., p. 212.

28 S. Beavis, 'Slow Start in View for Digital Television', *Guardian*, 25 March 1998.

29 E. Bell, 'Can Cable Reach For the Sky', *Observer*, 22 March 1998.

30 M. Tran, 'Time-Warner Buys Second Cable Firm', *Guardian*, 8 February 1995.

31 J. Davis, 'TCI Deal May Speed PC-TV Marriage', *CNET News*, 24 June 1998. Available on-line at http://www.news.com/News/Item/0,4,23528,00.html (5 June 1998).

32 F. Kramer, 'Murdoch Reportedly Reaches Tentative Deal with Primestar', *Nando.net*, May 1997. Available on-line at http://www.nando.net/newsroom/ntn/info/052797/info7_27632.html (10 May 1997).

33 AT&T press release, 'AT&T and DIRECTV Partner for Broadcast Satellite Service and Equipment', 22 January 1996. Available on-line at http://www.att.com/press/0196/960122.cha.html (11 August 1998).

34 P. Bacsich, 'Hughes DirecTV Makes Several Strategic Alliances', Open University, April 1996. Available on-line at http://www.de.infowin.org/ACTS/IENM/NEWSCLIPS/arch1996/030996uk.htm (6 June 1998).

35 C. Parkes, 'Murdoch Abandons United States Satellite Ambitions', *Financial Times*, 2 June 1997.

36 32.5 per cent – BSkyB; 32.5 per cent – BT; 20 per cent – Midland Bank; 15 per cent – Matsushita.

37 M. Doyle, 'Four Big Names Back Interactive Satellite TV', *Electronic Telegraph*, Issue 713, 8 May 1997. Available on-line at http://www.telegraph.co.uk:80/ (8 May 1997).

38 B. Potter, 'BIB Hits Technical and Price Snags', *Electronic Telegraph*, Issue 1184, 22 August 1998. Available on-line at http://www.telegraph.co.uk:80/ (5 October 1998).

39 M. Doyle, 'Digital TV Blow Hits BSkyB Shares', *Electronic Telegraph*, Issue 755, 19 June 1997. Available on-line at http://www.telegraph.co.uk:80/ (5 March 1998).

40 Select Committee on Culture, Media and Sport, *Fourth Report*, op. cit., Para. 75.

41 R. Gribben, 'C&WC to Offer Internet on TV', *Electronic Telegraph*, Issue 1020, 11 March 1998. Available on-line at http://www.telegraph.co.uk:80/ (5 August 1998).

42 Select Committee on Culture, Media and Sport, op. cit., Para. 75.,

43 European Commission, op. cit., I.3.

44 News Corporation Website. Available on-line at http://www.newscorp.com/public/pressdir/fbc.html (8 August 1998).

45 M. Tracey, op. cit., pp. 185–6.

46 S. Butterbaugh and F. Katz, 'Turner Pictures Being Integrated into Warner Bros', *Media Daily*, vol.4, no.223, 15 November 1996, published by Cowles New Media. Available on-line at http://www.mediacentral.com/Magazines/MediaDaily/index.html#01 (15 November 1996).

47 New York Staff, 'Fox Beats Turner on LA Dodgers', *Electronic Telegraph*, Issue 1029, 20 March 1998. Available on-line at http://www.telegraph.co.uk:80/ (9 September 1998).

48 Special correspondent, 'Billion-dollar United Top of Money League', *Electronic Telegraph*, Issue 1202, 9 September 1998. Available on-line at http://www.telegraph.co.uk:80/ (10 September 1998).
The blocking of BSkyB's bid was reported in A. Clark, 'City blasts Man United decision', *Electronic Telegraph*, Issue 1415, 10 April 1999. Available on-line at http://www.telegraph.co.uk:80/ (4 June 1999).

49 Herman and McChesney, op. cit., p. 118.

50 Tim Clark, 'The Battle for Digital Images', *CNET News*, 10 February 1998. Available on-line at http://www.news.com/News/Item/0,4,19030,00.html (3 March 1998).

51 J. Wallace, 'The Sleeping Giant Awakens to a New Dawn', extracted from J. Wallace, *Overdrive: Bill Gates and the Race to Control Cyberspace*, John Wiley, 1997; in *Electronic Telegraph*, 27 May 1997. Available on-line at http://www.telegraph.co.uk:80/ (4 August 1997).

52 Ibid.

53 M. Tran, 'Bill Gates Has Outgrown the PC Industry. Now He's Staring Into Space', *Guardian OnLine*, 21 May 1997. Available on-line at http://go2.guardian.co.uk/theweb/864227431-gates.html (21 May 1997).

54 S. Butterbaugh and F. Katz, 'TCI Pulls Out of MSN Partnership', *Media Daily*,

vol.4, no.223, 15 November 1996. Available on-line at http://www.mediacentral.com/Magazines/MediaDaily/index.html#01 (20 November 1996).

55 J. Wallace, op. cit.,

56 S. Somogyi and T. Standage, 'Why Java Changes Everything', *Electronic Telegraph*, Issue 399, 5 June 1996. Available on-line at http://www.telegraph.co.uk:80/ (9 September 1998).

57 D. Goodin and B. Heskett, 'Java Suit Hearing Under Way', *CNET News*, 8 September 1998. Available on-line at http://www.news.com/News/Item/0,4,26078,00.html (10 September 1998).

58 European Commission, op. cit.

59 Herman and McChesney, op. cit., p. 121.

60 J. Kornblum, 'Sprint Tries Net Phone Service', *CNET News*, 12 August 1998. Available on-line at http://www.news.com/News/Item/0,4,25215,00.html (21 August 1998).

61 Ibid.

62 S. Anderson, 'United States Coup Puts C&W Among Internet Stars', *Electronic Telegraph*, Issue 1099, 29 May 1998. Available on-line at http://www.telegraph.co.uk:80/ (5 June 1998).

63 Ibid.

64 Ibid.

65 J. Pelline, 'Cable Modems Fight for Lead', *CNET News*, *Special Report*, 20 November 1997. Available on-line at http://www.news.com/SpecialFeatures/0,5,16615,00.html (5 December 1997).

66 Select Committee on Culture, Media and Sport, op. cit., Para. 48.

67 E. Bell and E. Hellmore, 'Whose On-line Service Is It Anyway?', *Observer*, 29 September 1996.

68 P. Bacsich, 'Hughes DirecTV Makes Several Strategic Alliances', Open University, April 1996. Available on-line at http://www.de.infowin.org/ACTS/IENM/NEWSCLIPS/arch1996/03099 6uk.htm (5 June 1998).

69 J.V. Evans, 'New Satellites for Personal Communications', Wireless Technologies Special Report, *Scientific American*, April 1998, pp. 60–7.

70 Ibid., p. 63.

71 M. Tran, 'Bill Gates Has Outgrown the PC Industry', op. cit.

72 Evans, op. cit., p. 63.

73 T1 refers to the cables used by telecoms companies to transmit digital signals at a rate of 1.544 Mbytes. R. Mansell, *The New Telecommunications. A Political Economy of Network Evolution*, London, Sage, 1993, p. 237.

74 C. Lo, 'Get Wireless', *Wired*, Issue 5, 4 April 1997.

75 Select Committee on Culture, Media and Sport, op. cit., Para. 54.

76 Ibid., Para. 54.

77 Ibid., Para. 42.

78 Ibid., Para. 45.

79 M. Tran, 'Bill Gates Has Outgrown the PC Industry', op. cit.

80 J. Pelline and A. Lazarus, 'MS Invests $1 Billion in Comcast', *CNET News*, 9 June 1997. Available on-line at http://www.news.com/News/Item/0,4,11315,00.html (5 March 1998).

81 Ibid.

82 J. Davis, 'PC-like Cable Boxes Coming', *CNET News*, 11 July 1997. Available

on-line at http://www.news.com/News/Item/0,4,12350,00.html
(12 July 1997).

83 J. Davis, 'TCI Keeping Microsoft at Arm's Length', *CNET News*, 1 April 1998.
Available on-line at http://www.news.com/News/Item/0,4,20672,00.html
(6 April 1998).

84 M. Bracken, 'The BBC Goes Portal', *Wired News*, 21 July 1998. Available on-line
at http://www.wired.com/news/news/politics/story/13871.html (5 August 1998).

85 W. Wyatt quoted in WebTV Networks press release, 'Microsoft's WebTV
Networks and BBC Announce Services in the United Kingdom', 1 July 1998.
Available on-line at http://webtv.net/tv/corporate/media/bbc.html
(5 September 1998).

86 WebTV Networks press release, 'Microsoft WebTV Networks and BT Begin
Trial in United Kingdom', 18 March 1998. Available on-line at
http://webtv.net/ns/corporate/media/bt.html (5 August 1998).

87 W. Poel, 'BT and Microsoft to Get it Together?', March 1998, at PS
Consultants Website. Available on-line at
http://www.ps-consultants.co.uk/featurearticles/98–2.htm (3 April 1998).

88 R. Gribben, 'No BT Takeover, Says Microsoft', *Electronic Telegraph*, Issue 974,
24 January 1998. Available on-line at http://www.telegraph.co.uk:80/
(5 August 1998).

89 OECD, *Webcasting and Convergence: Policy Implications*. Available on-line at
http://www.oecd.org/dsti/sti/it/cm/prod/e_97–221.pdf (5 September 1998).

90 Ibid.

91 Ibid.

92 Herman and McChesney, op. cit., p. 125.

93 Ibid., p. 128.

94 G. Gilder, 'Life After Television, Updated', *Forbes ASAP*, 23 February 1994.
Available on-line at http://www.forbes.com/asap/gilder/ (5 May 1996).

95 G. Gilder, 'From Wires to Waves', *Forbes* ASAP, 23 February 1994. Available
on-line at http://www.forbes.com/asap/gilder/telecosm13a.htm
(5 August 1994).

96 R. Smith, Paper delivered to *Information Superhighway Conference*, sponsored by
National Communications Union, BT, National Consumer Council and 3Com,
at Cumberland Hotel, London, 24 October 1994.

97 J-C. Burgelman,'Convergence and Trans-European Networks: Some Policy
Problems', in K. Bjerg and K. Borreby, *Proceedings of the International Cross-
disciplinary Working Conference on Home-Orientated Informatics, Telematics &
Automation*, Copenhagen, University of Copenhagen, 1994, p. 19.

98 Staff Reporters, 'Massive Job Cuts For TCI Houston', *Houston Chronicle Online*,
5 December 1996. Available on-line at http://www.chron.com (5 May 1997).

99 N. Munford, L. Kolbe and W. Brenner, 'Convergence of Media, Machines and
Messages', *Convergence*, vol.3, no.1, 1997, p. 116.

100 J. Eakin, 'The Market: BICC Falls 8pc to 10-year Low', *Electronic Telegraph*,
Issue 841, 13 September 1997. Available on-line at
http://www.telegraph.co.uk:80/ (5 October 1997).

101 R. Gribben, 'Piped TV "a Turn-Off" for BT', *Electronic Telegraph*, Issue 994,
13 February 1998. Available on-line at http://www.telegraph.co.uk:80/
(4 April 1998).

102 Ibid.

103 G. Zorpette, 'A New Fat Pipe', *Scientific American*, April 1998, p. 26.

104 Ibid.
105 A. Barron and R. Uhlig, 'Hurry Up and Wait', *Electronic Telegraph*, Issue 384, 15 May 1996. Available on-line at http://www.telegraph.co.uk:80/ (3 September 1998).
106 N. Duffy, J. Davis and A. Daum, 'The Economics of Digital Television', in J. Steemers (ed.), *Changing Channels*, Luton, University of Luton Press, 1998, p. 47.
107 Ibid., pp. 45–6.
108 R. Allen, 'This is Not Television . . . ', in J. Steemers (ed.), op. cit., p. 65.
109 N. Munford, L. Kolbe and W. Brenner, op. cit., p. 117.
110 M. Tran, 'Time-Warner launches interactive TV system', *Guardian*, 15 December 1994.
111 E.R. Meehan, 'Technical Capability versus Corporate Imperatives: Towards a Political Economy of Cable Television and Information Diversity', in V. Mosco and J. Wasko (eds), *The Political Economy of Information*, Madison Wisconsin, University of Wisconsin Press, 1988, pp. 167–86.
112 N. Munford *et al.*, op. cit., p. 112.
113 Ibid., pp. 114–15.
114 M. Tran, 'Time-Warner launches interactive TV system', *Guardian*, 15 December 1994.
115 Ibid.
116 N. Munford *et al.*, op. cit., p. 115.
117 Ibid., p. 116.
118 Ibid., p. 115.
119 Ibid., p.116.
120 Ibid., pp. 116–17.
121 C.P. Taylor, 'Time-Warner Pulls Plug On Interactive TV Trial', *Inter@ctive Week*, 6 May 1997. Available on-line at http://www5.zdnet.com/zdnn/content/inwk/0414/inwk0028.html (11 December 1997).

Chapter 7

Privacy and censorship

Practical issues in the ethics of information

Peter Dean

> Like a force of nature, the digital age cannot be denied or stopped.
> It has four very powerful qualities that will result in its ultimate
> triumph: decentralizing, globalizing, harmonizing, and
> empowering.
>
> Nicholas Negroponte, Director of the Media Lab, Massachusetts
> Institute of Technology[1]

The four features identified by Negroponte as the driving force behind
the move to an information (and as Negroponte also suggests a post-
information)[2] age raise many ethical questions that are often overlooked in
a utopian view of the digital era. It is not that an increased dependency
on digital information gives rise to fundamentally new ethical questions, but
that information and communications technology can change the balance of
power between holders of information. As a result previously accepted norms
in the ethics of information are challenged and require re-evaluation.

Negroponte's four qualities of the digital age can be seen as polarising
the control of information between individuals and large organisations
(particularly governments and commercial organisations). Decentralisation
and empowerment give individuals greater ownership and control of information about themselves and their lives. The wider availability of information
can potentially allow an individual to make more informed choices either as a

voter or as a consumer. This is balanced by globalisation and harmonisation which make it easier for the state and private companies to collect and process information about individuals. They may then use that information to exploit and control individuals.

Most of the practical ethical problems that have arisen from the wider adoption of information and communication technologies are a symptom of the central question: who should control information? To formulate an answer to this question societies often turn to their legal system. However, there are a number of factors that make new technologies particularly difficult to regulate in this way.

This chapter begins by looking at some of the problems that can arise in trying to control new media technologies using traditional legislative processes. This is followed by a consideration of two of the most widely debated ethical issues in the new media – privacy and freedom of speech. Both these issues are examined as examples of a challenge to the accepted norms in the ethics of information brought about by the availability of new digital media technology. An analysis of these issues using a four-dimensional model of the information age based on Negroponte's categorisation can then highlight some of the ways in which new technology is influencing societies.

Jurisdiction

Traditionally legal systems have been based around the nation state. Differing cultural and political backgrounds have given rise to differing systems of jurisprudence and so actions that are legal in one country may be illegal in another. There has, however, been a growth in international legislation, particularly in support of bodies such as the United Nations, but this usually covers the relationships between nations rather than attempting to harmonise differing legal systems.

The jurisdiction of a particular legislature and court is therefore limited to a single country. This is in stark contrast to the global nature of digital telecommunications which can undermine national attempts at legislation. Through the adoption and propagation of a single set of base-level protocols, the Internet is now available on a global scale. As a result, the physical location of material published on the Internet becomes irrelevant to the reader, but this gives rise to problems in electronic publishing. For example, it is easy to circumvent the law of a particular country by moving the publishing operation (for example, the web server) 'off-shore'. This can bring a law into disrepute by making it unenforceable.

An example of this was the unauthorised publication on the Internet of a report into alleged ritual child abuse.[3] After a particularly difficult court case in Nottinghamshire, UK (the 'Broxtowe case'), Nottinghamshire Police and Social Services commissioned a joint investigation in 1989 into claims of widespread satanic abuse of children – the Joint Enquiry Team (JET). The full report was completed by the end of 1989, but for legal reasons (it named the children involved and the alleged abusers) it could not be published. The authors were then commissioned to produce a shorter, publishable report summarising the findings, but publication was suppressed by Social Services. The authors were forbidden to discuss it by their employers. Allegedly, this was because the conclusions contradicted the views held by Social Services who were keen to maintain their authority as experts in this particular field.

In 1997 journalists with the support of the original authors published the report on the Internet from the UK. They argued that publication of the report was in the public interest and should be available as a contribution to the debate. Nottinghamshire County Council took action and obtained a court order citing copyright infringement that required the removal of the report from the UK server. The publishers did this, but by this time a copy of the report had been downloaded in Canada and re-published from there. The original UK publishers simply provided a web page containing links to the report in Canada and so circumvented the court order. A subsequent order forced the UK group to remove the links to the material. The group then published the solicitor's letter that they had received on the Internet. The letter contained the Internet address of the relevant material in Canada and so readers could simply 'cut and paste' the address into their browser and still obtain the report. As UK courts have no jurisdiction over publication in Canada they were unable to enforce the order. Eventually the injunction was lifted as it was impossible to prevent the material spreading worldwide.

Conversely, actions in one country can prevent citizens in another from exercising their legal rights. The content of around 200 Internet Usenet newsgroups carried by the CompuServe on-line service provider was declared illegal in Germany by the German authorities in 1996 because of porno-graphic and neo-Nazi content. As a result CompuServe's German subsidiary was required to remove access to the appropriate groups.[4] However, CompuServe argued that the integrated, global nature of its network made it impossible to restrict access in Germany only, and that it would have to cut access worldwide. This prevented people in many countries from accessing the material even though it may have been legal in their country. There was severe criticism from the civil liberties lobby[5] and CompuServe later restored access to most of the material.

Privacy

According to Steven Miller, 'privacy is the power of information self-determination'.[6] If a person has control over the information that exists as a result of their interaction with other individuals, commercial organisations and the state, they can avoid unwanted commercial exploitation, political suppression or any unwanted intrusion into their lives. However, while appearing to be a highly desirable right of the individual, privacy has not been established as an absolute right, even in the US, a country with a written constitution. In the UK the lack of a written constitution renders the right to privacy even more tenuous. It was not until 1890 that an attempt was made to define privacy in legal terms, in an article entitled 'The Right to Privacy',[7] by Samuel Warren and Louis Brandeis. The authors defined privacy as 'the right to be left alone',[8] and they argued that it was unprotected by various property rights and so required additional legal protection, but it took until the late 1950s for the US Supreme Court to adopt this general principle. Even so, there is no explicit right to privacy contained within the US Constitution.

While governments have always monitored their citizens for political and law enforcement purposes, and commercial organisations have always collected information about potential customers for marketing purposes, the tools available to both invade and protect privacy have increased in power and sophistication. In an escalating 'arms race' governments have attempted to regulate the use of privacy tools while individuals, political groups and civil liberties campaigners have sought to defend and enhance the privacy of the individual.

Privacy tools

It's personal. It's private. And it's no one's business but yours. You may be planning a political campaign, discussing your taxes, or having an illicit affair. Or you may be doing something that you feel shouldn't be illegal, but is. Whatever it is, you don't want your private electronic mail (e-mail) or confidential documents read by anyone else. There's nothing wrong with asserting your privacy. Privacy is as apple-pie as the Constitution.[9]

Some encryption products put at risk efforts by federal, state and local law enforcement agencies to obtain the contents of intercepted communications by precluding real-time decryption. Real-time decryption is often essential so that law enforcement can rapidly respond to criminal activity and, in many instances, prevent serious and life-threatening criminal acts.[10]

As these two quotes demonstrate, the availability of cryptographic tools has been the subject of fierce debate, particularly in the US. The question of who should be able to use these tools is of major importance because the power of modern encryption techniques allows communications in almost complete privacy.

Whilst cryptography is often discussed in terms of one-to-one personal communication and the right to privacy, it is also the underlying technology for on-line financial transactions. This involves the secure transmission of credit card details, but increasingly supports other features such as authentication ('digital signatures') and digital cash transactions. Authentication allows the origin of messages and transactions to be verified. Digital cash allows on-line purchases to be made anonymously, like real cash but unlike credit-card purchases. This means that there are powerful commercial reasons for using cryptography as well as reasons associated with civil liberties issues. Indeed, commercial pressure is more likely to persuade governments to permit strong encryption than any argument based on a citizen's right to privacy.

The term cryptography has Greek origins and means 'secret writing'. It involves the concealment of information to prevent unauthorised access, particularly during communication when information is at its most vulnerable. The use of codes and code-breaking, first by governments and the military and then by commercial organisations, has a long history (see Chapter 1). However, it is only recently that effective cryptography has become readily available to individuals.

To send a confidential message the sender creates the message (the plaintext) and then applies a particular cryptographic process (encryption), producing a coded version (the ciphertext). The ciphertext, which is unreadable by humans, is then sent to the recipient who then reverses the cryptographic process (decryption) and recovers the plaintext. The encryption and decryption processes involve the application of a mathematical algorithm to the text. There are a wide range of different algorithms and many of these are very complex. Fortunately, most cryptographic software does not require a detailed knowledge of the algorithm in order to use it. Although encryption is a mathematical process, it is not only applicable to numerical messages. Text messages are easily converted into a numerically coded form for encryption and back again after decryption using, for example, the ASCII code.

For example, the following plaintext was encrypted using PGP ('Pretty Good Privacy'),[11] a popular cryptography package:

'Ask not what Microsoft can do for you,' Eddie said, 'ask what you can do for Microsoft.'[12]

This resulted in the following ciphertext:

——-BEGIN PGP MESSAGE——-
Version: PGPfreeware 5.0 for non-commercial use
<http://www.pgp.com>
MessageID: V8nzwc93N72oZatdUGUQz2OyMT4zRisA

qANQR1DBwU4Dkr/hJ0LwoKAQB/9vJYeKpkY0OkYKS1n0MUMN17
QuRJTbMHSlWVdS3RSQ2JhCDr0YwXHHVUtCzN0NdpBWiZ9O8Neg
06SQQsGqVZLvWXMLExA4JbZhsDUYrRJU53bqq2TtZWjdVz4ZADqT
6Y98MXv6DaTpvOEI4JaBx/I9Nzxz6OjJXY/doelb2nPS2D2WNol4iM
g4RvK+KVrni5V9o/PEV+I7dcedGeo3KkM0o8rTrRwonquUnfcL5Yf7zZ
GFg1AtrQvknxs9BK3qWayTuGDlgDAl6jJrPKAgbjHYriDL0YJ5R0d+NR
SVxwt0yPzgW4Mel1qjbNpMPnqua1IhbasvaQoWOfCbHI9F+rLAB/9
+tDFVT3Y7/esBQNIR3u3nR3lmv8pV+fjy16t9O5HN0Kz3blDoWctgHR
p6xr65Mb+LgEFk1CWu0grN6aO7q24RbG6w9qDs6RRDrR4673hz8p
F/36yYGoSxG1o3+IGZlifuL/zTCU0Ftrm0sh/ATZCm3/K1Gj4VYMmJ
HUVLwbidEV/u+9pmqR02h1UClcQDsvT6+1dllH30UVmlN45Yu4f4YJ
W/hZgRJFb/9Opl989v11SSg4Pg3hdo6bgUMz4+M6PZBqo/3bozuKi
h2TaZgoTdoGXyanxCWicNLSS3SSPUh82lM0DTeigOrc8pmtO636n5b
8SYtRgpYnueD79SFRqHyWigjSqOEah8tvCX0ayVOeEZSK4WW8kv3k
TLvM0A7Rw/zElnoa7S2bToeCDpXG0uW2Ua8YfmGztZiL/GCPB15KC
rcrzRF1Yuo4Gl/kfMs6WFeKGWdQrJhq5E1Ktw6Ql+1BeW/UBBXFZK
+A==
=eHHh
——-END PGP MESSAGE——-

This would then be sent to the recipient where it would be decrypted back into the plaintext.

An essential feature of this system is that both the sender and the recipient must have information about the cryptographic process; the sender in order to encrypt the message and the recipient in order to decrypt it. This information is usually in the form of a 'key'. A key is a piece of data that is combined with the plaintext in accordance with the cryptographic algorithm to produce the ciphertext. The use of cryptographic keys allows the algorithm to be distributed and used widely while at the same time providing the owners of information with the means of keeping control by keeping the keys secret.

An unauthorised recipient of an intercepted message may know the algorithm that has been used but cannot decrypt the message easily without the key. The process of trying to recover the plaintext without the key is called cryptanalysis. Cryptographic algorithms always have one distinctive property. They employ mathematical processes that operate very easily in one direction, but are very difficult to reverse. This is easily seen using the multiplication of prime numbers as an example: if the chosen encryption method is multiplication, the key is a number, and the plaintext is coded as a number then: plaintext × key = ciphertext.

For example, if the plaintext is 13 and the key is 11:
$13 \times 11 = 143$.

This is a simple operation that makes encryption easy and efficient. If the key is known then decryption is also easy as it just involves the reverse operation, i.e. division: Ciphertext ÷ key = plaintext.

For example, if the ciphertext is 143 and the key is 11:
$143 \div 11 = 13$. In this way the plaintext is recovered.

However, if the key is not known (for example by a cryptanalyst attempting an unauthorised decryption), the reverse operation, the factoring of a number back into its component factors, is much more difficult, especially if the numbers involved are large. The question 'What's eleven multiplied by thirteen?' is much easier to answer than 'Which two numbers were multiplied together to get 143?'. Such methods are referred to as 'one-way', and cryptographic algorithms are designed to exhibit this property so that encrypting and decrypting the message is easy with the key and difficult without it. Of course, factorisation of small numbers is not much more difficult than multiplication, and this is therefore not a practical method. As a result, the cryptographic algorithms in common use are made much more complicated to make cryptanalysis as difficult as possible.

The system described so far is called 'symmetric cryptography' as the key that encrypts the message must also be used to decrypt it. An example of this is the Data Encryption Standard (DES) algorithm;[13] a widely-implemented US government standard published in 1975 by the National Bureau of Standards (now the National Institute of Standards and Technology), and developed by the US National Security Agency and IBM. The problem with any symmetric method is that before any secure communications can take place, the sender and recipient must exchange the key. The key must be kept secret in order to keep the messages secret, and so it must be transmitted from sender to recipient securely. But if a secure means of transmitting the key is available then you don't need cryptography. In practice, it may be very difficult to exchange keys securely and so symmetric methods are not very useful for securing communications. However, they are still widely used where the encryption and decryption is local and carried out by the same person, for example in locking the contents of a computer disk while leaving it unattended.

Whitfield Diffie and Martin Hellman proposed an ingenious solution to the problem of exchanging keys in the mid-1970s.[14] Their system used asymmetric cryptography to avoid the problem completely. The system is asymmetric because the encrypting and decrypting keys are different. The process begins with an algorithm to generate a pair of keys. The keys are related by the fact that plaintext encrypted by one key (called the public key) can only be decrypted using the other key in the pair (called the private key). Note that the public key can only encrypt; it will not decrypt the message. That must be done using the private key. 'One-way' algorithms are used in key generation so that it is almost impossible to deduce the private key from the public key.

To use public key cryptography the recipient of the message first sends their public key to the sender. This can be over an insecure channel as the public key can only encrypt messages and is therefore of no use to a cryptanalyst. The sender than encrypts the message in plaintext using the public key to produce the ciphertext and sends it to the recipient. The recipient then uses their private key to decrypt the message and recover the plaintext. This can be an extremely secure means of communication, and has led to a fierce debate about the desirability of making such a system widely available.

The first practical implementation of public key cryptography, RSA, was developed and patented[15] by Ronald Rivest, Adi Shamir and Leonard Adelman. The patent is held by the Massachusetts Institute of Technology (MIT). The company RSA Data Security Inc.[16] has been set up to exploit this and other patents.

Cryptographic strength

Whilst all the cryptographic methods that have been described here are secure against simplistic attempts to break them, they are not all equally robust against a concerted effort to break them. The ability of a cryptographic method to withstand cryptanalysis (its cryptographic strength) is determined by two factors: the size of the key(s) and the mathematical structure of the algorithm. It is possible to use the same algorithm with a range of different key sizes and so it is a combination of these factors that sets the strength. A strong algorithm will provide the maximum cryptographic strength while keeping the key size as small as possible. A small key size improves the efficiency of encryption so keys are not usually any larger than necessary.

Keys are simply large numbers used as one input to the encryption process (the plaintext being the other input). The size is usually expressed as the number of binary digits (bits) required to represent the largest value the key can take. The higher the number of bits used to represent the key, the larger the number of possible keys and therefore the more resistant the key is to an exhaustive search (usually called a 'brute-strength' attack). For example, a 2 bit key has 2×2 (2^2) combinations, giving 4 possible keys:

00	Key 1
01	Key 2
10	Key 3
11	Key 4

A 3 bit key has $2 \times 2 \times 2$ (2^3) combinations, giving 8 possible keys:

000	Key 1
001	Key 2
010	Key 3
011	Key 4
100	Key 5
101	Key 6
110	Key 7
111	Key 8

The important feature of this arrangement is that adding one extra bit to the key doubles the number of possible keys and so doubles its strength for use with a given algorithm. One extra bit has little effect on the encryption efficiency, but has a large effect on the strength. By increasing the size of the key the cryptographic process can be made as strong as necessary. Practical keys are usually at least 40 bits long and so have at least 2^{40} possible keys (1099511627776)[17] to try in a 'brute-strength' attack by a cryptanalyst. To appreciate this number of possible keys consider that if a cryptanalyst could try one key per second then it would take over 34,000 years to try them all. However, a 41 bit key would have twice as many possible keys and so would be twice as strong. The set of all possible keys is called the key space.

Cryptography relies on keeping the key required to decrypt the ciphertext secret rather than keeping the algorithm secret. All the common algorithms are known in the public domain (although patents may control their use). Therefore cryptanalysts can analyse an algorithm and possibly develop short cuts that eliminate a subset of the key space from a 'brute-force' search. This has the effect of reducing the effective key size. Cryptographers can counteract this by increasing the key size appropriately, leaving a safety margin against possible short cuts.

Although it would appear to be the case that cryptography can be made arbitrarily strong, it is important to note that cryptographic strength decays over time. As computing power increases and cost decreases a 'brute-strength' attack against a given key size becomes more feasible. The empirical Moore's Law[18] predicts that computational speed doubles every eighteen months. To counteract this, key lengths need to be gradually increased. An extra bit per year would maintain the strength of any particular key.

In a move primarily to promote debate in this area, RSA Inc. has issued a number of cryptographic challenges.[19] The contests offer cash prizes to anyone who can decrypt messages without the key. Each contest uses a particular algorithm and key length to give increasing cryptographic strength for each contest. A number of groups have entered the contests and have found the keys using a 'brute-strength' attack. The weaker algorithms DES and RC5 56 bit were cracked by a loose collection of internet users[20] using a distributed system of clients and servers which used the idle time of large numbers of networked computers to search the key space. The group is currently working on RC5 64 bit, but this is 256 times stronger than RC5 56 bit and progress is very slow. After 302 days of searching the group had checked 370,085 trillion keys at a rate of 14,230,540 keys/sec without finding the key. However, that is only about 2 per cent of the keyspace. Cryptanalysts expect to search an average of 50 per cent of the keyspace to find a randomly chosen key. The DES II challenge was won by the Electronic Frontier Foundation using custom-built specialist hardware.[21] It found the correct key in less than three days. There is now a general consensus that DES does not provide secure encryption.

Regulation of cryptography

The free availability of a highly secure means of communication has led to concern within governments and law enforcement agencies. They argue strongly that the requirement to detect and prevent law breaking should override any absolute right to privacy for individuals. Appearing before a US House of Representatives sub-committee considering security issues relating to computers and communications, James Kallstrom of the FBI said that,

> without law enforcement's ability to effectively execute court orders for
> electronic surveillance, the country would be unable to protect itself

against foreign threats, terrorism, espionage, violent crime, drug trafficking, kidnapping, and other crimes. We may be unable to intercept a terrorist before he sets off a devastating bomb; unable to thwart a foreign spy before he can steal secrets that endanger the entire country; and unable to arrest drug traffickers smuggling in huge amounts of drugs that will cause widespread violence and death. Court-approved electronic surveillance is of immense value, and often is the only way to prevent or solve the most serious crimes facing today's society.[22]

This is a good example of the implications of new technology challenging current ethical practice. There is a well-established tradition of electronic surveillance (normally telephone tapping) of suspects by law enforcement agencies. It is subject to regulation and judicial review, but is quite a widespread practice. In 1994, US courts[23] authorised 1,154 surveillance orders (and denied none). This led to 2,852 arrests and 772 convictions. The average cost of each wiretap was about US$50,000.

Electronic surveillance is therefore an established part of law enforcement activity and so the potentially widespread availability of technology to prevent eavesdropping is seen by governments as a threat to a traditional means of information gathering. As a means of controlling the availability of strong encryption, the US government has considered two main policy instruments – export controls and key escrow.[24] Strong encryption is defined by US government agencies as asymmetric systems (e.g. RSA, PGP) which use key sizes greater than 512 bits, and symmetric systems (e.g. DES) which use key sizes greater than 40 bits.[25]

Export controls

US export controls have their origins in the First World War, but it was the Export Control Act of 1949 which allowed the executive arm of the US government to create and enforce export controls on any products it thought necessary. The process was exempt from judicial review. The Export Administration Act of 1969 included provision for the Commerce Control List (CCL), administered by the Department of Commerce. This was an attempt to balance the potentially conflicting demands of commercial exporters with national security concerns. Some cryptographic products were placed on this list, meaning that an export licence is required, but that one is likely to be granted provided it does not 'make a significant contribution to the military potential of any other country which would prove detrimental to the national security of the United States'.[26] However, strong cryptographic systems are also on the US Munitions List (USML) along with overtly military hardware – guns, tanks and so forth. The export of items on this list is controlled by the Department of State under the Arms Export Controls

Act and is much stricter. The National Security Agency advises both the Department of State and the Department of Commerce on the licensing of cryptographic products. It is much more difficult to obtain a licence to export items on the USML list. A side-effect of these regulations is that strong encryption is less readily available within the US as software producers are unwilling to develop and support two versions of a product, one for domestic use and one for export, and so they release a single version employing weak encryption.

Two cases show how blunt an instrument export control can be. In June 1991 Phil Zimmermann released PGP ('Pretty Good Privacy'), a public key cryptography package for personal computers based on RSA's patented algorithms, in the US.[27] He distributed the software at no charge as a political act. Within days the program was distributed widely and, through a Usenet newsgroup, was available worldwide. This gave rise to two problems for Zimmermann; RSA accused him of violating their intellectual property rights and the Department of Justice began a criminal investigation into whether he had violated the export controls covering strong encryption. Zimmermann was very careful to always include a note with the package stating that PGP should not be exported outside the US, but this was widely ignored by the user community. He also arranged for a subsequent version of the package to be released in New Zealand so that it was imported into the US rather than exported. Faced with the charge of patent infringement, Zimmermann argued that as he was distributing PGP free of charge he was not profiting from RSA's patents. This argument was hard to sustain as PGP could be depriving RSA of revenue. After a protracted investigation the Department of Justice wound up the case without bringing charges in January 1996.[28]

Paradoxically, Steven Levy has argued that the raising of public awareness of cryptography and regulation by the PGP affair was the best thing that could have happened to RSA.[29] By the time the Department of Justice investigation finished the patents were due to expire anyway, and Zimmermann was able to incorporate a range of different algorithms into the latest version of PGP. At the time of writing (1998), he is also making the full source code for PGP available so that anyone can check that there are no 'back door' weaknesses in the program. This independent public scrutiny of the algorithms within PGP by the cryptographic community means that users can be confident that the package provides a high degree of security.

Another example of the use of export control to regulate the availability of cryptographic products is the case of Bruce Schneier who wrote a book titled *Applied Cryptography*.[30] The book contained the source code for a functional cryptographic program as printed text. This could be typed into a computer and compiled into a working program. To make this stage easier for the reader the book included a floppy disk that also contained the same source code and so obviated the need for the data entry stage. A ruling was requested on the exportability of the book, and permission was granted to export the book, but not the accompanying disk! This brought export controls into disrepute and led to such comments as 'They think that terrorists can't type'.[31]

Key Escrow

The second major policy instrument that has been applied to cryptography is escrowed encryption. This form of regulation assumes the widespread availability of strong encryption, but aims to provide limited third party access to encrypted messages. This regulatory framework is attractive to government and law enforcement agencies as it allows encrypted communication to be subject to a similar surveillance regime as conventional communications, for example telephone tapping. The system relies on the adoption of a standard cryptographic system by everybody. The system would be similar to the symmetric methods described in this chapter, but with the addition of 'back door' access for law enforcement agencies. The US National Security Agency has developed a cryptographic algorithm called 'Skipjack'[32] that, in addition to encrypting and decrypting communications, takes the key and splits it into two. The end user retains the whole key and so can freely encrypt and decrypt messages, but the two halves are separated and kept in escrow. Neither part will decrypt the ciphertext, but each is lodged with a different government agency (an escrow agent). If a law enforcement agency wishes to intercept and decrypt the message then they can apply to the escrow agents for the two key halves, combine them and then decrypt the message. Two escrow agents are used rather than one to prevent abuse of the system by a single government agency. The Skipjack algorithm was implemented on a chip (called 'Clipper') designed for use in telephones. In 1993 the US government pressed for its adoption as a standard across the telephone system. Similar chips were designed for computers ('Capstone' and 'Tessera').

The adoption of 'Clipper' was strongly opposed by a wide range of different groups, both commercial and civil liberties/privacy campaigners, and for different reasons. For the system to work the 'Skipjack' algorithm must remain secret. If it were public, anyone could implement a version of 'Clipper' without registering the key with the approved escrow agents. If the algorithm is classified then its security cannot be independently verified. Any cryptographic algorithm can only acquire public confidence after extensive examination by the cryptographic community. The National Security Agency was heavily criticised[33] for not allowing this peer review of 'Skipjack'. A small panel of independent analysts was allowed to examine and verify the algorithm after agreeing not to disclose the details.[34] They concluded that 'Skipjack' was secure apart from the escrowed key access. However, the weakness of using a small closed review group was shown a short time later when a computer scientist at AT&T discovered a flaw in the design. The user could circumvent the mechanism that allows law enforcers to determine which escrowed key they need to retrieve in order to intercept the communication. As one commentator pointed out:

> I certainly don't trust a classified algorithm like SKIPJACK, even without a back door which everyone can see. I think I'll stick to systems which have been properly vetted to be clear of such compromises, like RSA. I hope others will do likewise and that RSA will become the standard which Clipper shouldn't be.[35]

This view is an example of the concern shared by some people that escrowed keys may not be held securely, and while such a back door exists then communications will always be vulnerable. To provide the access a government requires, escrowed encryption must be the only kind of encryption in use and this means that a government has to consider banning other forms of encryption. Other non-escrowed strong encryption is already freely available, and thus 'the genie is out of the bottle'.[36] Criminals therefore who are already involved in illegal activity would have no reason not to employ additional layers of strong encryption before communicating over escrowed communication channels. On retrieving the 'Skipjack' key and decrypting the message, the police may just find a PGP ciphertext. Opposition to 'Skipjack' has been so strong that the US government have so far failed to make progress in persuading the communications industries to adopt it. FIPS 185, the Federal Information Processing Standard describing 'Skipjack', is not an enforceable standard, even on other federal agencies.

In an attempt to clarify the confused situation regarding the regulation of encryption the US Congress requested the National Research Council to undertake an in-depth study of US encryption policy and to make recommendations.[37] This study was completed in 1996, and it supported the use and free availability within the US of strong encryption and the relaxation of export controls. It also identifies the problems with key escrow. The US government has not universally adopted the recommendations, primarily because of lobbying by the National Security Agency.

Steganography

The possibility that the use of strong encryption could be banned irrespective of the contents of the messages has led to major developments in the area of steganography. As we have already seen, the contents of a PGP encrypted message are highly secure, but there is no doubt that it is encrypted – the message is preceded by a plaintext header indicating which version of PGP has been used and the ciphertext is unreadable by humans. An interceptor can see that the message is encrypted even if they cannot decrypt it. If the act of encryption was in itself an offence, then merely the interception of the encrypted message could result in arrest even if the contents remained secret. Steganography is the study of techniques for hiding one message within another. It relies on stealth – fooling an interceptor into thinking they are looking at one kind of message when really it is another. This is different to encryption. If the interceptor realises a message is hidden, then it is fairly easily recovered. However if encryption is combined with steganography then extremely secure communication is possible. It is possible to encode a message into the letters which make up a paragraph of text or a message can be encoded on the pixels of a digital photograph as minute colour variations that are invisible to the viewer. One of the most popular steganography tools is Stego, developed by Romana Machado.[38]

Free speech and censorship

Probably the most widely debated issue arising from new technology for electronic publishing and distribution is the relationship between free speech and censorship. Prior to the widespread adoption of the Internet for worldwide publication, the dissemination of information via the print media, television or radio was a fairly complex, industrial and capital intensive process requiring printing presses, studios, transmitters, and so forth. The ability of any personal computer permanently connected to the Internet, combined with the bundling of web space with dial-up accounts from most Internet Service Providers (ISPs), means that many more people now have the opportunity to become worldwide publishers at very low cost. Alongside this, the development of sophisticated searching and indexing software for the Internet has provided a powerful means of searching many millions of published pages by keyword. It has never been easier to publish material, and it has never been easier for consumers to locate material. This is another example of advances in technology shifting the balance of power between publishers and consumers of information. The consequence is the need for a fresh evaluation of the right to free speech and the ethics of censorship.

Inevitably, some subject matter gives rise to controversy over whether it should be available on the Internet. As with traditional media, sexually explicit content, the depiction of violence, racist and sexist material and extreme political views are often the subject of debate.[39] Once again, however, the traditional equilibrium between publishers and potential censors has been upset. The Internet has provided much easier access to more extreme content in all these areas. Hard-core pornography, autopsy photographs, anti-Semitic and white supremacist views are now all much more freely available.

There are groups campaigning from both extremes of the free-speech/ censorship debate. The Electronic Frontier Foundation campaigns for free speech:

> EFF, the Electronic Frontier Foundation, is a non-profit, non-partisan organization working in the public interest to protect fundamental civil liberties, including privacy and freedom of expression, in the arena of computers and the Internet.[40]

Alternatively, the American Family Research Council[41] asserts that:

> With the reach of the Internet continually expanding into every aspect of our culture, it will become critical that electronic communication service providers bear some burden to protect children. The Internet has become a critical link in the apprehension of child abusers because child pornographers and paedophiles often use the Internet to transmit and sell their illegal images. However, it is difficult for law enforcement to police the Internet effectively without the assistance of service providers. Mandatory reporting legislation will provide our nation's law enforcement agencies with this much needed assistance.[42]

In areas such as child pornography there is almost universal agreement that such material should not be published electronically or otherwise. The debate is then centred on the best means of tackling the problem. In the long term, is the danger from censorship and the invasion of privacy greater than the danger from providing paedophiles with an additional means of communication?

Although the World Wide Web provides a simple and powerful means of worldwide publishing it is a model based on a clearly defined client-server paradigm. The material is published from reasonably easily identified physical web servers. Law enforcers can, in principle, identify the servers involved and their physical location. They can then take action and possibly apprehend those responsible and impound the hardware providing the web service. They may also be capable of severing the network connection. This fits well with a traditional publishing model where illegal printing may be stopped by seizing printing equipment and arresting the people operating it. So whilst there may be a difference of scale, web publishing can be regulated by existing legal frameworks. There have been many instances of web publishing being stopped either by law enforcement or by a corporate body responsible for a server that is being used by individuals contrary to corporate policy.[43]

A more problematic technology for lawmakers and enforcers is Usenet.[44] Usenet is a system of thousands of distributed on-line discussion groups. Each group provides a forum for the discussion of subject matter outlined in its charter. Whilst originally designed primarily for text-based messages, Usenet can be used to distribute any digital medium – pictures, video, sound, etc. A number of features of Usenet make it a powerful worldwide medium for someone with a particular message to propagate and consequently make it extremely difficult to regulate and censor for the following reasons:

- Usenet operates through the complete distribution and propagation of posted messages. There is no strict hierarchy of news group servers. Each server takes its incoming news from a reasonably adjacent server and sends any locally posted messages back where they are then propagated from server to server. This is extremely quick and efficient so copies of a posted message will exist on thousands of news servers within a few hours. Once posted, it is almost impossible for any agency to suppress it. Unlike web publishing, there is no central point that can be 'raided'.

- The Usenet system does not operate any strong form of authentication of message posters. Coupled with the availability of systems that can strip out any identification information, this means that people can post messages to Usenet in almost complete anonymity.[45] Having failed to suppress a Usenet posting it may not even be possible to trace the author.

- Usenet discussion groups are organised into a hierarchy by subject content. For example, the names of all groups relating to the UK begin 'uk', all groups relating to the UK media begin 'uk.media', all groups relating to radio in the UK begin 'uk.media.radio' and the specific group for discussion of BBC Radio Four is called 'uk.media.radio.bbc-r4'. This provides a simple, powerful means of organising the content. By clearly flagging the area of discussion it should be easy for users to avoid content which they do not wish to see. Organisations providing a Usenet feed to users have tried to use the subject-based hierarchy as a means of censoring Usenet content. For example, by blocking access to groups in the 'alt.sex.*' hierarchy, organisations can prevent access to sexually explicit material. However, this can sometimes be fairly naïve and rather heavy-handed. Anyone can post any message to any group, so sexually explicit material can be posted to any group, whatever the title. This may cause more offence than keeping it in an identifiable area, particularly if the target group chosen is sensitive to such material, for example, some religious groups or those frequented by children. In attempting to restrict access to sexual material, some organisations have even blocked access to groups legitimately discussing health issues by a crude choice of criteria for blocking groups by keyword. America Online received a deluge of complaints from breast cancer patients and researchers when it banned the word 'breast' from subscriber profiles. It was forced to reverse the decision.[46] And even if an organisation does prevent access through the news servers it manages, there are many free, uncensored news feeds around the world that users can connect to.

The difficulty of tracing and apprehending the originators of controversial material has resulted in the focus shifting to service providers. As the above quote from the Family Research Council demonstrates, service providers are seen as tangible corporate bodies that are susceptible to the legal process and who care about their public image. Some Internet service providers have come under considerable pressure to censor the network traffic they handle. In the UK, the *Observer* newspaper ran a front page headline: 'The pedlars of child abuse: We know who they are. Yet no one is stopping them'.[47] The report was directed at Demon Internet,[48] one of the UK's oldest and largest Internet service providers. The report criticised Demon as a company that 'provides access to thousands of illegal photographs of young children being sexually assaulted'.[49] This gives the impression that Demon is the originator of the material. However, most of the material concerned was carried on Usenet groups with Demon's Usenet server acting only as a relay in the worldwide propagation of the material. This incident illustrates an attempt to treat new media technologies differently to the more established forms. If a subscriber makes an offensive telephone call then there is no question of holding the telephone service provider liable for that call – the telephone company is seen as an innocent disseminator of information. Internet service providers should be treated in the same way.

Self-regulation

As an alternative to external regulation and censorship, service and content providers have developed systems of self-regulation and classification. Most service providers have developed an 'Acceptable Use Policy' (AUP). This sets out legitimate activities and content for subscribers. Acceptance of the AUP is normally a condition of registration with a service provider. Demon Internet has developed clear guidelines on the use of Usenet by their customers and reserves the right to terminate a connection.[50] This policy enables them to demonstrate a responsible attitude and to discourage more stringent regulation.

A popular form of self-regulation of content has been developed by the Recreational Software Advisory Council on the Internet (RSACi).[51] The RSACi was set up in 1994 by a group of trade organisations led by the Software Publishers Association. It is a non-profit organisation sponsored by content providers (from Pornotopia to the Birdville Church of Christ!) and software developers (Microsoft, IBM). This system revolves around the classification of content. A website publisher completes an on-line RSACi questionnaire that asks the publisher to classify the content according to the language used, depiction of violence, depiction of sex and nudity, etc. The publisher is then given a digital code based on the responses and this in turn is invisibly incorporated into the pages. Browser software can be configured by end users to only display pages that conform to particular content criteria, using the embedded code to identify the content. It is intended that parents, teachers or other responsible adults should configure the browsers used by children to restrict access to material they feel is inappropriate. However, such a system is dependent on sites registering with the service and on their accurate description of the content. Browsers can be configured to only allow access to RSACi classified sites, but until the system becomes more prevalent that would seriously restrict access to a large amount of uncontroversial material.

Other forms of content control are based on filtering access to content according to site name and keywords. These systems use locally installed software to monitor Internet usage, to block access to particular sites, and to pages containing words from a prescribed list.[52] The administrator of the system can modify the lists of sites and words, and regular updates are available by subscription to the original supplier. Such systems depend on the presence of recognisable words in the address and content of the material to determine access. Innocuously named material, especially photographs, can bypass such systems. There have been attempts to develop algorithms for analysing photographic images to determine whether they are pornographic. These rely on very crude measures such as the percentage of pixels with flesh tones. However, access to a great amount of classical art would be restricted by such a system.

Conclusions

As the increasing number of clashes between the users of new technologies and the legislators show, the rapid development of new means of disseminating and controlling information has challenged many previously accepted principles. Many legal and regulatory frameworks are constructed around a pre-digital view of information. These problems are compounded by the rate of development of new technology. Placing a high priority on rigour and enforce-ability often causes legislatures to work comparatively slowly. This means that changing technological factors alter the balance of power in information control faster than laws can be enacted to maintain the equilibrium.

The main issues considered in this chapter highlight the value of a four-dimensional view of an information age based on the characteristics identified by Negroponte:

Balance of Power in an Information Age	
Individual	**State/Commerce**
Negroponte characteristics:	
Globalisation →	
Harmonisation →	
← Decentralisation	
← Empowerment	
Practical Examples:	
Export controls on cryptography → (Globalisation – US policy becomes de facto world policy)	
Key Escrow → (Harmonisation – everybody must use 'Clipper')	
← Usenet (Decentralisation – no single source of publication)	
← PGP (Empowerment – brings strong encryption free to individuals)	

A partial solution to the problem of legislating in such a complex and rapidly changing area may lie in better technical education of lawmakers, thus promoting a greater understanding of the implications of new technology. There are some encouraging signs that governments are recognising the difficulties associated with the tight central control of information and are considering self-regulation as a more practical means of ensuring the responsible use of information. The UK House of Commons Select Committee on Culture, Media and Sport has observed that:

> The Government's approach to Internet regulation is to encourage voluntary action backed up by the full force of the existing law, based on the application of the general law on-line as off-line.[53]

Societies also need to explicitly confirm general principles on the ethics of information. These could then be applied to new technological developments without continual re-evaluation. The result might be information-based societies underpinned by the responsible use of information by individuals, commercial organisations and governments.

Notes

1 N. Negroponte, *Being Digital*, London, Hodder and Stoughton, 1995, p. 229.
2 Ibid., pp. 163–5.
3 The details of this case are available from the Cyber-Rights & Cyber-Liberties (UK) group, Centre for Criminal Justice Studies, University of Leeds, UK. Available on-line at http://www.leeds.ac.uk/law/pgs/yaman/yaman.htm (6 September 1998).
4 S. Ascarelli, 'Two On-Line Services Investigated in Racial Hatred Case', *Wall Street Journal*, 22 January 1996, p. B13.
5 Ibid.
6 S. Miller, *Civilizing Cyberspace: Policy, Power, and the Information Superhighway*, New York, ACM Press and Addison-Wesley Publishing Company, 1996, p. 264.
7 S. Warren and L. Brandeis, 'The Right to Privacy', *Harvard Law Review*, vol.4, 1890, p. 193.
8 Ibid.
9 P. Zimmermann, 'How PGP Works/Why Do You Need PGP?', in P. Ludlow (ed.), *High Noon on the Electronic Frontier – Conceptual Issues in Cyberspace*, Massachusetts, MIT Press, p. 182. Zimmermann is the creator of PGP (Pretty Good Privacy) encryption software. It is available worldwide and there is a version that is licensed to users at no cost.
10 Statement by James K. Kallstrom, Special Agent in Charge, Special Operations Division, New York Field Division, Federal Bureau of Investigation (FBI), on 'Special Issues in Computers and Communications', before the Subcommittee on Science, Space, and Technology, US House of Representatives, 3 May 1994.
11 Pretty Good Privacy, Inc. Home Page. Available on-line at http://www.nai.com/default_pgp. asp (6 September 1998).
12 K. Kelly, 'The Software Developer', in J. Brockman (ed.), *Digerati – Encounters With the Cyber Elite*, London, Orion Business, 1997, p. 95.
13 FIPS (Federal Information Processing Standards) 46, 46–1 and 46–2, National Institute of Standards and Technology, December 1993. Available on-line at http://csrc.ncsl.nist.gov/fips/fips46–2.txt (6 September 1998).
14 W. Diffie and M. Hellman, 'New Directions in Cryptography', *IEEE Transactions on Information Theory*, vol.IT–22, 1976, pp. 644–54.
15 US Patent 4,405,829.
16 RSA Data Security Inc. Home Page. Available on-line at http://www.rsa.com/ (6 September 1998).
17 $2^{40} = 2 \times 2 = 1099511627776$.
18 What is Moores Law? Available on-line at http://www.intel.com/intel/museum/25anniv/hof/moore.htm (6 September 1998).

19 The RSA Data Security Secret-Key Challenge. Available on-line at
    http://www.rsa.com/rsalabs/97challenge/ (6 September 1998).
20 Distributed.Net – Node 0. Available on-line at http://www.distributed.net/
    (6 September 1998).
21 EFF DES Cracker Project. Available on-line at
    http://www.eff.org/descracker.html (6 September 1998).
22 Kallstrom, op. cit.
23 Administrative Office of the US Courts, *Wiretap Report for the Period January 1,
    1994 to December 31, 1994*, US Government Printing Office, Washington, DC,
    1995.
24 National Research Council, *Cryptography's Role in Securing the Information Society*,
    Washington, National Academy Press, 1996, Chapters 4–5, pp. 113–215.
25 RSA Data Security, Inc., *Answers to Frequently Asked Questions About Cryptography
    Export Laws*. Available on-line at http://www.rsa.com/PUBS/exp_faq.pdf
    (9 September 1996).
26 National Research Council, op. cit., p. 118.
27 J. Schwartz, 'Privacy Program: An On-Line Weapon?', *Washington Post*, 3 April
    1995, p. A1.
28 E. Corcoran, 'US Closes Investigation in Computer Privacy Case', *Washington
    Post*, 12 January 1996, p. A11.
29 S. Levy, 'Crypto Rebels' in P. Ludlow (ed.), op. cit. p. 192.
30 B. Schneier, *Applied Cryptography*, New York, John Wiley & Sons, 1994.
31 National Research Council, op. cit., p. 164.
32 FIPS (Federal Information Processing Standards) 185, National Institute of
    Standards and Technology, February 1994. Available on-line at
    http://csrc.ncsl.nist.gov/fips/fips185.txt (6 September 1998).
33 J. Perry Barlow, 'Jackboots on the Infobahn' in P. Ludlow (ed.), op. cit., pp.
    207–13.
34 E. Brickell, D. Denning *et al.*, SKIPJACK Review – Interim Report. Available
    on-line at
    http://www.cosc.georgetown.edu/~denning/crypto/clipper/SKIPJACK.txt
    (6 September 1998).
35 J. Perry Barlow, 'The Denning-Barlow Clipper Chip Debate', in P. Ludlow (ed.),
    op. cit., p. 223.
36 S. Baase, *A Gift of Fire – Social, Legal and Ethical Issues in Computing*, New Jersey,
    Prentice Hall, 1997, p. 106.
37 National Research Council, *Cryptography's Role in Securing the Information Society*,
    Washington, National Academy Press, 1996.
38 Stego Online by Romana Machado. Available on-line at http://www.stego.com/
    (6 September 1998).
39 Yahoo UK and Ireland Index to Censorship and the Net. Available on-line at
    http://www.yahoo.co.uk/Society_and_Culture/Issues_and_Causes/Civil_Rights/
    Censorship/Censorship_and_the_Net/ (6 September 1998).
40 About the Electronic Frontier Foundation. Available on-line at
    http://www.eff.org/EFFdocs/about_eff.html#INTRO (6 September 1998).
41 Family Research Council. Available on-line at http://www.frc.org/
    (6 September 1998).
42 The Family Research Council – Frequently Asked Questions. Available on-line at
    http://www.frc.org/faq/faq20.html (6 September 1998).
43 Limits to freedom of expression are monitored by the Electronic Frontier

Foundation. Available on-line at http://www.eff.org/~declan/global/
(6 September 1998).

44 M. Hauben, R. Hauben, *Netizens: On the History and Impact of Usenet and the
Internet.* Available on-line at http://www.columbia.edu/~hauben/netbook/
(6 September 1998).

45 Yahoo UK and Ireland Index to Privacy Policy. Available on-line at
http://www.yahoo.co.uk/Computers_and_Internet/Internet/Policy/Privacy/
(6 September 1998).

46 *Associated Press and New York Times Press Service*, 'Cybercensors Reverse Ban on
"Breast"', 2 December 1995.

47 D. Connett, J. Henley, 'The Pedlars of Child Abuse: We Know Who They Are.
Yet No One is Stopping Them', *Observer*, 25 August 1996, p. 1, pp. 19–21.

48 Demon Internet Home Page. Available on-line at http://www.demon.net/
(6 September 1998).

49 D. Connett, J. Henley, op. cit.

50 Demon Internet Acceptable Use Policy. Available on-line at
http://www.demon.net/services/news/newsaup. html (6 September 1998).

51 Recreational Software Advisory Council Home Page. Available on-line at
http://www.rsac.org/ (8 September 1998).

52 Internet Parental Control Frequently Asked Questions. Available on-line at
http://www.vtw.org/ipcfaq (8 September 1998).

53 *The Multi-Media Revolution – Volume 1, The Fourth Report of the Culture, Media and
Sport Select Committee.* Available on-line at
http://www.parliament.the-stationery-office.co.uk/pa/cm199798/cmselect/
cmcumeds/520-vol1/52007.htm#a33 (6 September 1998).

Chapter 8

Spectacle as commodity

Special effects in feature films

Luke Hockley

Introduction

If you look through any of the personal computer magazines on sale you might be forgiven for thinking that it is now possible to create broadcast-quality special effects on your desktop computer. The magazines are full of advertisements for the latest versions of image manipulation software that suggest the ease and power of such programmes. The situation is exacerbated by the hype which can surround a television science fiction series like *Babylon 5*. This might lead the naïve consumer to believe that the Amiga computers used to generate the special effects for *Babylon 5* are the same machines that can be bought off the shelf. Both software and hardware producers have an obvious motive for promoting such myths, but the advances made in personal computing in terms of both power and speed do mean that it is possible to produce special effects similar to those used by film-makers and television producers. However, they are still a long way from the type of work stations used in the film industry, where machines such as those produced by Silicon Graphics and software such as NewTek's LightWave 3D and AliasWavefront's PowerAnimator dominate. While it is true that the cost of hardware continues to decrease, the software costs remain too high for most home users. For example, the new Maya software that supersedes PowerAnimator costs a minimum of £1,000 per copy per year.

The aim of this chapter is to present a critique of two differing positions concerned with special effects: the first explores the economics of special effects while the second locates their significance within television and film fictions. But rather than seeing these as diametrically opposed elements, this chapter aims to devise a way of analysing special effects that regards them as both economic and textual commodities. This will provide a perspective on special effects that takes account of their technological sophistication, economic significance and their role as an important element within film and television narratives.

However, before we begin, it is important to establish a working definition, or at least a common understanding, of what is meant by the seemingly unproblematic term 'special effect'. Questions of definition are essentially historical. Without reference to the historical discourse of the image (and when all is said and done special effects are only images and sounds) it is impossible to articulate the relationship of an image to its technology and its society. Images need to be seen in a definitional historical relationship with their antecedents, in relation to the technology that enables their reproduction, and with reference to their value as a commodity. This commodification of the image is addressed by cultural critics such as Herbert Schiller[1] and Bernard Edelman.[2] Schiller's exploration of the role of marketing and advertising in special effects clearly resonates with the political economy approach to the analysis of moving images. This mode of analysis was pioneered to great effect by the British movement of screen studies in the 1970s, and was exemplified by SEFT (Society for Education in Film and Television) and *Screen* (a leading British critical journal of film and television studies with a worldwide influence). As a counterpoint to this theme, Philip Hayward has suggested that the value of special effects lies not so much in the commodification of the image but with the creation of spectacle.[3] He suggests that the images in and of themselves are unremarkable. The prosaic discourse of televisual and filmic imagery needs something to step outside the everyday image and present itself as exceptional. The special effect, whether it is in a music video or feature film, presents itself as extraordinary.

One of the remarkable things about special effects is that they are clearly the product of capitalism, but at the same time they threaten to subvert the economic rationalism of movie-making. As a percentage of the total film budget, special effects have a disproportionate significance. *Star Wars* (George Lucas, 1977) cost around US$9 million, of which US$2.5 million was spent on special effects.[4] As an investment in the narrative of the film this is a remarkable proportion of the total budget. However, the film brought in around US$200 million in profits. The aim of this chapter is therefore to identify two theoretical axes with which to analyse special effects. Following the argument suggested by Schiller, special effects can be thought

Table 8.1 Model for the analysis of special effects in feature films

	Discourse	*Reception*
Narrative	Location in the internal narrative. Historical dimensions (direct and indirect reference to similar previous uses of special effects).	Expectation of audience (based on genre, star and director). Effect on audience (emotional, psychological, sociological). Sub-cultural exploitation by audience (appropriation of media artefacts and reading against the grain).
Industrial	Techniques used in production. Cost of production (as a factor in production budgets against eventual box-office gross).	Patterns of distribution (releasing conventions, cuts and phased world releases). Merchandising.

of as a materialist commodity. On the other hand, as suggested by Hayward, they are also a piece of industrial magic.

One way of presenting this interrelationship is as a grid. Table 8.1 provides a conceptual schema for the analysis of special effects. It suggests that the connected nature of the industrial production of film narratives and the historical and contemporary contexts within which they are viewed are particularly important.

Table 8.1 shows that special effects can be located as part of a complex system of historical and contemporary relationships. This chapter will introduce some of the implications of these intersections, but it cannot present a detailed exposition. These theoretical concerns are addressed directly towards the end of this chapter. But before we engage with these issues it is important to have a reasonably clear understanding of what is meant by the term 'special effect'.

The background – before the computer

In an interview in 1970 between Ivan Butler and Ray Harryhausen, the leading exponent of stop-frame model animation, Harryhausen commented that 'the term "special effects" is probably confusing to an audience. It means so many things that in the end it means nothing specific.'[5] At least from an academic position that is concerned with questions of definition and subsequent problems of evaluation, this is a rather depressing comment. Historically Harryhausen's observation came some two years after *2001: A*

Space Odyssey (Stanley Kubrick, 1968) which gave the first truly believable depiction of life in outer space, and seven years before *Star Wars* which was the first film to use the ground-breaking special effects technique of motion control photography. As his remark suggests special effects was already a complex business.

Harryhausen's films are instantly recognisable through the mythological scenes and monsters that he brought to life in his stop-frame animations. This ability of the cinematic medium to take something extraordinary and to make it seem believable has fascinated film-makers and illusionists from the early days of the moving image. The Victorians in particular had a passion for this type of entertainment and one of the most popular of these was the diorama. Created by Daguerre, the first diorama opened in Paris in 1822 and was such a success that he opened a second in London in 1823. This optical special effects-based entertainment utilised complex purpose-built auditoria with large realistic paintings. The aim was to produce a greater verisimilitude than just viewing a single large canvas painting. With his background in designing sets and complex visual effects for opera and theatre, Daguerre created in the diorama a heightened sense of movement and realism. In short he created a technological spectacle that was to last until 1851 when the last one closed. Daguerre's subjects were varied but included the re-creation of a number of famous buildings and natural landmarks including *The Basilica of St Paul* and *A View of Mont Blanc*. (The latter had the rather dubious 'added value' of using live goats to aid the realism of the scene.) Watching a diorama sounds like a remarkably cinematic experience. As Don Slater notes,

> Daguerre could alter the lighting to dissolve from one scene to the next. The dissolve – much like the cinema fade – could be experienced by the audience as both magical and technological, a wonder of scientific know-how which could transport the audience from one place or time to another. The technology was a commercial secret: mysterious science producing spectacular magic.[6]

Subsequent optical effects in film were based on similar techniques to those invented by Daguerre and had a similar purpose. The creation of mattes and the use of double exposure (in which two separate elements are combined into a single image) were both pioneered by Georges Méliès in his film *A Trip to the Moon* (1902). This film was ambitious and innovative in its use of special effects processes. Like Daguerre, Méliès used stage techniques (his father had been a stage magician) and combined them with various camera effects including tracking, model work, stop camera, double exposure and photography with black background.[7] Even today these remain some of the fundamental techniques used in the creation of special effects.

These effects, which rely on the physics and chemistry of film-making, are sometimes referred to as 'opticals'. In addition there are 'physical' effects. Models, or miniatures, explosions and crashes form an important part of the spectacle created by special effects. In part, the appeal of 1950s epics like *The Ten Commandments* (Cecil B. DeMille, 1956) does not lie in the story, which presents a rather austere view about the necessary rules for righteous living. Instead there is a rather more compelling sensation in the cinematic magic that gives Charlton Heston as Moses the power to part the Red Sea. (The notion of effect and sensations as commercial commodities will be returned to shortly.)

After the computer

With the passage of time matters of definition have if anything got worse not better. The development of 'motion control' photography by George Lucas' special effects company Industrial Light and Magic brought to the screen a realism in special effects that had previously been impossible. The technique uses a computer to control the movements of cameras, models and backgrounds so that intricate changes in the position of any of the elements can be achieved in a highly accurate and repeatable manner. According to Douglas Trumbull, a leading special effects supervisor, the motion control rig used on *Close Encounters of the Third Kind* (Steven Spielberg, 1977) enabled movements to be repeated to within ten-thousands of an inch.[8] This enabled different elements to be combined in a moving shot while maintaining control of the perspective that realism requires. Thus the sequence in *The Empire Strikes Back* (Irvin Kershner, 1980) in which the Millennium Falcon flies through an asteroid belt, consists of over forty shots with up to twenty-eight individually filmed elements.

In subsequent years computers were used not only to control the mechanical elements of image-making but also to generate images them-selves. As with all 'firsts' it is difficult to pin down the exact date of the first appearance of computer-generated imagery in film, but *Alien* (Ridley Scott, 1979) was certainly among the first.[9]

The advent of digital technology influenced the methods by which cameras could be controlled and the processes by which images could be generated. Both of these developments have now entered the mainstream of television and film production practice, and audiences have come to expect a high standard of special effects work, even in relatively low-budget television productions. The days of wobbly spaceships on BBC science fiction series such as *Dr Who* and *Blake's Seven* are well and truly over. In part, improvements in the quality of special effects come from developments in the field of computing. Faster desktop machines mean that for a few thousand pounds it is possible to produce cheap and cheerful special effects that previously would have required a detailed knowledge of the film production process. Animation techniques, such as laser fire, can be cheaply achieved on a desktop station whereas previously each blast had to be painstakingly animated by hand.

However, because such production technology is now relatively affordable, feature film production has had to develop increasingly impressive effects to keep ahead of television. The digital technology used to animate the dinosaurs in *Jurassic Park* (Steven Spielberg, 1992) is not available on anything remotely like a PC. The consequence of using cutting-edge technology is that it is expensive and a growing proportion of the production budget can, or has to be devoted to 'effects'.

But does this bring us closer to a working definition of what is meant by 'special effects'? As suggested above there is a close relationship between the chemistry and physics of film and the techniques used in creating special effects. As Martin Barker suggests,

> In one sense, it could be said that the whole of cinema is one century long special effect. The moment we pass beyond pointing a camera and microphone at a space and recording what ever passes in front of them, construction of effects is taking place . . . [but] In another way, too, special effects can't be the whole of cinema. Effects are only meaningful by virtue of being set against another measure in a film.[10]

Special effects, then, are different to the other aural and visual elements of film. They are moments of spectacle that present the extraordinary and impossible as believable. As Colin Brown puts it,

> There are two types of effect. There's the visible effect which carries the wow factor which basically is in your face. It's the dinosaur in *Jurassic Park*, it's the alien in *Aliens IV* . . . Then there's the invisible effect. It adds a huge amount to the story-telling in the film . . . and a good example . . . would be that incredible camera move,[11] and when I say incredible, I mean impossible, where Leonardo DiCaprio and his buddy are standing on the prow of the ship [*Titanic*] where the camera actually pulls back maybe 2 or 3 miles and does so seamlessly.[12]

Of course, this is not truly an 'invisible effect'[13] because at some point in the shot the viewer will recognise that what is happening is impossible. Just because a digital effect is apparently woven seamlessly into the fabric of the film does not mean that viewers will not recognise it for what it is. Audiences understand that films are constructed artefacts and that special effects are distinctive elements. On recognising a special effect for what it is, viewers move from an engagement with the film narrative as real, to enjoying the spectacle and techniques of cinema.

To develop Barker's and Brown's points, special effects are part of, and embedded into, the narrative of the film. They may by 'visible' or 'invisible'; or, as in the above example from *Titanic* (James Cameron, 1997), somewhere between the two. They represent the spectacular elements of a narrative, whether they are visible to the film viewer or go unnoticed.

Political economy – a theory of special effects

Film producers have not been slow to notice that the pleasure derived from watching such effects has a commercial value in excess of less effects-based films. This, combined with the increasing percentage of production budgets devoted to special effects, has led some theorists to focus on the economics of film production and the significant role played by special effects. The American cultural critic, Herbert Schiller, is at the forefront of such analysis and has suggested that special effects can best be understood as an integral part of the capitalist system. He argues that as a device they aim to add value to what is becoming a devalued artefact – the film.[14]

But to conceptualise special effects in such a steadfast economic manner fails to recognise the multifaceted nature of the spectacle of special effects and fails primarily to understand their narrative as well as industrial dimensions. His argument, which sees capital as the locus of desire, and hence pleasure, seems out of touch with the extraordinary developments in special effects in which the image as icon has reinvented itself as digitally re-created simulacra. The most obvious example of this has been the development of virtual characters such as the 500 digital extras that inhabit the *Titanic* in James Cameron's film of the same name. Such narratively-driven realist elements must be examined when looking at the role of special effects. Virtual actors are not created to save money, not at the moment anyway, but to add novelty and an element of spectacle to films. It has the added purpose of conferring on the film a 'hi-tech' status.

Yet Schiller is surely on to something with his argument that capitalist society has an almost Darwinian drive to perpetuate and protect itself and that films are symptomatic and supportive of this venture. In fact he goes so far as to suggest that special effects can only be understood if they are seen not just as an element within the media production process itself but as constituting a new sphere of economic activity. He therefore suggests that special effects can be abstracted from the television/film discourse and turned into commodities in their own right. Which is to say that the spectacle can of itself have a monetary value. He notes: 'Indeed, an entirely new economic sphere emerged, the special effects industry, difficult as it is to place into the standard industrial classification.'[15]

However, this assertion is problematic from a number of stand-points. First, as we have already suggested, the film industry, and by extension television, has no problem in seeing the role that special effects has in the traditional/industrialised hierarchy of the production process. However, unwittingly Schiller does make an historical observation which is that special effects as an identifiable, and hence commodifiable element, did not fully emerge until the 1930s.[16]

Thus definitions of special effects are bound up with and part of the materialist base that forms the elements of production. As Butler comments,

> The special effects department is concerned with the PHYSICAL side of the particular action sequence involved. . . . The OPTICAL work, matting, double printing, comes under the heading of special effects, though the laboratory side is usually referred to as process work.[17]

Such distinctions are helpful only in so much as they assist in locating the nexus of production within a material process to which value can be ascribed. However, within the work of digital images and sounds such definitions seem highly problematic. Here physical and optical processes can be subsumed into a single digital process, as in the later example from *Titanic*. Thus the physical and the optical are intertwined and indeed, in the world of the digital image such distinctions no longer seem helpful or valid.

In attempting to pin special effects to a specific economic practice Schiller could be accused of taking a reductionist view of seeing films in purely economic and historical terms. Schiller actually acknowledges the impossibility of this, but none the less wants to identify a moment in history when special effects can be seen as fracturing the complacent materialist discourse of feature film consumption. He writes,

> But the elevation of special effects into a primary constituent of film and general entertainment is much more recent. It can probably (and arbitrarily) be assigned to their use in *Star Wars*, produced in 1977. A case can also be made for Stanley Kubrick's *2001*; when it was made in 1970[18] it achieved a startling pseudo-environment.[19]

It seems as though Schiller is looking for milestones. But there are no milestones. Rather, after time it may be possible to identify cultural indicators that are the result of a particular conjunction of social, economic, historical and psychological forces. It is actual film and television productions that subsequently become regarded as landmark events – an attribution that reflects only a part of their role in the cultural and historical practices of film-making. Of course there is often a disjunction between the historical condition of production and subsequent recognition.

An example of this can be seen in John Brosnan's book *Movie Magic: The Story of Special Effects in the Cinema* (1974), which is a collection of reflections on the state of the British and American special effects industry. The interviews with special effects technicians, integrated into a commentary by the author, present a generally pessimistic view of the future of special effects, particularly in the UK. In the book, Douglas Trumbell, a special effects supervisor, expresses doubts that a special effects film would be made in the UK again.[20] The reason given for this was that 2001 had proved so difficult and costly that it seemed difficult to believe that such a complex feat of film-making would be attempted again. As Brosnan summarises,

> 2001 lifted the field of special effects onto a completely new plane of achievement. It proved that, given a director with the drive of Stanley Kubrick, a team of top experts, and a considerable amount of time and money, special effects can be used to create unique and powerful images. Unfortunately, with the film industry in its present grim state, it may be a long time before we see its like again.[21]

Another weakness in Schiller's approach can be seen in his use of the term 'pseudo-environment'[22] to describe the futuristic worlds created through the use of special effects – specifically the world of 2001. While being careful not to create a direct relation between reality and its on-screen depiction he none the less momentarily gives in to the seductions of naturalistic film-making – something that he is seemingly against. He assumes that some films are more realistic than others and that this can be a factor in their financial success. However, the quality of the special effects in a film does not necessarily determine box-office success. For example, Tron (Steven Lisberger, 1982) had both ground-breaking special effects and computer-generated imagery, yet it was a critical and financial failure, as were Dune (David Lynch, 1984) and Waterworld (Kevin Reynolds, 1995).

Within this model of analysis realism as a mode of representation is part of the cycle of production and consumption. Be it 'startling pseudo-environment', rendered textures or virtual reality, the pervasive drive to realism remains constant. Thus special effects have a role and value only in so much as they are an integral part of the realist narrative structure. Recent CGA (computer-generated animation) films such as Toy Story (John Lasseter, 1995) and Antz (Eric Darnell, 1998) illustrate this point superbly. A digitally-created explosion is of itself of no value; it is unlikely that any one would pay to see a film consisting entirely of such images, but as part of a 'believable' narrative the image has a value. Yet Schiller suggests that this is precisely what is happening; that special effects in themselves have value and that as they increase in value the narrative content of film is diminished. He argues that, 'The utilization of special effects, especially those of the most recent vintage, seems to lead to a reduction in the creative substance of the project.'[23]

An earlier version of this argument can be found in the writings of Karl Marx and subsequent commentators who question what is produced and how economic value can be attached to it. As Raymond Williams points out:

> There is a difficult passage in the *Grundrisse* in which he argues that while the man who makes a piano is a productive worker, there is a real question whether the man who distributes the piano is also a productive worker; but he probably is, since he contributes to the realizations of surplus value. Yet when it comes to the man who plays the piano, whether to himself or to others, there is no question: he is not a productive worker at all.[24]

This is quite clearly wrong. Whether materialist criticism likes it or not something has been produced and this may or may not have an economic value. What is important is that value is dependent on the discourse within which the act of production takes place. The image of the Star Ship *Enterprise NCC1710D* flying across the galaxy has little value, but placed within a television or film narrative it acquires a value not just to itself, but a value that is accrued to, and by, the film/television programme as a whole.

In a paradoxical way Schiller is both wrong and right. He is wrong to suggest that special effects do not have an easily identifiable place in the hierarchy of production roles, but he is right to suggest that special effects, as part of the overall filmic experience, have a value. And no matter if this is an artistic, creative or technological value it means that it also has an economic value, but only in so much as they exist within a broader filmic discourse.

The spectacular

Philip Hayward in his article on special effects and pop music video takes a very different tack to Schiller and engages directly with the notion of 'discourse'.[25] He locates a differentiated use of special effects and tracks their increasing use in promotional video. In this respect his argument is not unlike Schiller's, for Hayward also suggests that special effects have had a key role in developing science fiction genres. However, he does not argue that their influence has been detrimental. Of particular interest to Hayward is the emergence of the special effects company Industrial Light and Magic, who first came to the notice of the public in 1977 with their work on *Star Wars*. Hayward writes,

> As the title of the leading Hollywood special effects company 'Industrial Light and Magic' suggests, the commercial success of these genres was substantially premised on the exploitation of the 'wonder-factor' generated by successive elaborations of special effects technology.[26]

However, Hayward goes on to argue that music video as a form, borrowed some of the stylistic conventions of science fiction and horror to produce striking visual imagery which relies on technologically-complicated images. The most remarkable manifestation of this was the establishing of the music video TV channel, MTV. Interestingly, Hayward suggests that the lure of the music video lies not just in the band or its music, but in the images that surround the music. Central to this is what he calls 'impact aesthetics'. Despite the two writers' different approaches, this could almost be a term culled from Schiller. However, Schiller describes things rather differently when he notes that 'Special effects sound and imagery short circuit the brain and hit the gut'.[27] Hayward adopts a more gentlemanly approach, and is more concerned with identifying the reasons for the appeal of the form and suggests that 'visual effects technologies have been utilised to develop SPECTACULARITY as a key element of the form's appeal'.[28]

The notion of spectacularity alludes to Guy Debord's influential work *The Society of the Spectacle*. In this short book, Debord suggests that society is moving to a point where the contemplation of the image replaces other forms of consumption. He argues that '[the principal of commodity fetishism] . . . is absolutely fulfilled in the spectacle, where the perceptible world is replaced by a set of images . . . [and] reaches its absolute fulfilment in the spectacle, where the tangible world is replaced by a selection of images'.[29]

The dramatic nature of special effects would appear to support this argument. The images of fire in *Backdraft* (Ron Howard, 1991), the sight of the Star Ship *Enterprise* entering warp drive, or the sight of the *Titanic* sinking all have an appeal. They hit you 'in the gut', they offer a sensuous delight that lets us indulge in a veritable orgy of images and sounds. As Hayward puts it,

> Their [special effects'] arguable excess has supplied us with particularly intense demonstrations of technology employed to produce dazzle and impact – a return to childhood wonder akin to that aimed at by *Star Wars et al.* and which bypasses concern with textual profundity in favour of technological 'magic'.[30]

Hayward is right to draw our attention to the spectacular nature of special effects. But it is important not to treat special effects as though they had a meaning and value independent of their use in each media artefact. Instead it is crucial to see them as a part of media discourses. The same special effect in a pop video and in a movie can mean two very different things. In the post-modern world where images and sounds slip from one genre to another and one medium to the next, they evade our best attempts to ascribe a meaning to them. To remark that context is a determinant of meaning may sound like an old fashioned truism, but it none the less has an element of truth about it. Humpty Dumpty in *Through the Looking Glass* instructs Alice that,

'When I use a word . . . it means just what I choose it to mean, – neither more nor less.'[31] There is a tendency for us to treat images in the same way.

But we don't live in a looking glass world and images can and should have specific meanings attributed to them. The validity of an interpretation (for in ascribing a meaning to an image we are engaging in the interpretative act) is determined by several factors. As suggested by the model at the start of this chapter these include: the denotative and connotative; the text and discourse; viewer expectation; and generic convention.

Towards a conclusion

There are several significant areas that neither Hayward nor Schiller develop. Because of his assertion that narrative sophistication exists in an inverse relationship with technological complexity, Schiller marginalises narrative. The problem with this is that to prove his point it would be necessary to develop a comprehensive theory of narrative aesthetics that allowed for a comparative analysis of a variety of film narratives. The problems here are enormous. First, it presupposes that narrative exists primarily within the structure of the film. While this is in part correct it ignores a substantial body of theory from French Structuralism, reception theory and psychoanalysis. All of these suggest that narratives are the products of complex interrelations between viewer and film.[32]

Second, there is a rather élitist subtext to Schiller's argument that implicitly assumes that narrative sophistication should be valued over the more visceral appeal of special effects. To adopt this position is to devalue popular culture. Special effects movies are not evidence of an international 'dumbing down' of cultural values. Instead audiences and sub-cultural movements take ownership of images and re-contextualise them into new sets of meanings. For example, 'Trekkies' (fans of the television series *Star Trek*) take the images and sounds of their fictional universe and, with a detailed knowledge of the programmes, assume the role of key characters. They attend conventions to discuss character and narrative developments, they learn and converse in the fictional languages of the series, they socialise with like-minded fans who aim to escape from the mainstream discourse of television consumption and become active agents of deconstruction and displacement.[33]

However, what Schiller does succeed in doing is to bring the industrial and economic perspective to the fore. But in doing this he underplays the importance of production processes and hierarchies. None the less he does usefully draw attention to the increasing percentage of production budgets that are devoted to special effects. Colin Brown is a Production Executive at Cinesite. Founded in 1992 they are currently one of the largest digital effects studios in the world. He confirms the observation that special effects are becoming an ever more significant part of production budgets:

We can get anything up to 50 per cent of a film's overall budget. In 1993 a film might have five 5-second [special effects] shots in it which is a considerable film in terms of computer-generated imagery. The film that we've done most recently had 800 shots in it.[34]

Hayward concentrates on the special effect as a sensation or spectacle. This helpfully identifies spectacle as a key factor within the narrative that functions in two contradictory ways. First, as an object of 'the gaze' (the image to be looked at), the special effect draws the viewer into the narrative. Undoubtedly one of the functions of special effects is to make the narrative more believable and as such they are a 'realist' device. This is particularly the case with 'invisible' effects that go largely unnoticed by the viewer. More obvious effects are determined by the needs of the narrative and seek to enhance its believability. Second, Hayward is keen to draw attention to the differing nature of various audio-visual discourses. He notes that the same stylistic conventions (by which he means effects) function quite differently for horror-film audiences than they do for audiences for pop videos. He gives the example of Michael Jackson's *Thriller*.

Thus while Hayward and Schiller have elements in common, they actually represent quite different critical traditions. Schiller sees the production and consumption of special effects in economic terms, while Hayward adopts a more textual focus in his analysis.

In order to move the debate forward it is necessary to develop a model for the analysis of special effects that locates them as both a site of narrative interest and economic activity and this is where we started. To understand these two spheres, the textual and the economic, both must be placed within current industrial contexts and seen as part of an unfolding discourse. When this is done the strengths and limitations of each can be identified with greater ease. This is an attempt to develop a position that sees special effects in contemporary terms as existing within a set of social, industrial, (sub-)cultural and economic relationships, and at the same time as part of an unfolding historical discourse. To borrow linguistic terms from Saussure, this type of special effects analysis would aim to take a synchronic contemporary cross-section through a society with shared psychological and logical relations, and combine it with a diachronic awareness of the developing nature of 'media' discourse.[35]

Notes

1 H. Schiller, *Information Inequality: The Deepening Social Crisis in America*, London, Routledge, 1996.
2 B. Edelman, *Ownership of the Image: Elements for a Marxist Theory of Law*, London, Routledge, 1979.
3 P. Hayward, 'Industrial Light and Magic – Style, Technology and Special Effects

in the Music Video and Music Television', in P. Hayward (ed.), *Culture, Technology and Creativity in the Late Twentieth Century*, London, John Libbey and Company, 1990.

4 M. Sadler, 'The British Empire Strikes Back', *The Movie*, Orbis Publishing Ltd, 1982, p. 1830.

5 I. Butler, *The Making of Feature Film: A Guide*, Harmondsworth, Penguin, 1971, p. 146.

6 D. Slater, 'Photography and Modern Vision: The Spectacle of "Natural Magic"', in C. Jenks (ed.), *Visual Culture*, London, Routledge, 1995, p. 218.

7 Depending on the exact nature of the effect that was being attempted, other background colours gradually came into use including blue, red and green, although the illusion of one image superimposed on another remained the same.

8 M. Sadler, op. cit., p. 1832.

9 P. Hayward and T. Wollen (eds), *Future Visions: New Technologies of the Screen*, London, BFI Publishing, 1993, p. 33. The reference to computer-generated imagery refers to images in the body of the film itself and not to the title sequence.

10 M. Barker, *The Awkward Audiences of Judge Dredd*, Luton, University of Luton Press, 1998, p. 283.

11 Brown is referring to the sequence in the 1997 film *Titanic*, directed by James Cameron.

12 'The Computer That Ate Hollywood', transcript of BBC *Horizon* Documentary, pp. 5–6. Transmitted 30 April 1998. Available on-line at http://www.bbc.co.uk/horizon/specialfxtran.shtml (19 May 1998).

13 Invisible effects also include optical enhancements of colour – for example, to make a sky bluer or a sunset redder. They also include audio effects that provide extra ambience to the sound.

14 H. Schiller, *Information Inequality: The Deepening Social Crisis in America*, London, Routledge, 1996, pp. 59–74.

15 Ibid., p. 63.

16 Incidentally, this is true of most of the specialisations that combine to form the production process. These separate 'trades' emerged as the result of two developments. The first was a change in technology. By this point sound films were well established and the need to synchronise sound with picture bought with it some complexities. Filming had to take place in conditions where sound and lighting could be controlled. This requirement could most easily be fulfilled by shooting in purpose-built structures that excluded daylight and ambient noise – these came to be known as sound stages. On these new stages cameras had to be much quieter than before or they had to be 'blimped' (muffled). The early blimps were little more than soundproof boxes which had the undesirable side-effect of preventing camera movement. Thus it was necessary to have sound technicians to advise on microphones and cameramen to control the visual elements of the film. With this change came the second and important development, namely the emergence of the Hollywood Studio System. As its name suggests the studio system embodied a formula that was both technical and aesthetic for the production of feature films. This relied on differentiated production tasks, hence the development of specific production roles.

17 Butler, op. cit., p. 139.

18 Schiller gets the date wrong; *2001: A Space Odyssey* was released in 1968.

19 Schiller, op. cit., p. 64.

20 M. Sadler, op. cit, pp. 1830–4.
21 J. Brosnan, *Movie Magic: The Story of Special Effects in the Cinema*, London, Macdonalds and Jane's, 1974, p. 229.
22 Schiller, op. cit., p. 64.
23 Ibid., pp. 65–9.
24 R. Williams, 'Base and Superstructure in Marxist Cultural Theory', *New Left Review*, 82, 1973, p. 6.
25 Hayward, op. cit.
26 Ibid., p. 128.
27 Schiller, op. cit., p. 65.
28 Hayward, op. cit., p. 125.
29 G. Debord, *The Society of the Spectacle* (trans. Donald Nicholson-Smith), New York, Zone Books, 1997 (3rd edn), p. 26.
30 Hayward, op. cit., p. 132.
31 L. Caroll, *Through the Looking Glass*, Harmondsworth, Penguin, 1872, (this edition, 1954), p. 116.
32 The relationship between psychoanalytic theory and special effects forms the basis for Steven Neal's article, 'Hollywood Strikes Back: Special Effects in Recent American Cinema', Screen, vol.21, no.3, 1980, pp. 101–5.
33 For a detailed study of this type of fan culture, see M. Barker, op. cit.
34 'The Computer That Ate Hollywood', op. cit.
35 F. Saussure, *Course in General Linguistics* (trans. Wade Baskin), New York, McGraw Hill, 1966, pp. 99–100.

Chapter 9

The myth of cyberspace

The central criterion of a critical viewpoint is very simple: Any scientific theory or position which looks like a metaphor of the social ideology, or which can be construed as contributing to the psychological, social, or material alienation of any class or group in the society, is automatically suspect. It must therefore be subject to a metascientific evaluation before being accepted as valid, or useful or 'true'.[1]

Introduction

In the closing years of the twentieth century the advanced capitalist nations appear to be on the brink of a new multimedia age. More and more households are adopting digital television and connecting to the Internet and the technical ingenuity of these devices is impressive. Yet, powerful as these technologies are, of equal, if not greater importance is their symbolic dimension. Digital technologies have become a potent symbol in a discourse that sees the inhabitants of the advanced capitalist world as living through a new era: the Information Age. Implicit in this perspective is an optimism that celebrates current innovations in media and network technologies as heralding a new and hopeful period.

When the technologies developed by the military, described in Chapter 1, were adopted for non-military purposes they took on a symbolic role as well as a practical one. To the computer counter-culture of the 1960s – as outlined in Chapter 2 – the computer represented a revolutionary means of both empowering individuals against the 'system' and unlocking their full potential as humans. For telephone, cable, movie, computer, publishing and broadcasting corporations converging digital technologies represented an opportunity, albeit uncertain and risky, to expand markets and cut costs. For governments these technologies have been seen as the rationale for the deregulation and privatisation of much of the telecommunications and media industries. All share the belief, expressed by British Prime Minister Tony Blair in 1998, that:

> information is the key to the modern age. The new age of information offers possibilities for the future limited only by the boundaries of our imaginations. The potential of the new electronic networks is breath-taking – the prospect of change as widespread and fundamental as the agricultural and industrial revolutions of earlier eras.[2]

Blair is here subscribing to an ideology[3] that has been propagated by a group of writers who believe that we have left the 'industrial age'. They can be categorised as 'post-industrialists'. The post-industrialists proclaim the information age and hold that 'in the current era the entire business of man becomes learning and knowing [and] all forms of wealth result from the movement of information'.[4] Theirs is an ideology that, ignoring any social or historical context, sees media technology as an autonomous agent of social change. It is, as Raymond Williams has put it, a position which is 'not only a ratification, indeed a celebration, of the medium as such, but an attempted cancellation of all other questions about it and its uses'.[5] Moreover, in identifying information as the source of value in the post-industrial era, the ideology of information commits the epistemological error of conceptualising it as some 'thing' that can be quantified independently of its content or meaning. This position has the effect of legitimising the increasing commercialisation of media with detrimental consequences for democracy.

The ideology of cyberspace

Recent versions of the ideology of the information age have stressed the power of computer networks and in particular the Internet to create a new domain for human activity: cyberspace. This ideology of cyberspace attempts to synthesise two distinct intellectual perspectives. On the one hand there is a rationalistic approach which stresses how technology can make society materially better off by enabling more output to be obtained from fewer inputs.[6] This view, with its roots in the English empiricist tradition of the application of reason to economic productivity,[7] sees digital technology as the foundation of a new era of economic growth and prosperity. The other strand comprises a quasi-spiritual technological utopianism that regards media technologies as a force for democracy and personal, social and spiritual liberation (computer power to the people). The result of this synthesis is, as Campbell and Barbrook have put it, 'a hybrid ideology . . . an unexpected collision of right-wing neo-liberalism, counter-culture radicalism and technological determinism'.[8]

Technology and consciousness

A number of cyberspace ideologues proclaim the spiritually transforming nature of media technologies – a theme first introduced, as we saw in Chapter 2, by Marshall McLuhan who believed that the computer might enable the human race to achieve higher levels of spirituality leading to a new age of harmony.[9] McLuhan saw electronic media as having the potential to create a new and better phase in human relations which would '[compel] commitment and participation'.[10]

McLuhan's notion of the 'global village'[11] has became a slogan for advocates and promoters of network technologies in the 1980s and 1990s. Symptomatic of this new interest in McLuhan has been his adoption by *Wired* magazine as its patron saint. The introduction to *Wired*'s first issue in 1992 quoted the opening paragraph of McLuhan's *The Medium is the Massage*, and the magazine's layout and typography is a conscious emulation of *The Medium is the Massage*'s innovative visual style.[12] McLuhan's quasi-theological perspective has given a millenarian tinge to the discourse around new media technologies. Characteristic of the spiritual view of those who promote the ideology of cyberspace is that the spread of a planetary computer network prefigures a quasi-mystical 'neo-biological civilization'.[13] Kevin Kelly, an editor of *Wired* magazine, sees a new 'global mind' emerging out of digital networks. For Kelly 'the global mind is the union of computer and nature – of telephones and human brains and more'.[14] Kelly sees this global mind as developing a level of intelligence and consciousness 'out of our control and beyond our understanding. Thus network economics will breed a new spiritualism.'[15]

Information and productivity

Another intellectual dimension of the ideology of information is a faith in free-market capitalism which has its roots in an Anglo-American intellectual tradition concerning the application of systematic knowledge to the processes of expanding material well-being. The influence of this materialist approach is clear in an essay titled *Cyberspace and the American Dream: A Magna Carta for the Knowledge Age*.[16] In this manifesto, written by four of the leading proponents of the doctrine and published in 1994 by the right-wing 'Progress and Freedom Foundation',[17] 'cyberspace' is seen as 'the latest American frontier'.[18] Ignoring the role of military expenditure in the development of multimedia technologies (see Chapter 1), they claim that the

> reason for America's victory in the computer wars of the 1980s is that dynamic competition was allowed to occur.[19]

The principle of free-market capitalism is further affirmed in the explicit identification of 'ownership by the people' with 'private ownership'.[20] King John's *Magna Carta* of 1215 was concerned with delineating the rights of the feudal barons. The *Magna Carta for the Knowledge Age* is concerned with asserting the property rights of the modern media and telecommunications barons and putting the case for easing the 'burden' of taxation on them. While proclaiming the benefits of competition, *Magna Carta for the Knowledge Age*, at the same time, advocates that media corporations should be permitted to engage in alliances and mergers since: 'contrived competition between phone companies and cable operators will not deliver two-way multimedia [nor a] more civilized tele-society'. Most of these ideas were, not surprisingly, incorporated into the US Telecommunications Reform Act of 1996.

Origins of the information theory of value

The intellectual basis of the notion that value resides in information, lies in a philosophical tradition going back to the European Enlightenment of the seventeenth and eighteenth centuries and given a distinctive Anglo-American free-market bent in the nineteenth century. At the heart of this tradition are two related ideas: the progress of humanity and the belief that this can be achieved by means of the application of systematic knowledge. It was in the seventeenth century that the idea that technology could achieve a better life on earth began to gain currency. One of the first to propose this was the English philosopher Francis Bacon (1561–1626) who argued that knowledge was power and that man's lot could be improved by the application of reason and technology. In his book *New Atlantis*[21] (1627), Bacon described an imaginary society based on the technological application of knowledge gained through systematic investigation.[22] This belief was continued and elaborated in the eighteenth and nineteenth centuries by such philosophers as Turgot[23] (1727–81) and Saint-Simon[24] (1760–1825) in France and the political economists Adam Smith (1723–90) and Charles Babbage (1792–1871) in Britain.[25] In his classic work, *An Inquiry into the Wealth of Nations* (1776), Smith had paid particular attention to how rational organisation alone could increase the amount that a given number of workers could produce.[26] Smith argued further that the general application of these principles could increase the total output of society. This belief in the efficacy of the systematic analysis and organisation of economic activity was most fully developed by the American engineer F. W. Taylor (1856–1915) in his book *The Principles of Scientific Management* (1911). Taylor claimed that the efficiency of every task a worker performed could be improved by a close analysis and redesign of that task. Taylor's method involved a time and motion study in which an observer with a stop-watch would measure a worker's performance to improve it, i.e. enable each worker to produce more in less time. Both Henry Ford and Lenin were great admirers of Taylor. Taylor's management techniques were incorporated into the technologies of the mass-production lines of Ford and General Motors.

From this tradition comes the belief that, in a post-industrial society, 'a country's store of information is . . . its greatest potential source of wealth'.[27] This idea was given wide currency by the American sociologist Daniel Bell during the 1960s and 1970s. Bell, who claims to have been the first to have used the term 'post-industrial' in the 1960s,[28] described how the post-industrial society had come into being as the consequence of technological innovation enabling more to be produced by fewer workers.[29] (The terms 'post-industrial society' and 'information society' are synonymous here since for Bell 'post-industrial society is organised around knowledge'.)[30] The post-industrialist assertion that we are entering an information society rests on the measurement of economic statistics. For example, Bell bases his thesis on post-war US occupational distribution statistics that show a shift from manufacturing to 'information' occupations. Works such as Machlup's *The Production and Distribution of Wealth in the United States*[31] and Porat's *The Information Economy: Definition and Measurement*[32] seemed to confirm Bell's hypothesis that productivity due to technological innovation in one sector allows workers to move into other occupations without material disadvantage. As a consequence the occupational distribution of the population changed from one where manufacturing workers were in a majority to one in which information workers became the largest category in the workforce.[33]

Furthermore, in the emerging post-industrial society, there has been 'a change in the character of knowledge itself'.[34] Uniquely in our age, Bell contends, systematic abstract 'theory' is replacing the 'rule-of-thumb empiricism'[35] of the pioneers of industrialism. Bell suggests this change can be seen in: the rise of scientifically-based industry;[36] Keynesian macro-economic demand management;[37] and the development and application of new 'intellectual technologies'[38] such as information theory and cybernetics.[39] According to Bell, theoretical knowledge is the key 'strategic resource' of the post-industrial economy; scientists, economists, engineers and computer scientists have become the key personnel; and universities and research institutes the key institutions. Above all this approach stresses the rationality of economics and the identification of the public interest with the maximisation of economic value.

Economic value

In discussing value a distinction must be made between value as an ethical concept and value as an economic concept. As an ethical concept value refers to that which has intrinsic worth and is esteemed for its own sake. But in economic theory, value has the technical meaning of a unit of measurement in a formal abstract economic model. The debate about economic value is complicated because in politico-economic discourse the maximisation of particular economic values, in the technical sense, is usually identified with an enhancement of value in the ethical sense. This becomes clear from a historical survey of previous theories of economic value. The problem of the location of economic value has been at the centre of economic thought since its beginnings in the seventeenth century and the information theory of value is but the latest in a 300-year history of such theories. Theories of value have always arisen as a generalised set of logically related principles whose purpose is to legitimise the claims to public resources of particular sectional interests. The first economists, the mercantilist writers of the seventeenth century, tended to be merchants who wrote pamphlets trying to persuade the public and politicians that their sectional interest and the national interest were the same. Championing the cause of the new merchant-venturer corporations and joint stock companies, they reasoned that value resided in the precious metals that they acquired in the course of their trading. Such precious metal benefited everyone, they claimed, because it acted as an incentive to production, and could be converted into armies and national power. The mercantilist writers were trying to persuade politicians to grant privileges to the merchant's companies and protect their overseas interests with military power by clothing their rhetoric with the precise language of the sciences.[40]

In the same manner the classical economists Adam Smith and David Ricardo championed the nineteenth-century manufacturing interest and set out to demonstrate, in a systematic and logical way, the benefits of removing existing trade restrictions on industrial capitalists. In order to do this they needed to construct conceptual models that ascribed objective measurable values to economic activity. Ricardo's theories of value underpinned the political cause of the factory owners against the landed interest in the Corn Laws controversy of the early nineteenth century. Ricardo was concerned with demonstrating how taxes on imported grain led to a misallocation of national wealth away from productive workers and entrepreneurs to unproductive landowners. To do this, he constructed a mathematical model of how wealth was distributed between the different classes. The difficulty involved finding a unit by which the amount to be distributed could be measured. In order to analyse the distribution of output between the social classes it was necessary to have a theory of value that provided a consistent measure of the surplus that was distributed. The measure of value Ricardo chose happened to be labour (or rather an abstraction of labour) that only existed as a term in his conceptual model of the economy.

Each of these theories located value in a category which, if maximised, would benefit a particular commercial interest and the information theory of value fits into this tradition. By emphasising the value of information to national economies and society in general, the information theory of value has been effective in persuading governments to institute policies for the benefit of the computer and media industries in particular. It is a doctrine that has worked to the advantage of those whom Kroker and Weinstein have described as the 'virtual class'[41] – the social strata who own and operate the multimedia technologies. Such a doctrine has provided the intellectual rationale for state policies in the 1980s and 1990s which have increased the power and profitability of global media conglomerates in the name of the general good of society.

Critique of post-industrialist historicism

For information age ideologues what makes the present epoch different from all previous ones is the role of knowledge in the economic process. Characteristic of this approach is Alvin Toffler's periodisation of history into 'waves' of technological innovation.[42] Toffler sees the current age, with its computer and information-based economy, as a distinct historical era, a 'Third Wave' coming after the first two 'waves' of agriculture (10,000 years ago) and industry (300 years ago).[43] The reason that it is possible for Toffler, Bell and other post-industrialist writers to claim that information has a uniquely important role in the current age is that they have conceptualised it as an economic phenomenon. Having done this it is possible for them to claim that we are becoming an information society by measuring the increase in the money value of a range of phenomena which are said to constitute this society. These phenomena include personal computers sold, the volume of telephone and data traffic, the number of people in information occupations, the number of people connected to the Internet, pay-per-view TV transactions and so on.

It is in fact difficult to demonstrate that 'information' *per se* is a unique new factor in contemporary society. Indeed, there has been no period in human history when knowledge has not formed an integral part of any economic activity. As Wilden has pointed out even the most primitive tools used in antiquity were repositories of information:

> Tools are artefacts but they are not in essence objects. Since they qualitatively increase a species' possibility of organising and controlling the matter-energy in the ecosystem, their primary characteristic is that of information. They are forms which inform; they are informed because they remember the past and make possible new types of projection into the future.[44]

Information necessarily plays a vital part in the activities of even traditional pre-industrial societies in which 'priests and shamans . . . have occult expertise for advising believers on auspicious times and procedures for conducting their lives' tasks'.[45]

Even the 'information explosion' of the late twentieth century has a historical precedent in Europe where, after the introduction of the printing press in the sixteenth century, it is estimated, the volume of books printed doubled approximately every seven years.[46] If these estimates are reasonably correct, the growth of recorded information is a historical phenomenon, not unique to the late twentieth century.

Historians have also challenged the idea that economic activity in the current era is unique in its reliance on information as the primary source of value. Research has shown how information networks were established to support the nascent commercial capitalism of medieval European city states such as Venice.[47] It has been claimed that even the late twentieth-century dependence on electronic computers has its origins in a 'control crisis' which occurred in industrial production between 1870 and 1910 as a result of the rapid increase in the speed and scale of operation. A principal proponent of this view, James Beniger, argues that an extensive information-processing apparatus was a necessary precondition for the large-scale industrial operations of the nineteenth century. For example, the development of railway systems would not have been possible without an army of clerks and other 'information workers' to compile timetables and monitor the movements of rolling-stock. For Beniger, the great innovations of information processing were not so much machines as procedures: standardisation, interchangeable parts, printed forms, record-keeping, regularity, management and marketing. According to this analysis computers have not created a new information economy in the late twentieth century. They have rather filled existing niches which were previously occupied by nineteenth-century information-processing tools such as adding machines, switching circuits, typewriters, punch-card tabulators and human computers. Beniger concludes that 'microprocessor and computer technologies, contrary to currently fashionable opinion are not new forces only recently unleashed upon an unprepared society'.[48]

Cyberdemocracy and the Public Sphere

The development of global networks of computer mediated communications has prompted the claim that society is on the verge of a new era of democracy. There is a direct link here with the idealism of the computer counter-culture of the late 1960s and early 1970s that we examined in Chapter 2. Pioneers of the computer counter-culture movement have been at the forefront in arguing that computer mediated communications have created the possibility of a revitalisation of democracy by creating a new 'commons of information'.[49] This new space is seen as the electronic equivalent of the Greek agora, the New England town meeting or the café society of Enlightenment Paris.[50] On the other side there are those who argue that the democratic potential of these technologies is being limited by 'the rapid colonisation of cyberspace by capital'[51] that we traced in Chapters 3, 4 and 5. In the following section we shall examine this debate.

The Public Sphere

Much of the current theorising about the democratic implications of the new digital technologies centres on the German philosopher Jürgen Habermas's concept of a 'Public Sphere'.[52] Habermas traces the origins of our current media world in the development of a democratic Public Sphere from the seventeenth century, arguing that the development of early modern capitalism brought into being an autonomous arena of public debate. During this period, Habermas argues, the economic independence provided by private property, the critical reflection fostered by letters and novels, the flowering of discussion in coffee houses and salons and the emergence of an independent, market-based press, created a new public engaged in critical, political discussion. From this was forged a reason-based consensus which shaped the direction of the state.[53]

Habermas saw the ideal Public Sphere as being a space distinct from both the state and the market[54] where citizens could exchange views on matters of importance to the common good, so that public opinion could be formed. Some have criticised Habermas's historical account for concentrating on the activities of bourgeoise men to the exclusion of women and the poor as well as presenting an inaccurate interpretation of the role of the eighteenth-century press.[55] Habermas has also been criticised for appearing to privilege the 'masculine' communication mode of rational, logical deliberation, over the 'feminine' emotional way of knowing.[56] Whatever the truth of this, and it is now widely accepted that Habermas's historical account of the Public Sphere is probably wrong,[57] the idea of a Public Sphere provides a framework for thinking about the role of computer mediated communications in furthering democracy. Thus, although the ideal of a genuine Public Sphere has never been achieved in practice, we should not underestimate the

importance of the idea since, as Dahlgren argues, 'support for such fundamental principles has . . . an important moral authority, and . . . in the present
context, rather radical implications'.[58]

Decline of the Public Sphere

It is a crucial part of Habermas's position that public communication
was degraded from the nineteenth century by the rise of commercial mass
media. With commercialisation the Public Sphere became 'enmeshed with
discourses from entertainment and advertising'[59] and the public came to
be seen as media consumers to be manipulated and delivered to advertisers.
In this new situation large organisations achieve political compromise behind
closed doors and gain popular approval through public relations and media
events involving staged publicity and manipulation.[60] This has meant that
only the wealthiest corporations have an effective voice in the Public Sphere
which has been transformed from a 'culture-debating' space to a 'culture-
consuming' one. In this new situation, according to Habermas, the media are
no longer agents of empowerment and rationality, but instead sell politics as
entertainment and promote the passivity of their audiences. Modern media,
for Habermas, thus become a sphere for the exercise of power rather than a
forum for rational discussion among free and informed citizens.

Computer mediated communications and the Public Sphere

Cyberspace enthusiasts claim that computer mediated communications can
reverse this erosion of the Public Sphere and return us to a lost age of
democratic discourse. This nostalgia is exemplified by the front cover of the
December 1997 issue of *Wired* which, instead of the usual cutting-edge
graphics, displays a 1943 picture entitled *Freedom of Speech* by the American
painter Norman Rockwell. The picture advertises a story, entitled the *Digital
Citizen*,[61] based on the results of a survey of 'the attitudes and beliefs of
individuals who are at the leading edge of the digital revolution'.[62] The
picture shows a scene from the America of the 1930s or 1940s. A man in
work clothes is standing up and speaking at a public meeting. He is clearly
addressing some figure of authority and his demeanour is dignified and
resolute. His seated neighbours gaze up at him with respect. In his pocket is
an official looking document which, we may infer, he has read and mastered.
This nostalgic notion, that there is some lost golden age of democracy that
computerised media technology will allow us to recover, is characteristic of
the ideology of cyberspace. It can be seen for example in John Perry Barlow's
grandiose *Declaration of the Independence of Cyberspace*, a pastiche of the 1776
American Declaration of Independence written in response to restrictions on
expression contained in the US Telecommunications Reform Act of 1996.[63]

For Mark Poster the Internet is important because, as a decentralised communications system, it questions the assumptions of older positions: 'if the technological structure of the Internet institutes costless reproduction, instantaneous dissemination and radical decentralisation, what might be its effects upon the society, the culture and the political institutions?'[64] Such commentators point to the 'virtual communities' which have come into being on the Internet centred around news groups, Multi-User Domain (MUD) games and other forms of networking. These, it is claimed, give a voice to previously excluded groups such as women, gays and greens,[65] enabling them to disseminate their views to wider audiences. With the advent of new media technologies, audience segmentation and the advent of alternative political movements, Dahlgren sees 'the contours of historically new conditions for the Public Sphere' emerging.[66] This development, according to Dahlgren, could be as important as that chronicled by Habermas and could herald an era when alternative political movements like greens and feminists are able to transmit their views to the dominant media.[67]

De-massification of the media

Cyberspace enthusiasts assert that computer mediated communications are creating a new Public Sphere because, in contrast to the passive and isolated consumption of 'old' mass media, the new media technologies encourage interaction and community. For Howard Rheingold the political significance of computer mediated communications lies in their capacity to challenge the existing political hierarchy's monopoly on powerful communications media.[68] In a similar vein the post-industrialist writer Ithiel De Sola Pool[69] (1917–84) contends that new media and communications technologies have the potential to facilitate a 'great renaissance' in which multimedia technologies could create the conditions that might lead to 'an efflorescence in science, culture and the arts'.[70] According to Pool, the significant features of new media technologies are that they are more interactive, they demand more from the user than passive television consumption, and that they offer the viewer/user more diversity and the opportunity to produce and disseminate their own work.[71] Toffler describes this process as the de-massification of the media, and sees it as bringing into being 'a truly new era [that] will have a far reaching impact on the most important sphere of all, the one inside our skulls . . . these changes revolutionise our image of the world and our ability to make sense of it'.[72]

With the establishment of the Internet and a proliferation of channels these writers believe that there is now the potential to create new democratic spaces in which a diversity of voices may be heard leading to a more informed citizenry and an enhanced democratic process.

Electronic democracy

According to Friedland, 'the concept of "electronic democracy" connotes a radically new form of democratic practice modified by new information technologies'.[73] Through the technology of the Internet, people have greater access to government agencies and information. They also have the ability to disseminate that information rapidly to large numbers of people – thus promoting grass-roots organisations and activism. A host of political and interest groups ranging across the political spectrum from the Ku Klux Klan to revolutionary anarchists have established websites to propagate their views. Many see this as evidence that computer mediated communication will enhance the democratic process by making available large and up-to-date collections of factual information in conjunction with a medium that is also a forum for discussion and debate. For Rheingold such citizen-to-citizen discussion, backed up by facts available to all, is creating the basis for the electronic democracy of the future.[74] It is undoubtedly true that both public and voluntary organisations are making use of the Internet as an integral part of their activities. In all of the advanced capitalist nations political parties, politicians and departments of state have set up websites and electronic mail addresses. It is now possible to obtain details of a politician's political position, as well as detailed accounts of both legislative deliberations and administrative policy from the Internet.

Non-governmental organisations too have been establishing a presence on the Internet since the late 1980s.[75] Pioneers in this field have been GreenNet[76] in the UK, and the Institute for Global Communications[77] (IGC) in the US. In 1990 GreenNet and IGC joined with groups in other countries[78] to form a global network known as the Association for Progressive Communications (APC), all 'committed to making the Internet serve the needs of global civil society'.[79] By 1998 the APC was making information on human rights, labour issues and ecology available to activists throughout the world as well as administering over 900 computer conferences.[80]

Anarchic structure of the Internet

One of the features of the Internet often cited as being conducive to democracy is its decentralised and uncontrollable structure which is the legacy of its origins as a military command and control system designed to withstand nuclear attack. According to advocates of cyberdemocracy this structure means that communications on the Internet cannot be censored or controlled by state authorities. As Stonier puts it: 'No dictator can survive for any length of time in communicative society as the flows of information can no longer be controlled from the centre.'[81]

This feature of the Internet was emphasised by the inability of the Chinese government to stem the worldwide dissemination of dissident views during the Tiananmen Square pro-democracy protests of 1989. The Internet was first effectively used as an instrument of political dissent by the Zapatista insurgents in the southern Mexican state of Chiapas.[82] When in January 1995 the Mexican government moved against the Zapatistas, the rebels and their sympathisers used the Internet to inform and mobilise individuals and support groups worldwide. The result was that the Mexican and US governments were bombarded with messages arguing for negotiations rather than repression. The campaign was successful in as much as it embarrassed the Mexican government into starting talks with the rebels.[83] Similarly, in the May 1998 insurrection in Indonesia, which overthrew the dictator Suharto, student dissidents used the Internet to exchange information and co-ordinate tactics and strategies.[84] The potential of the Internet to aid activists in challenging big business was dramatised by the 'McLibel' trial. This ensued after the McDonalds restaurant chain served writs for libel on protesters handing out leaflets criticising the company's policies in 1990. During what turned out to be the longest civil trial in British history, supporters of the protesters set up a website on which were published the case against McDonalds' employment practices, farming and food-production methods.[85]

Cyberspace and capital

The commodification of the Public Sphere

The early development of the Internet, powered mainly by academics under the auspices of the National Science Foundation, had a culture which was strongly influenced by the values of the computer counter-culture. However, any hopes that the new information infrastructure may develop according to counter-culture values have been disappointed by the political triumph of the Right. During the 1980s and 1990s the multimedia conglomerates' passion for digital convergence has been encouraged by governments who saw market competition as the essential spur to the growth of the media and information industries.

On the face of it, far from creating a new Public Sphere, these developments might be said to work against the free communication and discussion of ideas that take place in an ideal Public Sphere. Critics have argued that the decline of the Public Sphere in the twentieth century is more likely to be accentuated than reversed by computer mediated communications. Such critics claim that these multimedia technologies might represent the latest phase in a process by which civic communication has been degraded by technologies in the service of profits.

As early as 1961, the American sociologist Daniel Boorstin[86] had located the beginning of this process of degradation of public discourse in the 'graphic revolution' that resulted from the proliferation of mechanically-reproduced commercial imagery. The graphic age, according to Boorstin, has led those who seek to influence public opinion, mainly politicians and commercial publicists, to create 'pseudo-events' – synthetic occurrences designed solely to be reported and enhance their image.[87]

The American educationalist Neil Postman points out that mass media, starting with the telegraph and photography in the nineteenth century and continuing with cinema, radio and television in the twentieth century, has, paradoxically, contributed to the degradation of public debate.[88] Postman contends that, during the nineteenth century, the process of reading had encouraged rationality and mature democratic discussion. However, with the coming of the telegraph, this began to change because telegraphy:

> gave . . . legitimacy to the idea of context-free information . . . the idea that the value of information need not be tied to any function it might serve in social and political decision making and action.[89]

This process accelerated with the development of photography which:

> like the telegraph, recreates the world as a series of idiosyncratic events. The world is atomised. There is only a present and it need not be part of any story that can be told.[90]

The process began in advertising. After the introduction of photo-gravure printing, which allowed the mass production of images, advertising relied less on propositions and more on images. Emotional appeal, not tests of truth became the basis of consumer decisions and, according to Postman, the process by which politics was to become a branch of show business had begun as the new focus on the image undermined traditional definitions of information and news. Postman sees the 'new imagery' as not just a supplement to language, but a bid to replace it as our dominant means for construing, understanding and testing our political situation. In a continuation of the trends described by Postman political parties and interest groups are increasingly using the Internet to put over their messages. Even where e-mail responses are elicited from the public, for example by the White House, replies tend to be formulaically composed by computer.[91] It is a political model in which citizens are conceived of as recipients of political messages rather than participants in a process of political discussion. This model is taken to its logical conclusion in proposals for direct electronic plebiscites. In this plebiscitary model, individuals would directly express their opinions by selecting from a range of screen options with a handset or similar device. Advocates of this form of cyberdemocracy such as the right-wing American politicians Ross Perot and Newt Gingrich[92] argue that, if the network is cast widely enough, the sum of individual opinions will allow for the rapid expression of the common will.[93] Whether this represents any kind of Public Sphere is doubtful however, since such a system not only prevents the process of discussion but will also tend to work to the advantage of those interests who have the money and influence to mobilise the mass media in support of their case.[94]

Corporate control

The New Right rhetoric associated with building 'information super-highways' has stressed that only unrestrained market forces will build the infrastructure that is predicted to bring so many benefits to the general population. From this perspective there is no contradiction between consumer capitalism and a democratic Public Sphere. However, it is just as likely that any democratic advantages of new communications technologies will be outweighed by the increasing domination of capitalist global multimedia oligopolies. The lesson of media history is that, in an unregulated or lightly regulated regime, what gets transmitted is primarily what is profitable rather than what is in the public interest.[95] Thus we have seen that what is being developed by the major corporate new media players is more of the same in the form of enhanced digital television rather than the creation of technologies for democratic interaction. Early evidence following the introduction of digital TV in the UK would appear to confirm this view. The hundreds of channels made available by digitisation are not being used to expand the range of political views but rather to establish commercial services such as home shopping and near-video-on-demand (where the same movie has staggered starting times across several channels).

Even the free-access culture of the Internet is being compromised by the proliferation of commercial sites, sustained by advertising, which have increasingly populated the World Wide Web. The consequences of such commercialism on the Internet were illustrated by the activities of Prodigy, one of the earliest commercial network services, which has been reported as censoring news group postings.[96]

Limited access

Another factor which diminishes the potential of cyberspace as a new global Public Sphere is that participation is overwhelmingly by white middle-class English-speaking males, most of whom live in the United States. Access is largely restricted either to those who can afford to own a personal computer and pay the connection charges or who are employed by institutions that provide such access. A 1995 NOP survey confirmed that it is the well-off who are most likely to be Internet users.[97] Even in the US no more than 9 per cent of the population regularly uses the Internet.[98] Furthermore these developments, which benefit the better-off, have been taking place at a time when the policies of neo-liberal governments have resulted in the running-down of the old informational resources which benefit the poor such as libraries and free-to-air TV.

The disparity between information haves and have-nots is even greater when one looks at the global situation. The vast majority of the world's population has not even got access to a telephone let alone a personal computer connected to the Internet. This was a point emphasised by the South African Deputy President Thabo Mbeki in 1995 when he observed 'there are more telephone lines in Manhattan, New York than in Sub-Saharan Africa'.[99] Even where individuals in poor countries do have Internet access they are generally obliged to communicate in English. Indeed the very fact that they have the on-line resources indicates that they are most likely to be members of a ruling élite, further accentuating existing social differences and power structures.

Information and power

In this chapter I have argued that the idea that advances in media technologies will herald an age of unprecedented prosperity and democracy is not supported either intellectually or in practice. In particular I would argue that the promise of more general access to information and democratic resources is more than offset by the increasing domination by monopolistic capitalist media conglomerates and increasing disparities in income which disenfranchise the majority from participating in cyberspace democracy. However, even if access to cyberspace was more equitable it is not clear that this in itself would result in a more democratic and responsive political system since power does not depend on information alone. In the end the crucial factors are who owns the infrastructure and who has the power to send in the police. The head of News Corporation, Rupert Murdoch, has often lauded the new media technologies as having the potential to empower people 'from the once powerful press barons'.[100] Yet, when the Chinese government objected to the BBC's coverage of their brutal suppression of pro-democracy protests, Murdoch did not hesitate to remove the BBC World service from his *Star* satellite, a move seemingly designed to placate a government with which he hoped to do business. If a government wishes it may send the police to close down an Internet service provider (ISP). In 1996 a number of Usenet newsgroups carried by the CompuServe ISP were declared illegal by the Bavarian authorities in Germany because of pornographic and neo-Nazi content.[101] In December 1998 the first case involving the use of the Internet for political purposes came before a Chinese court when a software engineer, Lin Hai, was accused of using the Net to 'subvert the socialist system'. The Chinese government, anxious to prevent the undermining of the state monopoly of news, stipulates that all connections to the Internet must go through one of four official ISPs.[102] These developments lead one to the melancholy conclusion that it is not knowledge but power and the drive for profit that is the problem and this will not be changed by a proliferation of digital channels or websites.

Challenging the ideology of cyberspace

Alternative traditions

The remarkable technologies devised for military purposes have taken on an ideological role and become currency in a discourse about the future of society. It is a discourse that has reflected a more general mechanistic paradigm sustained by: the idea of economic growth as the ultimate good, the self-serving interests of large corporations and an acceptance of Toffleresque technological determinism. But this discourse is not primarily about the future; it is also a matter of current politics since, as Robins puts it, '[that] which is generally presented in terms of technological futures is much more a matter of social relations and representations of social life in the present'.[103]

The ideology of the information age is a convenient myth for politicians since it explains current economic troubles (falling real incomes, job insecurity and unemployment) as the inevitable result of technological change while at the same time promising a better future without the need to change existing economic arrangements. It is thus an explanation that simultaneously absolves the politicians of responsibility and justifies the New Right settlement. However, the evidence to date is that, far from bringing unalloyed benefits as promised by the ideologues of cyberspace, the combination of free-market economics and new media technologies represents a way for monopoly capitalism to further invade our lives and suppress rather than encourage a critical engagement with society. Yet in the current political climate no scheme that does not conform to the prevailing free-market ideology is likely to appear on the agenda. It is argued here that the consequences of not finding alternatives to the market are so serious that we need to explore alternatives to the prevailing paradigm. This may be considered naïve but, as Jameson has argued, the proposition that 'the market is in human nature cannot be left to stand unchallenged ... it is the most crucial terrain of ideological struggle in our time'.[104]

In constructing these alternatives there are existing intellectual traditions that may be drawn upon. Specifically to counter the mechanistic philosophy of the conventional economic paradigm we should look to an approach grounded in the concept of 'convivial tools'. And to counter the model of a free market in information we should revitalise notions of public service broadcasting. This would support a philosophy that sees human value as residing in a state of being rather than having.[105]

Tools for conviviality

In his book *Tools for Conviviality* Ivan Illich posits a crisis of industrialism dominated by unbalanced and destructive economic growth and a subordination of people to technology.[106] To counter this trend Illich proposes that tools should be designed for 'conviviality' rather than economic efficiency. By 'conviviality' Illich meant: 'autonomous and creative intercourse among persons, and the intercourse of persons with their environment'.[107] For Illich 'convivial tools are those which give each person who uses them the greatest opportunity to enrich the environment with the fruits of his or her vision'.[108] Illich argues that tools have both political and ethical implications. They are political because 'as the power of machines increases, the role of persons more and more decreases to that of mere consumers'[109] and they are moral since, for Illich, conviviality is an 'individual freedom realised in personal interdependence and, as such, an intrinsic ethical value'.[110] (Clearly this is the same vision which inspired the computer counter-culture in their opposition to the technocratic 'machine' and which subsequently mutated to the debased consumerism of the 'California Ideology'.)

Illich's conception of the political and moral nature of tools provides us with a matrix within which to think about the future development of media technologies in terms that avoid the economic tunnel vision of the current dominant discourse. The critical issue is how to maximise the democratising and liberating potential multimedia while at the same time militating against its tendency to create apathetic, narcotised consumers.

Public service

Given the weaknesses of the free market model of communications in providing resources for democracy, there is scope to turn once more to ideas of public service broadcasting which have been devalued, but not entirely extinguished, during the 1980s and 1990s. Some have argued that, since the new technologies have undermined decisively the notion of state-structured and territorially-bound public life mediated by radio, television, newspapers and books, the conventional ideal of a unified Public Sphere and its corresponding vision of citizens striving to live up to some public good are obsolete.[111] However, the concepts of the Public Sphere and public service broadcasting do offer a way of conceptualising how multimedia technologies may be put to the service of an active participatory democracy.

It is true that recent developments in multimedia technologies have great potential for providing citizens with resources for democracy but only if these are provided in the context of some notion of a non-commercial public interest. The deregulation of communications by the New Right represents a threat to democracy which gives control over information vital for citizenship to capitalist multimedia conglomerates. This concurs with Garnham's view that:

> the public service broadcasting model is the best guarantor for rational and universalistic politics, but that, within a media landscape dominated by market-driven media and in a market characterised by high levels of concentration and advertising finance, public service broadcasting offers a viable alternative model that is closer to delivering on the promises of the Public Sphere than the bulk of market driven media; it is thus a model to be built upon, rather than to be destroyed in the name of consumer choice and freedom.[112]

We need to think in terms of building a public information utility that incorporates the principles of participatory democracy and conviviality. What might be the form that such an ideal information utility should take?

In the first place ownership of the means of transmission should again be public and financed by tolls on usage by commercial enterprises. One of the consequences of the growth of Internet commerce is likely to be that participants, both private and corporate, will increasingly be able to avoid paying indirect taxes to the state. This would have an adverse effect on the state's ability to finance public services. It is also an argument for states, acting in the common interest, to devise some method of taxing the increasing revenue-streams that migrate to cyberspace. There is a strong case for using general taxation for the creation of the all-fibre to-the-door network which private corporations, for reasons outlined, have been reluctant to construct. This should be done in the context of a Freedom of Information Act in which there is an obligation on both public and private organisations to make available on-line, at no cost to the citizen, such information as public statistics and company records.

Such a vision could, however, occur without a fundamental shift in prevailing political ideologies which at the time of writing (1998) seems increasingly remote. However, the important thing is to keep the debate alive and in this multimedia technologies such as the Internet will undoubtedly play their part.

Epilogue: empowerment real and virtual

At the end of this book we must conclude that the critical issues we have examined – the history of the medium, its commercial potential, and its implications for personal and public life – can only make sense in the context of old, perennial questions regarding the good society and what it is to be human. This is the context in which we must consider the question of whether multimedia technologies have value for us and our fellows. With regard to value we concur with Lewis Mumford's view that 'value comes into existence through man's primordial need to distinguish between life-maintaining and life-destroying processes and to distribute his interests and his energies accordingly'.[113]

Multimedia technologies may be judged to be valuable to the extent that they facilitate the conditions within which individuals may achieve their full physical spiritual and intellectual potential. However, this can never be achieved by technology alone, but must be in the context of changes in political and social institutions which bring about genuine, participatory industrial and political democracy. At present multimedia technologies can be seen to be amplifying the passive spectator-democracy of sound-bites and photo-opportunities rather than encouraging real participation. This will only change when citizens not only have adequate information but also know that their decisions are likely to have an effect. This state, contrary to the views of the ideologues of cyberspace, can never be brought about by multimedia technologies alone.

Notes

1 A. Wilden, *System and Structure. Essays in Communication and Exchange*, London, Tavistock Publications Ltd, 1977 p. xx.

2 T. Blair, *Forward to Our Information Age: The Government's Vision*, Cabinet Office, 1998.

3 Ideology is a difficult and ambiguous term. Its first use in English was in 1796 as a direct translation of *idéologie*, a word coined by the French philosopher de Tracey who had used it to denote a rational science of ideas which was distinct from ancient metaphysics. (R. Williams, *Keywords: A Vocabulary of Culture and Society*, London, Fontana, 1976, p. 126.) Inspired by the English empiricists, who held that only that which could be verified by the senses was true, de Tracey advocated a political programme that would harness scientific knowledge to the service of man. During the French Revolution when France was under the rule of the Directory, *idéologie* became the official state doctrine. ('Origins and Characteristics of Ideology', *Britannica CD98*, Standard edition 1994–8, Encyclopaedia Britannica Inc.) In 1812 the *idéologues* in the Directory came into conflict with Napoleon Bonaparte who reviled their beliefs as abstract, impractical and fanatical. (R. Williams, op. cit., p. 126.) In its modern sense the term 'ideology' has been greatly influenced by the ideas of Karl Marx. The term as used by Marx had echoes of Napoleon's pejorative meaning as in Marx's criticism of the Prussian ruling class in the 1840s '[who] live in a world situated beyond the real world'. (K. Marx, *Debates on the Freedom of the Press*, quoted in D. Mclennan, *Karl Marx: His Life and Thought*, St. Albans, Hertfordshire, Paladin, 1976, p. 490) Marx implied that ideology represents an illusion, a view of the world shaped by class interests that ignores the real processes of history.

There is also a more neutral sense, also used by Marx, of ideology as a set of ideas, ideals, beliefs and values associated with any particular group. (Williams, op. cit., pp. 128–9.)

4 M. McLuhan, *Understanding Media*, London, Sphere Books, 1973, p. 69.

5 R. Williams, *Television: Technology and Cultural Form*, Glasgow, Fontana/Collins, 1974, p. 126.

6 Ibid.

7 E. Meiksins Wood, 'Modernity, Postmodernity, or Capitalism', in R. McChesney, E. Wood, J. Foster (eds), *Capitalism and the Information Age: The Political Economy of the Global Communications Revolution*, New York, Monthly Review Press, 1998, p. 38.

8 R. Barbrook and A. Cameron, 'The Californian Ideology', *Mute*, Issue 3, London, Autumn 1995.

9 E. Norden, *Playboy*, March 1969, The Marshall McLuhan Center on Global Communications website. Available on-line at http://www.mcluhanmedia.com/mmclpb01.html (5 September 1998).

10 M. McLuhan, *The Medium is the Massage*, London, Penguin, 1967, p. 24.

11 Ibid., p. 63.

12 G. Wolf, 'The Wisdom of Saint Marshall, the Holy Fool', *Wired Archive*, 1 January 1996. Available on-line at http://www.wired.com/wired/archive/4.01/saint.marshal_pr.html (2 September 1998).

13 K. Kelly, *Out of Control: The New Biology of Machines*, London, Fourth Estate, 1994, p. 202.

14 Ibid.

15 Ibid.

16 E. Dyson, G. Gilder, G. Keyworth and A. Toffler, *Cyberspace and the American Dream: A Magna Carta for the Knowledge Age*, Release 1.2, 22 August 1994. Available on-line at http://alberti.mit.edu/arch/4.207/texts/cyberspace-dream.html (6 September 1998).

17 The Progress and Freedom Foundation is a 'not-for-profit research and educational organization'. Ibid.

18 Ibid.

19 Ibid.

20 Ibid.

21 F. Bacon, *The Advancement of Learning and the New Atlantis*, London, Oxford University Press, 1960.

22 Writing of Bacon, Lewis Mumford observed: 'At a moment when the bitter struggle within Christianity between contentious doctrines and sects had come to a stalemate, the machine itself seemed to offer an alternative way of reaching heaven. The promise of material abundance on earth, through exploration, organised conquest and invention, offered a common objective to all classes.' L. Mumford, *The Myth of the Machine*, London, Secker & Warburg, 1967, p. 283.

23 K. Kumar, *Prophesy and Progress*, London, Penguin, 1978, p. 17.

24 Ibid., p. 31.

25 H. Braverman, *Labour & Monopoly Capital*, New York and London, Monthly Review Press, 1974, p. 89.

26 Quoted in J.K. Gailbraith, *The Age of Uncertainty*, London, BBC/Andre Deutsche, 1977, p. 23.

27 T. Stonier, *The Wealth of Information. A Profile of the Post-Industrial Economy*, London, Thames Methuen, 1983, p. 12.

28 D. Bell, *The Coming of Post-Industrial Society: A Venture in Social Forecasting*, London, Penguin, 1976 p. xi.

29 Ibid., p. 191.

30 Ibid., p. 20.

31 F. Machlup, *The Production and Distribution of Wealth in the United States*, Princeton, New Jersey, Princeton University Press, 1962.

32 M. Porat, *The Information Economy: Definition and Measurement*, Washington, DC, US Department of Commerce, Office of Telecommunications, 1977.

33 Bell, op. cit., p. 15.

34 Ibid., p. 343.

35 Ibid., p. 20.

36 Ibid., pp. 21–2.

37 Ibid., pp. 22–5.

38 Ibid., p. 27.

39 Ibid., p. 29.

40 M. Dobb, *Studies in the Development of Capitalism*, London, George Routledge & Sons, 1947, p. 202.

41 A. Kroker and M. Weinstein, *Data Trash: The Theory of the Virtual Class*, Montreal, New World Perspectives, 1994, p.163.

42 Toffler's book *The Third Wave* was an instant best-seller when it was published in 1980, and it was serialised in several popular journals including *Reader's Digest* as well as being the selection of a number of book clubs. This is an indication of the keen public interest in such 'futurology'. See T.R. Young, 'Information, Ideology and Political Reality, Against Toffler', in J.D. Slack and F. Fejes (eds), *The Ideology of the Information Age*, Norwood, New Jersey, Ablex Publishing Corporation, 1987, p. 120.

43 A. Toffler, *The Third Wave*, London, Collins, 1980, pp. 29–30.

44 A. Wilden, *System and Structure, Essays in Communication and Exchange*, London, Tavistock Publications Ltd, 1977, p. 363.

45 C. Marvin, 'Information and History', in Slack and Fejes (eds), op. cit., p. 54.

46 'Information Processing and Information Systems', *Britannica CD98*, Standard edition 1994–8, Encyclopaedia Britannica Inc.

47 J.R. Beniger, *The Control Revolution. Technological and Economic Origins of the Information Society*, Cambridge, Massachusetts and London, England, Harvard University Press, 1986, p. 121.

48 Ibid., p. vii.

49 L. Felsenstein, *The Commons of Information, Dr. Dobbs' Journal*, May 1993, on Impact Web page. Available on-line at http://bliss.berkeley.edu/impact/speakers/speakers_page.html (2 February 1998).

50 Typical of those who take this approach is Howard Rheingold. See H. Rheingold, *Virtual Communities*, at Howard Rheingold Website: http://www.well.com/user/hlr/vcbook/ (7 June 1998).

51 L. Dahlberg, 'Cyberspace and the Public Sphere: Exploring the Democratic Potential of the Net', *Convergence*, vol.4, no.1, 1998, p. 70.

52 J. Habermas, *The Structural Transformation of the Public Sphere*, Cambridge, Polity Press, 1989.

53 J. Curran, 'Mass Media and Democracy: A Reappraisal' in J. Curran and

M. Gurevitch (eds), *Mass Media and Society*, London, Edward Arnold, 1991, p. 83.

54 N. Garnham, 'The Media and the Public Sphere', *Intermedia*, vol.14, no.1, January 1986, pp. 28–33.

55 C. Sparkes, 'Is There a Global Public Sphere?', in D.J. Thussu (ed.), *Electronic Empires: Global Media and Local Resistance*, London, Arnold, 1998, p. 104.

56 J. McGuigan, 'What Price the Public Sphere', in Thussu (ed.), op. cit., pp. 111–12.

57 Sparkes, op. cit., p. 112.

58 P. Dahlgren, 'Ideology and Information in the Public Sphere', in Slack and Fejes (eds), op. cit., p. 26.

59 P. Dahlgren and C. Sparks, *Communication and Citizenship*, London, Routledge, 1991, p. 17.

60 Garnham, op. cit., p. 30.

61 J. Katz, 'The Digital Citizen', *Wired*, 5 December 1997, p. 68.

62 The survey revealed that the 'digital class' is largely made up of well-off English-speaking white men who mostly live in the US and who are 'convinced that technology is a force for good and that our free-market economy functions as a powerful engine of progress'. See J. Katz, op. cit., p. 71.

63 J.P. Barlow, *Declaration of the Independence of Cyberspace*, 8 February 1996. Available on-line at http://www.tarleton.edu/~swarren/cyberspace.htm (5 December 1998).

64 M. Poster, *CyberDemocracy: Internet and the Public Sphere*. Available on-line at http://www.poster.democ.htm (9 May 1997).

65 E. Laclau, *New Reflections on the Revolution of our Time*, London, Verso, 1990.

66 Dahlgren and Sparks, op. cit., p. 14.

67 Ibid., p. 15.

68 H. Rheingold, *Virtual Communities, Introduction*, 1993. Available on-line at http://www.rheingold.com/vc/book/intro.html (10 June 1998).

69 I.S. Pool, *Technologies Without Boundaries. On Telecommunications in a Global Age*, Cambridge, Massachusetts and London, Harvard University Press, 1990.

70 Ibid., p. 240.

71 Ibid.

72 A. Toffler, p. 181

73 L.A. Friedland, 'Electronic Democracy and the New Citizenship', *Media Culture and Society*, vol.1, 1996, London, Sage, pp. 185–212, CPN website. Available on-line at http://www.cpn.org/sections/new_citizenship/e-dem&new_citizenship1.html (10 June 1998).

74 H. Rheingold, *Virtual Communities*. Available on-line at http://www.well.com/user/hlr/vcbook/vcbook3.html (6 June 1998).

75 *A Brief History of the APC*. Available on-line at http://www.apc.org/english/history.html (11 November 1998).

76 Ibid.

77 Friedland, op. cit.

78 Sweden (NordNet), Canada (Web), Brazil (AlterNex), Nicaragua (Nicarao) and Australia (Pegasus). See *A Brief History of the APC*, op. cit.

79 Ibid.

80 See APC home page. Available on-line at http://www.apc.org/index.html/#contents (11 November 1998).

81 T. Stonier, op. cit., p. x.
82 P. Barkham, 'Dissident and Defiant Slipping Through the Net', *Guardian*, 4 December 1998.
83 D. Kellner, *Theorising New Technologies*, January 1998. Available on-line at http://www.gse.ucla.edu/research/kellner/tnt.html (20 November 1998).
84 Barkham, op. cit.
85 Web pages dealing with the McLibel campaign may be found at http://burn.ucsd.edu/~mai/mclibel_kiosk.html, and http://www.McSpotlight.org/ (11 December 1998).
86 D. Boorstin, *The Image*, London, Pelican, 1963.
87 Ibid., p. 189.
88 N. Postman, *Amusing Ourselves to Death: Public Discourse in the Age of Show Business*, London, Methuen, 1987, p. 77.
89 Ibid., pp. 73–4.
90 Ibid.
91 K. Hacker, 'Missing Links in the Evolution of Electronic Democratisation', *Media, Culture and Society*, vol.18, no.2, 1996, pp. 213–232.
92 L.A. Friedland, op. cit., pp. 185–212.
93 Ibid.
94 Ibid.
95 E.S. Herman, 'Privatising Public Space', in Thussu (ed.), op. cit., pp. 127–9.
96 H. Rheingold, *Virtual Communities*, Chapter 10. Available on-line at http://www.rheingold.com/vc/book/10.htm (6 June 1998).
97 Quoted by P. Golding in 'Worldwide Wedge: Division and Contradiction in the Global Information Infrastructure', in Thussu (ed.), op. cit., p. 141.
98 Katz, op. cit., p. 71.
99 Quoted in P. Golding, op. cit., p. 146.
100 Quoted by Golding and Murdoch in J. Curran and M. Gurevitch (eds), *Mass Media and Society*, London, Arnold, 1996, p. 20.
101 S. Ascarelli, 'Two On-Line Services Investigated in Racial Hatred Case', *Wall Street Journal*, 22 January 1996, p. B13.
102 J. Gittings, 'Chinese Man on Trial for Bypassing Censor', *Guardian*, 4 December 1998, p. 16.
103 K. Robins, *Into the Image*, London, Routledge, 1996, p. 99.
104 Jameson, op. cit., p. 263.
105 E. Fromm, *To Have or to Be*, London, Jonathan Cape, 1978.
106 I. Illich, *Tools for Conviviality*, London, Calder & Boyars, 1973.
107 Ibid., p. 11.
108 Ibid., p. 21.
109 Ibid., p. 11.
110 Ibid.
111 J. Keane, 'Structural Transformations in the Public Sphere', *The Communications Review*, vol.1, no.1, 1995, p. 1.
112 N. Garnham, 'Comments on John Keane's "Structural Transformations in the Public Sphere"', *The Communications Review*, vol.1 no.1, 1995, p. 25.
113 L. Mumford, *The Condition of Man*, London, Martin Secker & Warburg, 1962, p. 270.

Bibliography

Books and Journals

Administrative Office of the US Courts, *Wiretap Report for the Period January 1 1994 to December 31 1994*, US Government Printing Office, Washington, DC, 1995.

Allen, R., 'This is Not Television . . . ', in Steemers (ed.), *Changing Channels: The Prospects for Television in Digital World*, Luton, University of Luton Press, 1998.

Ascarelli, S., 'Two On-Line Services Investigated in Racial Hatred Case', Wall Street Journal, 22 January 1996, p. B13.

Associated Press and New York Times Press Service, 'Cybercensors Reverse Ban on "Breast"', 2 December 1995.

Baase, S., *A Gift of Fire – Social, Legal and Ethical Issues in Computing*, New Jersey, Prentice Hall, 1997.

Bacon, F., *The Advancement of Learning and the New Atlantis*, London, Oxford University Press, 1960.

Baker, K., *Fibre Optics and Opto-Electronics*, London, HMSO, 1982.

Barbrook, R. and Cameron, A., 'The Californian Ideology', *Mute*, 3, Autumn 1995.

Barker, M., *The Awkward Audiences of Judge Dredd*, Luton, University of Luton Press, 1998.

Barkham, P., *Dissident and Defiant Slipping Through the Net, Guardian*, December 4 1998.

Barlow, P.J., 'Jackboots on the Infobahn', in Ludlow, P. (ed.), *High Noon on the Electronic Frontier – Conceptual Issues in Cyberspace*, Massachusetts, MIT Press, 1996.

Barlow, P.J., 'The Denning-Barlow Clipper Chip Debate', in Ludlow, P. (ed.), *High Noon on the Electronic Frontier – Conceptual Issues in Cyberspace*, Massachusetts, MIT Press, 1996.

Barnouw, E., *A Tower in Babel: A History of Broadcasting in the United States*, New York, Oxford University Press, 1966.

Beavis, S., 'Slow Start in View for Digital Television', *Guardian*, 25 March 1998.

Bell, D., *The Coming of Post-Industrial Society: A Venture in Social Forecasting*, London, Penguin, 1976.

Bell, E. and Hellmore, E., 'Whose On-line Service is it Anyway?', *Observer*, 29 September 1996.

Bell, E., 'Can Cable Reach For the Sky', *Observer*, 22 March 1998.

Beniger, J.R., *The Control Revolution. Technological and Economic Origins of the Information Society*, Cambridge, Massachusetts and London, Harvard University Press, 1986.

Bernal, J.D., *The Extension of Man*, St Albans, Hertfordshire, Paladin, 1973.

Bjerg K. and Borreby K., *Proceedings of the International Cross-disciplinary Working Conference on Home-Orientated Informatics, Telematics & Automation*, Copenhagen, University of Copenhagen Press, 1994.

Bookchin, M., *Post-Scarcity Anarchism*, Berkeley, Ramparts Press, 1971.

Boorstin, D., *The Image*, London, Pelican, 1963.

Braverman, H., *Labour & Monopoly Capital*, New York and London, Monthly Review Press, 1974.

Briggs, A., *The Birth of Broadcasting*, London, Oxford University Press, 1961.

Brittan, S., 'The Fight for Freedom in Broadcasting', *Political Quarterly*, vol.58, no.1, 1987.

Broadcasting Research Unit, *The Public Service Idea in British Broadcasting – Main Principles*, London, Broadcasting Research Unit, 1985.

Brosnan, J., *Movie Magic: The Story of Special Effects in the Cinema*, London, Macdonalds and Jane's, 1974.

Brunner, J., *Shockwave Rider*, New York, Harper & Row, 1975.

Burgelman, J-C., 'Convergence and Trans-European Networks: Some Policy Problems', in Bjerg, K. and Borreby, K., *Proceedings of the International Cross-disciplinary Working Conference on Home-Orientated Informatics, Telematics & Automation*, Copenhagen, University of Copenhagen Press, 1994.

Burgelman, J-C., 'The Future of Public Service Broadcasting: A Case Study for a "New" Communications Policy', *European Journal of Communication*, vol.1, 1986.

Bush, V., 'As We May Think', first published in *The Atlantic Monthly*, July 1945; reprinted in Nelson, T., *Literary Machines*, Sausalito, Mindful Press, 1983.

Butler, I., *The Making of Feature Film: A Guide*, Harmondsworth, Penguin, 1971.

Cain, J., *The BBC: 70 Years of Broadcasting*, London, BBC, 1992.

Carey, J., *Communication as Culture*, London, Routledge, 1989.

Carroll, L., *Through the Looking Glass*, Harmondsworth, Penguin, 1872 (this edition 1954).

Cawson, A., 'In Search of the Interactive Consumer. The Design and Development of Compact Disc-Interactive', in Bjerg, K. and Borreby, K., *Home-Orientated Informatics, Telematics & Automation*, Copenhagen, University of Copenhagen Press, 1994.

Collins, R., *Direct Broadcasting by Satellite in the UK*, London, ESRC, 1991.

Collins, R. and Murroni, C., *New Media, New Policies*, Cambridge, Polity Press, 1996.

Connett, D. and Henley, J., 'The Peddlers of Child Abuse: We Know Who They Are. Yet No One is Stopping Them', *Observer*, 25 August 1996, pp. 19–21.

Corcoran, E., 'US Closes Investigation in Computer Privacy Case', *Washington Post*, 12 January 1996, p. A11.

Cotton, B. and Oliver, R., *The Cyberspace Lexicon*, London, Phaidon, 1994.

Cotton, B. and Oliver, R., *Understanding Multimedia 2000: Multimedia Origins: Internet Futures*, London, Phaidon, 1997.

Council of the European Communities, *Council Directive On the Establishment of the Internal Market for Telecommunications Services Through Open Network Provision*, Brussels (90/387/EEC OJ L 192/10), 1990.

Crisell, A., *Understanding Radio*, London, Routledge, 1994.

Curran, J., 'Mass Media and Democracy: A Reappraisal', in Curran, J. and Gurevitch, M. (eds), *Mass Media and Society*, London, Edward Arnold, 1991.

Dahlberg, L., 'Cyberspace and the Public Sphere: Exploring the Democratic Potential of the Net', in *Convergence*, Luton, John Libbey Media at the University of Luton Press, vol.4, no.1, Spring 1998.

Dahlgren, P., 'Ideology and Information in the Public Sphere', in Slack, J.D. and Fejes, F., *The Ideology of the Information Age*, Norwood, New Jersey, Ablex Publishing Corporation, 1987.

Dahlgren, P., and Sparks, C., *Communication and Citizenship*, London, Routledge, 1991.

Darley, A., 'Abstraction to Simulation', in P. Hayward (ed.), *Culture, Technology and Creativity in the Late Twentieth Century*, London, John Libbey, 1990.

Debord, G., *The Society of the Spectacle*, New York, Zone Books (3rd edn), 1997.

Dejesus, E.X., 'How the Internet Will Replace Broadcasting', *Byte*, February 1996.

DeLanda, M., *War in the Age of Intelligent Machines*, New York, MIT Press, 1991.

Dickson, D., *Alternative Technology and the Politics of Technical Change*, London, Fontana/Collins, 1974.

Diffie, W. and Hellman, M., 'New Directions in Cryptography', *IEEE Transactions on Information Theory*, vol.IT-22, 1976, pp. 644–6, 54.

Dobb, M., *Studies in the Development of Capitalism*, London, George Routledge & Sons, 1947.

Duffy, N., Davis, J. and Daum, A., 'The Economics of Digital Television', in Steemers, J. (ed.), *Changing Channels: The Prospects for Television in the Digital Age*, Luton, John Libbey at the University of Luton Press, 1998.

Edelman, B., *Ownership of the Image: Elements for a Marxist Theory of Law*, London, Routledge, 1979.

Evans, C., *The Making of the Micro, A History of the Computer*, Oxford, Oxford University Press, 1983.

Evans, C., *The Mighty Micro*, Oxford, Oxford University Press, 1983.

Evans, J.V., 'New Satellites for Personal Communications', in 'Wireless Technologies Special Report', *Scientific American*, April 1998, pp. 60–7.

Feldman, T., *Multimedia in the 1990s*, London, Blueprint, 1991.

Ferguson, M. (ed.), *New Communication Technologies and the Public Interest: Comparative Perspectives on Policy and Research*, London, Sage, 1986.

Forrest, J., 'Views of the Future of Digital Terrestrial TV', Spectrum, Autumn 1993.

Fritz, M., 'Digital Video Disks. Compact Disks Pump Up', *Wired*, July 1996.

Fromm, E., *To Have or to Be*, London, Jonathan Cape, 1978.

Fuller, R. Buckminster, *Utopia or Oblivion. The Prospects for Humanity*, London, Penguin, 1972.

Gailbraith, J.K., *The Age of Uncertainty*, London, BBC/Andre Deutsche, 1977.

Garner, R., 'The Mother of Multimedia', *Wired*, April 1994.

Garnham, N., 'Public Service versus the Market', *Screen*, Jan–Feb 1983.

Garnham, N., 'The Media and the Public Sphere', *Intermedia*, vol.14, no.1, January 1986, p. 30.

Garnham, N., 'Comments on John Keane's "Structural Transformations in the Public Sphere"', *The Communications Review*, vol.1, no.1, 1995, p. 25.

Garratt, G.R.M., *The Communications Explosion in the Nineteenth Century: Some Contributions of Electrical Engineering*, Milton Keynes, Open University Press, 1973.

Geer, S., 'A Lifeline for CD-ROM', *Daily Telegraph*, 17 September 1996.

Gibbons, T., 'De/Re-regulating the System: The British Experience', in Steemers, J. (ed.), *Changing Channels: The Prospects for Television in a Digital World*, Luton, John Libbey at the University of Luton Press, 1998.

Gibson, W., *Neuromancer*, London, Grafton Books, 1986.

Gittings, J., 'Chinese Man on Trial for Bypassing Censor', *Guardian*, London, December 4, 1998.

Golding, P., 'Worldwide Wedge: Division and Contradiction in the Global Information Infrastructure', in Thussu, D.J., *Electronic Empires: Global Media and Local Resistance*, London, Arnold, 1998.

Gore, A., *Earth in the Balance : Ecology and the Human Spirit*, Boston, Houghton Mifflin, 1992.

Gross, L.S., *Telecommunications. An Introduction to Electronic Media*, Madison Wisconsin, Brown and Benchmark, 1995.

Habermas, J., *The Structural Transformation of the Public Sphere*, Cambridge, Polity Press, 1989.

Hacker, K., 'Missing Links in the Evolution of Electronic Democratisation', *Media, Culture and Society*, vol.18, no.2, London, Sage, 1996, pp. 213–32.

Hancock, D., 'Digital Television: A European Perspective', in Steemers, J. (ed.), *Changing Channels: The Prospects for Television in a Digital World*, Luton, John Libbey at the University of Luton Press, 1998.

Hayward, P., 'Industrial Light and Magic – Style, Technology and Special Effects in the Music Video and Music Television', in P. Hayward (ed.), *Culture, Technology and Creativity in the Late Twentieth Century*, London, John Libbey and Company, 1990.

Hayward, P. and Wollen, T. (eds.), *Future Visions: New Technologies of the Screen*, London, BFI Publishing, 1993.

Heilbroner, R.L., *The Worldly Philosophers: The Lives, Times, and Ideas of the Great Economic Thinkers*, New York, Simon & Schuster, 1953.

Heller, C., *Broadcasting and Accountability*, London, BFI Publishing, 1978.

Herman, E.S., 'Privatising Public Space', in D.J. Thussu, *Electronic Empires: Global Media and Local Resistance*, London, Arnold, 1998.

Herman, E.S. and McChesney, R.W., *The Global Media*, London, Cassell, 1997.

Hodges, A., *Alan Turing: The Enigma of Intelligence*, London, Counterpoint, 1983.

Hoffmann-Riem, W., 'New Challenges for European Multimedia Policy', *European Journal of Communications*, vol.11, 1996.

Hollins, T., *Beyond Broadcasting: Into the Cable Age*, London, BFI Publishing, 1984.

Home Office, *Direct Broadcasting by Satellite: Report of a Home Office Study*, London, HMSO, 1981.

Home Office, *Report of the Inquiry into Cable Expansion and Broadcasting Policy (the Hunt Report)*, London, HMSO, 1982.

Homer, S., 'Interactive Television For All', *Independent*, 5 April 1993.

Humphreys, P. and Lang, M., 'Digital Television Between the Economy and Pluralism', in Steemers, J. (ed.), *Changing Channels: The Prospects for Television in a Digital World*, Luton, John Libbey at the University of Luton Press, 1998.

Huxley, A., *The Doors of Perception and Heaven and Hell*, London, Penguin Books, 1963.

Illich, I., *Tools for Conviviality*, London, Calder & Boyars, 1973.

Information Technology Advisory Panel (ITAP), *Cable Systems: A Report by the ITAP*, London, HMSO, 1982.

ITV, *Television and the Role of ITV*, London, Spectrum Strategy Consultants, 1995.

Jameson, F., *Postmodernism or the Cultural Logic of Late Capitalism*, London, Verso, 1991.

Jeffcoate, J., 'Multimedia in the Business Market. Is There a Multimedia Market?', in *Information Management and Technology*, vol.26, no.5, 1993.

Jeffcoate, J. *Multimedia in Practice: Technology and Applications*, London, Prentice Hall, 1995.

Kaldor, M., *The Baroque Arsenal*, London, Abacus, 1982.

Katz, J., 'The Digital Citizen', *Wired*, December, 1997.

Keane, J., 'Structural Transformations in the Public Sphere', *The Communications Review*, vol.1, no.1, 1995, p. 1.

Kelly, K., *Out of Control: The New Biology of Machines*, London, Fourth Estate, 1994.

Kelly, K., 'The Software Developer', in Brockman, J. (ed.), *Digerati – Encounters with the Cyber Elite*, London, Orion Business, 1997.

Kroker, A. and Weinstein, M., *Data Trash: The Theory of the Virtual Class*, Montreal, New World Perspectives, 1994.

Kumar, K., *Prophesy and Progress*, London, Penguin, 1978.

Laclau, E., *New Reflections on the Revolution of Our Time*, London, Verso, 1990.

Leary, T., 'The Cyberpunk: The Individual as Reality Pilot', in McCaffrey, L., *Storming the Reality Studio*, Durham, North Carolina and London, Duke University Press, 1993.

Levy, S., *Insanely Great. The Life and Times of Macintosh, the Computer that Changed Everything*, London, Penguin, 1995.

Lo, C., 'Get Wireless', *Wired*, 4 April, 1997.

Ludlow, P. (ed.), *High Noon on the Electronic Frontier – Conceptual Issues in Cyberspace*, Massachusetts, MIT Press, 1996.

McCaffrey, L., *Storming the Reality Studio*, Durham, North Carolina and London, Duke University Press, 1993.

McGuigan, J., 'What Price the Public Sphere', in Thussu, D.J., *Electronic Empires: Global Media and Local Resistance*, London, Arnold, 1998.

Machlup, F., *The Production and Distribution of Wealth in the United States*, Princeton, New Jersey, Princeton University Press, 1962.

McLuhan, M., *The Medium is the Massage*, London, Penguin, 1967.

McLuhan, M., *Understanding Media*, London, Sphere Books, 1973.

Mansell, R., *The New Telecommunications. A Political Economy of Network Evolution*, London, Sage, 1993.

Marchand, P., *Marshall McLuhan: The Medium and the Messenger*, New York, Ticknor & Fields, 1989.

Marcuse, H., *One Dimensional Man*, London, Sphere, 1968.

Marks, P., 'Cue the Computer', *Guardian*, 16 May 1996.

Marks, P., 'The White City Heat of Technology', *Guardian*, 11 July 1996.

Marvin, C., 'Information and History', in Slack, J.D. and Fejes, F., *The Ideology of the Information Age*, Norwood, N.J., Ablex, 1987.

Marvin, C., *When Old Technologies Were New*, Oxford, Oxford University Press, 1988.

Meehan, E.R., 'Technical Capability versus Corporate Imperatives: Towards a Political Economy of Cable Television and Information Diversity', in Mosco, V. and Wasko, J. (eds), *The Political Economy of Information*, Madison Wisconsin, University of Wisconsin Press, 1988, pp. 167–186.

Meiksins Wood, E., 'Modernity, Postmodernity, or Capitalism', in McChesney Wood, R. and Foster, J. (eds), *Capitalism and the Information Age: The Political Economy of the Global Communications Revolution*, New York, Monthly Review Press, 1998.

Metcalfe, S., 'Information and Some Economics of the Information Revolution', in Ferguson, M. (ed.), *New Communication Technologies and the Public Interest: Comparative Perspectives on Policy and Research*, London, Sage, 1986.

Miller, S., *Civilizing Cyberspace: Policy, Power, and the Information Superhighway*, New York, ACM Press and Addison-Wesley Publishing Company, 1996.

Mosco, V. and Washo, J. (eds), *The Political Economy of Information*, Madison Wisconsin, University of Wisconsin Press, 1988.

Mulgan, G.J., *Communication and Control: Networks and the New Economies of Communication*, Cambridge, Polity Press, 1991.

Mumford, L., *The Condition of Man*, London, Martin Secker & Warburg, 1962.

Mumford, L., *The Myth of the Machine*, London, Secker & Warburg, 1967.

Munford, N., Kolbe, L. and Brenner, W., 'Convergence of Media Machines and Messages', *Convergence*, vol.3, no.1, 1997, p. 117.

National Research Council, *Cryptography's Role in Securing the Information Society*, Washington, National Academy Press, 1996.

Neal, S., 'Hollywood Strikes Back: Special Effects in Recent American Cinema', *Screen*, vol.21, no.3, 1980, pp. 101–5.

Negroponte, N., *Being Digital*, London, Hodder & Stoughton, 1996.

Nelson, T., *Computer Lib/Dream Machines*, Redmont, Microsoft Press, 1987.

Nelson, T.H., *Literary Machines*, Sausalito, Mindful Press, 1992.

Nyce, J.M. and Kahn, P., *From Memex to Hypertext*, Boston, Academic Press, 1991.

Parkes, C., 'Murdoch Abandons United States Satellite Ambitions', *Financial Times*, 2 June 1997.

Peasey, J., *Public Service Broadcasting in Transition*, unpublished PhD thesis, University of Bath, 1990.

Perry, R., 'The Rise and Rise of the Family PC', *Guardian*, 20 October 1994.

Phillips, T., 'Dial S for satellite', *Guardian*, 29 January 1998.

Pimentel, K. and Teixera, K., *Virtual Reality Through the New Looking Glass*, Pennsylvania, McGraw Hill, 1993.

Pool, I.S., *Technologies Without Boundaries. On Telecommunications in a Global Age*, London, Harvard University Press, 1990.

Porat, M., *The Information Economy: Definition and Measurement*, Washington, DC, US Department of Commerce, Office of Telecommunications, 1977.

Postman, N., *Amusing Ourselves to Death: Public Discourse in the Age of Show Business*, London, Methuen, 1987.

Quarterman, J.S., *The Matrix: Computer Networks and Conferencing Systems Worldwide*, Cincinnati, Digital Press, 1990.

Rickett, F., 'Multimedia', in Hayward, P. and Wollen, T. (eds), *Future Visions of the Screen*, London, BFI Publishing, 1994.

Robins, K., *Into the Image*, London, Routledge, 1996.

Roszak, T., *The Cult of Information*, London, University of California Press, 1994.

Roszak, T., *The Making of a Counter Culture. Reflections on the Technocratic Society and its Youthful Opposition*, Berkeley, University of California Press, 1995.

Rucker, R., *Mondo 2000. A Users Guide to the New Edge*, London, Thames and Hudson, 1993.

Sadler, M., *'The British Empire Strikes Back', The Movie*, Orbis Publishing Ltd, 1982.

Saussure, F., *Course in General Linguistics* (trans. Baskin, W.), New York, McGraw Hill, 1966.

Schiller, H., *Information Inequality: The Deepening Social Crisis in America*, London, Routledge, 1996.

Schneier, B., *Applied Cryptography*, New York, John Wiley & Sons, 1994.

Schwartz, J., 'Privacy Program: An On-Line Weapon?', *Washington Post*, 3 April 1995.

Slater, D., 'Photography and Modern Vision: The Spectacle of "Natural Magic"', in Jenks, C. (ed.), *Visual Culture*, London, Routledge, 1995.

Sparkes, C., 'Is There a Global Public Sphere?', in Thussu, D.J., *Electronic Empires: Global Media and Local Resistance*, London, Arnold, 1998.

Sparkes, V., 'Cable Television in the United States', in Negrine, R.M. (ed.), *Cable Television and the Future of Broadcasting*, London, Croom Helm, 1985.

Steemers, J., 'Broadcasting is Dead. Long Live Digital Choice', *Convergence*, vol.3, no.1, Spring 1997.

Steemers, J. (ed.), *Changing Channels: The Prospects for Television in a Digital World*, Luton, John Libbey at the University of Luton Press, 1998.

Steemers, J., 'Die terrestrische Fernsehsektor in Grossbritannien', *Media Perspektiven*, June 1998.

Steemers, J., 'On the Threshold of the "Digital Age": Prospects for Public Service Broadcasting', in Steemers, J. (ed.), *Changing Channels*, Luton, John Libbey at the University of Luton Press, 1998, pp. 97–124.

Sterling, B., *Mirrorshades, the Cyberpunk Anthology*, London, HarperCollins, 1986.

Sterling, B., *The Hacker Crackdown. Law and Disorder on the Electronic Frontier*, London, Penguin Books, 1992.

Stonier, T., *The Wealth of Information. A Profile of the Post-Industrial Economy*, London, Thames Methuen, 1983.

Thussu, D.J., *Electronic Empires: Global Media and Local Resistance*, London, Arnold, 1998.

Toffler, A., *The Third Wave*, London, Collins, 1980.

Tracey, M., *The Decline and Fall of Public Service Broadcasting*, Oxford, Oxford University Press, 1998.

Tran, M., 'Telecoms Space Race Starts', *Guardian*, 22 March 1994.

Tran, M., 'Time Warner Launches Interactive TV System', *Guardian*, 15 December 1994.

Tran, M., 'Time Warner Buys Second Cable Firm', *Guardian*, 8 February 1995.

Tran, M., 'Telecom Firms Ring No Changes', *Guardian*, 2 June 1997.

Veljanovski, C. and Bishop, W., *Choice by Cable*, London, Institute of Economic Affairs, 1983.

Veljanovski, C., *Commercial Broadcasting in the UK: Over-regulation and Misregulation*, London, Centre for Economic Policy Research, 1987.

Warren, S. and Brandeis, L., 'The Right to Privacy', *Harvard Law Review*, vol.4, 1980, p. 193.

Wilden, A., *System and Structure: Essays in Communication and Exchange*, London, Tavistock Publications Ltd, 1977.

Williams, R., *Communications*, London, Penguin, 1962.

Williams, R., 'Base and Superstructure in Marxist Cultural Theory', *New Left Review*, 82, 1973.

Williams, R., *Television: Technology and Cultural Form*, Glasgow, Fontana/Collins, 1974.

Wooley, B., *Virtual Worlds: A Journey in Hype and Hyperreality*, Oxford, Blackwell, 1992.

Young, P., *Person to Person: The International Impact of the Telephone*, Cambridge, Granta Editions, 1991.

Young, T.R., 'Information, Ideology and Political Reality, Against Toffler', in Slack, J.D. and Fejes, F., *The Ideology of the Information Age*, Norwood, New Jersey, Ablex Publishing Corporation, 1987.

Zimmermann, P., 'How PGP Works/Why Do You Need PGP?', in Ludlow, P. (ed.), *High Noon on the Electronic Frontier – Conceptual Issues in Cyberspace*, Massachusetts, MIT Press, 1996.

Zorpette, G., 'A New Fat Pipe', *Scientific American*, April 1998.

Electronic references

Anderson, S. (29 May 1998) 'United States Coup Puts C&W Among Internet Stars', *Electronic Telegraph*, Issue 1099. Available on-line at http://www.telegraph.co.uk:80/ (5 June 1998).

Anonymous, *Telecommunications History Timeline*, on Webb & Associates website. Available on-line at http://www.webbconsult.com/timeline.html#1800 (4 August 1998).

Associated Press (20 October 1997) 'AT&T Names Armstrong to Top Post', *The Seattle Times*. Available on-line at http://www.seattletimes.com/extra/browse/html97/att_102097.html (11 August 1998).

Association for Progressive Communications, *A Brief History of the APC*. Available on-line at http://www.apc.org/english/history.html (November 1998).

AT&T press release (22 January 1996) 'AT&T and DIRECTV Partner for Broadcast Satellite Service and Equipment'. Available on-line at http://www.att.com/press/0196/960122.cha.html (11 August 1998).

Bacsich, P. (April 1996) 'Hughes Directv Makes Several Strategic Alliances'. Available on-line at http://www.de.infowin.org/ACTS/IENM/NEWSCLIPS/arch1996/030996uk.htm (6 June 1998).

Barlow, J.P. (8 February 1996) *Declaration of the Independence of Cyberspace*. Available on-line at http://www.tarleton.edu/~swarren/cyberspace.htm (December 1998).

Barron, A. and Uhlig, R. (15 May 1996) 'Hurry Up and Wait', *Electronic Telegraph*, Issue 384. Available on-line at http://www.telegraph.co.uk:80 (August 1998).

BBC (April 1998) 'The Computer that Ate Hollywood', transcript of BBC *Horizon* documentary, pp. 5–6. Transmitted 30 April 1998. Available on-line at http://www.bbc.co.uk/horizon/specialfxtran.shtml (19 May 1998).

Bracken, M. (21 July 1998) 'The BBC Goes Portal', *Wired News*. Available on-line at

http://www.wired.com/news/news/politics/story/13871.html
(5 August 1998).

Brand, S. (December 1972) 'Spacewar: Fanatic Life and Symbolic Death Among the Computer Bums', *Rolling Stone*. Available on-line at http://www.baumgart.com/rolling-stone/spacewar.html (1 June 1998).

Brickell, E. and Denning, D. *et al.*, *SKIPJACK Review* – Interim Report. Available on-line at http://www.cosc.georgetown.edu/~denning/crypto/clipper/SKIPJACK.txt (6 September 1998).

British Telecom Online (1998) from BT website. Available on-line at http://www.education.bt.com/factfile/ff9text.htm (3 February 1998).

Browning, J. (April 1994) 'Universal Service (An Idea Whose Time is Past)', *Wired*. Available on-line at http://www.wired.com/wired/2.09/features/universal.access.html (May 1996).

Butterbaugh, S. and Katz, F. (15 November 1996) 'Turner Pictures Being Integrated into Warner Bros', *Media Daily*, vol.4, no.223, Cowles New Media. Available on-line at http://www.mediacentral.com/Magazines/MediaDaily/index.html#01 (12 November 1996).

Butterbaugh, S. and Katz, F. (15 November 1996) 'TCI Pulls Out of MSN Partnership', *Media Daily*, vol.4, no.223, Cowles New Media. Available on-line at http://www.mediacentral.com/Magazines/MediaDaily/index.html#01 (20 November 1996).

Clark, T. (10 February 1998) 'The Battle for Digital Images', *CNET News*. Available on-line at http://www.news.com/News/Item/0,4,19030,00.html (3 March 1998).

Cyber-Rights & Cyber-Liberties (UK) group, Centre For Criminal Justice Studies, University of Leeds, UK. Available on-line at http://www.leeds.ac.uk/law/pgs/yaman/yaman.htm (6 September 1998).

Davis, E. (July 1995) 'Technopagans', *Wired*. Available on-line at http://www.wired.com/wired/3.07/features/technopagans.html (16 July 1998).

Davis, J. (1 April 1998) 'TCI Keeping Microsoft at Arm's Length', *CNET News*. Available on-line at http://www.news.com/News/Item/0,4,20672,00.html (6 April 1998).

Davis, J. (11 July 1997) 'PC-like Cable Boxes Coming', *CNET News*. Available on-line at http://www.news.com/News/Item/0,4,12350,00.html (12 July 1997).

Davis, J. (June 24 1998) 'TCI Deal May Speed PC-TV Marriage', *CNET News*. Available on-line at http://www.news.com/News/Item/0,4,23528,00.html (5 June 1998).

Davis, J. (13 March 1998) 'Apple's Columbus a Bold Bet', *CNET News*. Available on-line at http://www.news.com/News/Item/0,4,20057,00.html (13 March 1998).

De Bra, P., *Hypertext Systems*, Eindhoven University of Technology Website. Available on-line at http://wwwis.win.tue.nl/2L670/static/zog.html (May 1998).

Doyle, M. (8 May 1997) 'Four Big Names Back Interactive Satellite TV', *Electronic Telegraph*, Issue 713. Available on-line at http://www.telegraph.co.uk:80 (5 May 1997).

Doyle, M. (19 June 1997) 'Digital TV Blow Hits BSkyB Shares', *Electronic Telegraph*, Issue 755. Available on-line at http://www.telegraph.co.uk:80 (5 March 1998).

Dyson, E., Gilder, G., Keyworth, G. and Toffler, A. (1994) *Cyberspace and the*

American Dream: A Magna Carta for the Knowledge Age, Release 1.2. Available
  on-line at http://alberti.mit.edu/arch/4.207/texts/cyberspace-dream.html
  (September 1998).

Eakin, J. (13 September 1997) 'The Market: BICC Falls 8pc to 10-Year Low',
  Electronic Telegraph, Issue 841. Available on-line at
  http://www.telegraph.co.uk:80 (October 1997).

Electronic Frontier Foundation, *DES Cracker Project*. Available on-line at
  http://www.eff.org/descracker.html (6 September 1998).

Electronic Frontier Foundation, *About the Electronic Frontier Foundation*. Available on-
  line at http://www.eff.org/EFFdocs/about_eff.html (6 September 1998).

European Commission (December 1997) *Green Paper on the Convergence of the
  Telecommunications, Media and Information Technology Sectors*, Brussels. Available
  on-line at http://www.ispo.cec.be/convergencegp/97623.html
  (11 August 1998).

The Family Research Council, *Frequently Asked Questions*. Available on-line at
  http://www.frc.org/faq/faq20.html (6 September 1998).

Felsenstein, L. (May 1993) 'The Commons of Information', *Dr. Dobbs' Journal*.
  Online. Available on-line at
  http://bliss.berkeley.edu/impact/speakers/speakers_page.html (February 1998).

FIPS (Federal Information Processing Standards), National Institute of Standards
  and Technology. Available on-line at http://csrc.ncsl.nist.gov/fips/fips185.txt
  (6 September 1998).

Friedland, L.A. (1996) 'Electronic Democracy and the New Citizenship', in *Media,
  Culture and Society*, vol.1, London, Sage, pp. 185–212. Available on-line at
  http://www.cpn.org/sections/new_citizenship/e-dem&new_citizenship1.html
  (June 1998).

Gilder, G. (7 December 1992) 'Into the Fibersphere', *Forbes Magazine*. Available on-
  line at http://www.forbes.com/asap/gilder/telecosm13a.htm (1 August 1998).

Gilder, G. (23 February 1994) 'Life After Television, Updated', *Forbes ASAP*.
  Available on-line at http://www.forbes.com/asap/gilder/ (5 May 1996).

Gilder, G. (5 June 1995) 'From Waves to Wires', *Forbes Magazine*. Available on-line
  at http://www.forbes.com/asap/gilder/telecosm13a.htm (1 August 1998).

Goodin, D. and Heskett, B. (8 September 1998) 'Java Suit Hearing Under Way',
  CNET News. Available on-line at
  http://www.news.com/News/Item/0,4,26078,00.html (10 September 1998).

Gribben, R. (24 January 1998) 'No BT Takeover Says Microsoft', *Electronic Telegraph*,
  Issue 974. Available on-line at http://www.telegraph.co.uk:80/ (5 August 1998).

Gribben, R. (13 February 1998) 'Piped TV 'a Turn-off' for BT', *Electronic Telegraph*,
  Issue 994. Available on-line at http://www.telegraph.co.uk:80/ (August 1998).

Gribben, R. (11 March 1998) 'C&WC to Offer Internet on TV', *Electronic Telegraph*,
  Issue 1020. Available on-line at http://www.telegraph.co.uk:80/ (August 1998).

Grossman, L.K. (Winter 1994) 'Reflections on Life Along the Electronic Superhighway', *Media Studies Journal*. Available on-line at
  http://www.gspa.washington.edu/Courses/Net/*grossman.html (8 July 1998).

Hauben, M. and Hauben, R., *Netizens: On the History and Impact of Usenet and the
  Internet*. Available on-line at http://www.columbia.edu/~hauben/netbook/
  (6 September 1998).

Hecht, J. (1994) *A Fiber-Optic Chronology*, New York, Delmar Publishers.
  Available on-line at http://www.sff.net/people/Jeff.Hecht/history.html
  (April 1998).

House of Commons, Culture, Media and Sport Select Committee (22 May 1998) *Select Committee on Culture, Media and Sport Fourth Report – The Multi-Media Revolution*, vol.1. Available on-line at http://www.parliament.the-stationery-office.co.uk/pa/cm199798/cmselect/cmcumeds/520-vol1/52003.htm (25 August 1998).

Kellner, D. (January 1998) *Theorising New Technologies*. Available on-line at http://www.gse.ucla.edu/research/kellner/tnt.html (November 1998).

Kornblum, J. (12 August 1998) 'Sprint Tries Net Phone Service', *CNET News*. Available on-line at http://www.news.com/News/Item/0,4,25215,00.html (August 1998).

Kramer, F. (May 1997) 'Murdoch Reportedly Reaches Tentative Deal with Primestar', *Nando.net*. Available on-line at http://www.nando.net/newsroom/ntn/info/052797/info7_27632.html (October 1997).

Krempl, S. (1998) *Newt Gingrich's Vision: An Interview with Mr. Speaker During his 'House Visit' at Oracle in Silicon Valley January 15th 1998*, Telepolis website. Available on-line at http://www.heise.de/tp/english/inhalt/te/1417/1.html (September 1998).

Leary, T., Timothy Leary's Biography. Available on-line at http://www.leary.com/Biography/QuickBio.html (7 July 1998).

Leary, T., *The Church of LSD*. Available on-line at http://leary.com/archives/text/Archives/Millbrook/ChurchofLSD.html (7 July 1998).

Machado, R., *Stego Online*. Available on-line at http://www.stego.com/ (6 September 1998).

New York Staff (20 March 1998) 'Fox Beats Turner on LA Dodgers', *Electronic Telegraph*, Issue 1029. Available on-line at http://www.telegraph.co.uk:80/ (9 September 1998).

News Corporation, Website. Available on-line at http://www.newscorp.com/public/pressdir/fbc.html (8 August 1998).

Nielsen, A.C. , 'Cable History'. Available on-line at http://www.classic-cable.com/history.html (20 July 1998).

OECD, *Webcasting and Convergence: Policy Implications* (February 1998). Available on-line at http://www.oecd.org/dsti/sti/it/cm/prod/e_97-221.pdf (5 September 1998).

Oftel, *A Brief History of Recent UK Telecoms Developments at Oftel*. Available on-line at http://www.oftel.gov.uk/history.htm (11 August 1998).

Oftel (March 1998) *Digital Television and Interactive Services: Ensuring Access On Fair, Reasonable and Non-Discriminatory Terms Consultative Document*. Available on-line at http://www.oftel.gov.uk/broadcast/dig398.htm (6 March 1998).

Pelline, J. (7 February 1997) 'The Old Guard: Telephone companies', *CNET News*. Available on-line at http://www.news.com/SpecialFeatures/05773000.html (March 1998).

Pelline, J. (20 November 1997) 'Cable Modems Fight for Lead', *CNET Special Report*. Available on-line at http://www.news.com/SpecialFeatures/0,5,16615,00.html (5 December 1997).

Pelline, J. and Lazarus, A. (9 June 1997) 'MS Invests $1 Billion in Comcast', *CNET News*. Available on-line at http://www.news.com/News/Item/0,4,11315,00.html (5 March 1998).

Pilgrim, K. (2 April 1996) 'Merger May Create Static for Tele-TV', *Cable News*

Network. Available on-line at http://www.cnnfn.com/news/9604/02/tele_tv/ (4 August 1998).

Poel, W. (March 1998) 'BT and Microsoft to Get it Together?', PS Consultants Website. Available on-line at http://www.ps-consultants.co.uk/featurearticles/98-2.htm (7 August 1998).

Poster, M., *CyberDemocracy: Internet and the Public Sphere.* Available on-line at www.poster.democ.htm (May 1997).

Potter, B. (22 August 1998) 'BIB Hits Technical and Price Snags', *Electronic Telegraph*, Issue 1184. Available on-line at http://www.telegraph.co.uk:80 (October 1998).

Pretty Good Privacy Inc, P.G.P. Home Page. Available on-line at http://www.nai.com/default_pgp. asp (6 September 1998).

Pretzlik, C. (23 April 1996) 'Bell Atlantic Swallows Nynex in $23bn Deal', *Electronic Telegraph*, Issue 368. Available on-line at http://www.telegraph.co.uk (5 May 1998).

Pretzlik, C. (11 November 1997) 'WorldCom Wins Battle for MCI', *Electronic Telegraph*, Issue 901. Available on-line at http://www.telegraph.co.uk (5 January 1998).

Recreational Software Advisory Council Home Page. Available on-line at http://www.rsac.org/ (8 September 1998).

Rheingold, H. (1985) *The Virtual Community.* Available on-line at http://www.well.com/user/hlr/vcbook/vcbook3.html (4 April 1998).

RSA Data Security Inc. (1996) *Answers to Frequently Asked Questions about Cryptography Export Laws.* Available on-line at http://www.rsa.com/PUBS/exp_faq.pdf (September 1998).

Somogyi, S. and Standage, T. (5 June 1996) 'Why Java Changes Everything', *Electronic Telegraph*, Issue 399. Available on-line at http://www.telegraph.co.uk (9 September 1998).

Spalte, M., (1996) BT Website. Available on-line at http://www.btinternet.com/~fyneview/light.straw/about.html (1 August 1998).

Special Correspondent (9 September 1998) 'Billion-dollar United Top of Money League', *Electronic Telegraph*, Issue 1202. Available on-line at http://www.telegraph.co.uk:80/ (10 September 1998).

Staff reporters (5 December 1996) 'Massive Job Cuts for TCI Houston', *Houston Chronicle Online.* Available on-line at http://www.chron.com/ (5 May 1997).

Taylor, C.P. (6 May 1997) 'Time Warner Pulls Plug on Interactive TV Trial', *Inter@ctive Week.* Available on-line at http://www5.zdnet.com/zdnn/content/inwk/0414/inwk0028.html (December 1997).

Tran, M. (21 May 1997) 'Bill Gates Has Outgrown the PC Industry. Now He's Staring into Space', *Guardian OnLine.* Available on-line at http://go2.guardian.co.uk/theweb/864227431-gates.html (5 May 1997).

US Government (1996) *Realizing the Information Future: The Internet and Beyond.* Available on-line at http://nii.nist.gov/nii/niiinfo.html (6 July 1996).

US Government (1996) *Telecommunications Act of 1996, Establishment of Open Video Systems.* Available on-line at http://thomas.loc.gov/cgi-bin/query/z?c104:s.652.enr: (8 October 1998).

Wallace, J. (1997) 'The Sleeping Giant Awakens to a New Dawn', extracted from Wallace, J., *Overdrive: Bill Gates and the Race to Control Cyberspace*, London,

John Wiley, in *Electronic Telegraph*, 27 May 1997. Available on-line at http://www.telegraph.co.uk:80/ (4 August 1997).

Webb & Associates, *Telephone History Time Line*. Available on-line at http://www.webbconsult.com/timeline.html#1800 (8 July 1998).

WebTV Networks press release (18 March 1998) *Microsoft WebTV Networks and BT Begin Trial in United Kingdom*. Available on-line at http://webtv.net/ns/corporate/media/bt.html (5 August 1998).

Wolf, G. (1996) 'The Wisdom of Saint Marshall the Holy Fool', *Wired Archive* 4, 1 January 1996. Available on-line at http://www.wired.com/wired/archive/4.01/saint.marshal_pr.html (September 1998).

Woodyard, C. (December 1995) 'Bill Will Decide Industry's Future', *Houston Chronicle*. Available on-line at http://www.chron.com/5 (12 August 1996).

Index

Milton Keynes UK
Ingram Content Group UK Ltd.
UKHW042324061024
449327UK00004B/36

9 780415 121507